Woodfield, Ian.

English musicians in the age of exploration.

$48.00

DATE			

English Musicians in the Age of Exploration

Frontispiece: The voyage of Jacob Mahu in 1598. Five trumpeters accompany their captain during a stop on the African coast.

English Musicians in the Age of Exploration

Ian Woodfield

SOCIOLOGY OF MUSIC NO. 8

PENDRAGON PRESS
STUYVESANT, NY

Other Titles in the series SOCIOLOGY OF MUSIC

No. 1 *The Social Status of the Professional Musician from the Middle Ages to the 19th Century*, Walter Salmen, General Editor (1983) ISBN 0-918728-16-9

No. 3 *A Music for the Millions: Antibellum Democratic Attitudes and the Birth of American Popular Music* by Nicholas Tawa (1984) ISBN 0-918728-38-X

No. 4 *Music in Society: A Guide to the Sociology of Music* revised edition in English by Ivo Supovic (1987) ISBN 0-918728-35-5

No. 5 *Excelsior: Journals of the Hutchinson Family Singers, 1842–1846* edited and annotated by Dale Cockrell (1989) ISBN 0-918728-65-7

No. 6 *Music For Hire: A Study of Professional Musicians in Washington, 1877–1900* by Katherine K. Preston (1991) ISBN 0-918728-66-5

No. 7 *Concert Life in Haydn's Vienna: Aspects of a Developing Musical and Social Institution* by Mary Sue Morrow (1989) ISBN 0-918728-83-5

Library of Congress Cataloging-in-Publication Data

Woodfield, Ian.
English Musicians in the age of exploration / Ian Woodfield.
p. cm.—(Sociology of Music ; no. 8)
Includes index and bibliographical references.
ISBN 0-945193-59-9
1. Expatriate Musicians—Social conditions. 2. Music and Society. 3. Music—16th century—History and criticism. 4. Music—17th century—History and criticism. I. Series.
ML3795.W574 1995
780'.89'21--dc20

94-46265
CIP
MN

Contents

List of Illustrations

Acknowledgements

It is firstly a pleasure to acknowledge the generous financial support given to my work over several years by the Queen's University of Belfast. I am similarly indebted to the British Academy for a grant which enabled me to travel to Holland to study depictions of naval trumpeters in Dutch maritime paintings.

I am grateful to several colleagues (past and present) in the Department of Social Anthropology at Queen's, in particular Rembrandt Wolpert and Martin Stokes, for the loan of books and for directing my attention to sources which I would otherwise have missed.

For permission to reproduce works of art, thanks are due to: Her Majesty the Queen; The British Library; The Rijksmuseum, Amsterdam; The Nederlandsch Historisch Scheepvaart Museum; The Ulster Museum, Belfast; The National Maritime Museum, London; and the Fitzwilliam Museum, Cambridge.

Chapter 13 was first published in 1990 in the *Journal of the Royal Musical Association* under the title: "The Keyboard Recital in Oriental Diplomacy, 1520–1620." I am grateful to the editors for permission to reprint the material here.

This book is dedicated to my wife Thérèse for her constant support and encouragement, and to our three children—Rebecca, Jonathan, and Anna (aged two), who is just reaching her own "Age of Exploration."

Abbreviations

AHSI	*Archivum Historicum Societatis Iesu*
ASB	*Asiatic Society of Bengal*
BRS	*British Record Society*
Chelys	*Chelys: Journal of the Viola da Gamba Society*
CS	*Camden Society*
CSP	*Calendar of State Papers*
EHR	*English Historical Review*
EIU	*Erudición Ibero-Ultramarino*
EM	*Early Music*
HLB	*Huntingdon Library Bulletin*
HLQ	*Huntingdon Library Quarterly*
HMC	*Historical Manuscripts Commission*
HMYB	*Hinrichsen's Musical Year Book*
HS	*Hakluyt Society*
IJNA	*International Journal of Nautical Archaeology*
JAMS	*Journal of the American Musicological Society*
JMH	*Journal of Modern History*
JLSA	*Journal of the Lute Society of America*
JRMA	*Journal of the Royal Musical Association*
LSR	*Luttrell Society Reprints*
LV	*Linschoten Vereeniging*

MHSI	*Monumenta Historica Societatis Iesu*
ML	*Music and Letters*
MM	*Mariners Mirror*
MQ	*Musical Quarterly*
MT	*Musical Times*
NA	*Norfolk Archaeology*
NRS	*Navy Records Society*
PRSAM	*Publications of the Royal Swedish Academy of Music*
RMARC	*Royal Musical Association Research Chronicle*
VRS	*Van Riebeeck Society*

Introduction

When Sir Francis Drake (1540–1596) set sail from Plymouth on 15 November 1577 at the start of his epic circumnavigation of the world, he had with him on board the *Pelican* four professional musicians and at least one trumpeter. Preparations for the voyage were made in great secrecy to prevent news from reaching the ears of Spanish informers, and for this reason the musicians were almost certainly kept in ignorance of their destination. It is from subsequent accounts of the voyage that we learn of the presence of musicians and trumpeters on board, of their varied and active life at sea, and of their return to Plymouth in the renamed *Golden Hind* in September 1580. Simon Wood, Thomas Meckes, Richard Clarke and one "George" (the professional consort), together with the trumpeters led by John Brewer, thus became the first English musicians to pass through the Straits of Magellan into the Pacific Ocean.

This study takes as its central theme the part played by English musicians in the growth of the overseas interests of their country, from the accession of Elizabeth I to the end of the seventeenth century. The great period of expansion in English exploration and overseas trade begins with the early voyages to the New World of Sir John Hawkins, Sir Francis Drake, Sir Martin Frobisher and Sir Humphrey Gilbert, includes the founding of the Russia Company, the Levant Company, and the Barbary Company, and ends with the development of eastern trade on a large scale by the East India Company. All aspects of music associated with these developments are discussed.

Part 1 focuses upon the musical community of the long-distance sailing ship: the recruitment, training, and conditions of service of the professional musicians, the trumpeters, and the drummers; and musical life on board—the psalm singing, the military and ceremonial duties of the trumpeters, the activities of amateur musicians, and the special musical and theatrical entertainments devised for the pleasure of all on board.

In Part 2, the work of musicians in the two major theatres of English overseas enterprise is assessed. In North America, the vital role of musicians as ambassadors during tense periods of initial contact is emphasized, and their subsequent contribution to the process of exploration, conquest, and settlement analyzed. The important contributions made by musicians working for the eastern trading companies in establishing staging posts along the trade routes and in gaining permission to open factories is considered, and leads to an account of musical life in eastern settlements during the seventeenth century.

In Part 3, reactions to these developments are discussed. Few English composers showed any interest in the newly discovered parts of the world, a notable exception being Thomas Weelkes in his geographical madrigal "Thule." A new interpretation of this piece is given. The attitudes of English travelers to the indigenous musical cultures of America, Africa, and Asia are assessed. Finally, an interesting example of the process of acculturation in the English sphere of influence is presented. Rarely in the course of this study is it possible to consider English musicians in isolation. The other leading maritime nations of Europe—Portugal, Spain, France, and Holland—all made use of musicians in their own spheres of influence, and it is often revealing to make comparisons.

The literature of Renaissance exploration, together with that of the related fields of naval, military, economic, and early colonial history, is vast in scope. It is not my intention here to attempt a systematic survey of the original sources, even those most closely related to the history of English exploration; however, since readers whose interests lie chiefly in the history of music may well be unfamiliar with even the basic literature of sixteenth- and seventeenth-century exploration, some remarks on the most significant sources consulted in this study may be helpful.

The most valuable sources for the Elizabethan voyages are Hakluyt's two great collections. The first of these, entitled *The Principall Navigations, Voiages, and Discoveries of the English Nation,* was published in 1589. A facsimile edition was produced for the Hakluyt Society by Cambridge University Press in 1965.[1] A second, enlarged edition of the collection was published in three volumes in 1598, 1599

[1]The facsimile has an introduction by D. B. Quinn and R. A. Skelton and an index by A. Quinn.

and 1600. The title was that of the earlier work (note, however, the change of spelling—*The Principal Navigations*), but the new edition was more than twice the size of its predecessor. Unless otherwise indicated, all references to Hakluyt in this study are to the widely available edition of the 1598 collection, published in twelve volumes by James MacLehose (Glasgow, 1903–1905). For some details it will be necessary to consult the earlier edition, since Hakluyt pruned certain accounts for the 1598 edition. After his death in 1616, Hakluyt's work was continued by Samuel Purchas, whose *Hakluytus Posthumus, or Purchas His Pilgrimes, Contayning a History of the World in Sea Voyages and Land Travells by Englishmen and Others* (London, 1625) is a vast compilation of material. The editorial techniques employed by Purchas have been widely criticized (and with justice), but his great collection contains much of value, especially on the early years of the East India Company. References to Purchas in this study are to the edition published in twenty volumes by James MacLehose (Glasgow, 1905–1907). The journals of voyages contained in these three major collections rarely include much detail about musicians, but there is enough material to provide, at least in outline, a history of English musicians and the voyages of exploration.

Archival material concerning the Elizabethan voyages is only occasionally of direct use in the study of musicians. Lack of detail is the usual problem. Two sources, however, are of sufficient value to merit mention here: the financial accounts of Frobisher's three voyages to the Northwest, preserved in the Public Record Office (E 164/35 and 36), which contain details of payments to named trumpeters and of the purchase of bells for barter with the Eskimos[2]; and the Exchequer accounts of the last voyage of Drake and Hawkins to the West Indies in 1595 (E 351/2233), which contain details of payments to the musicians engaged for the expedition.[3] The particular value of sources of this type is that they provide information rarely found in journals, concerning the recruitment and payment of musicians.

For the seventeenth century, a wealth of material survives in the archives of the East India Company which are preserved in the

[2]A selection of the accounts for the 1576 voyage is in D. B. Quinn, *New American World: A Documentary History of North America to 1612*, Vol. 4: *Newfoundland from Fishery to Colony. Northwest Passage Searches* (London, 1979), 193–200.

[3]These accounts have been abridged in K. R. Andrews, *The Last Voyage of Drake and Hawkins* (*HS*, 2nd series, vol. 142, Cambridge, 1972).

India Office Library in London. Four extensive series of records contain information relevant to this study: (i) the Court Books—minutes of the meetings of the Company in London, which include information on matters such as the employment of musicians and the purchase of instruments for presentation in the East;[4] (ii) the Original Correspondence—letters received by the Company from its servants in the East, which occasionally include comments on the activities of musicians and reports on the success of their presentation instruments;[5] (iii) the Marine Records—the journals that the Company required all its captains to keep, which range from mere logs of weather, wind speed, and direction, to diaries of considerable significance, such as the journal of John Saris; (iv) the Factory Records—an extensive series of documents, which comprise the records of the consultations that took place in the overseas factories.[6] Potentially useful documents relating to the employment of musicians by the East India Company are the wills of individuals who died in the Company's service overseas or on board ship during the long voyages to and from India. The early seventeenth-century wills in the Commissary Court of London (London Division) are of particular interest as they include those of two musicians whose activities are described elsewhere.[7]

Taken together, the extant records of the East India Company give us an excellent impression of the ways in which England's largest overseas trading organization made use of musicians to further its ends in the Indian subcontinent. They provide us with a much better sense of continuity than is possible with the relatively patchy documentation of the earlier Elizabethan ventures.

[4]The Court Books and the Original Correspondence of the East India Company are calendared in W. N. Sainsbury, *CSP, Colonial Series, East Indies, China and Japan*, 5 vols. (London, 1862–1892). See also G. Birdwood and W. Foster, *The First Letterbook of the East India Company 1600–1619* (London, 1893).

[5]An edition of the early correspondence was begun by F. C. Danvers (vol. 1) and continued by W. Foster (vols. 2–6) as *Letters Received by the East India Company from its Servants in the East, 1602–1617* (London, 1896–1912).

[6]W. Foster, *The English Factories in India, 1618–69*, 13 vols. (Oxford, 1906–1927). C Fawcett, *The English Factories in India, 1670–1684* (new series), 4 vols. (Oxford, 1936–1955).

[7]M. Fitch, *Index to Testamentary Records in the Commissary Court of London (London Division), now preserved in Guildhall Library, London: Volume III, 1571–1625* (*BRS*, vol. 97; London, 1985).

Mention must be made of the publications of three societies. Easily the most valuable modern series in the field of Renaissance exploration is published under the auspices of the Hakluyt Society, which was founded in 1846 for the specific purpose of making available scholarly editions and translations of accounts of discovery and exploration. Over 250 volumes have appeared to date. The inclusion of so many translations in the series enhances its value and is particularly apt, given Hakluyt's very influential role in encouraging the translation of accounts of Portuguese, Spanish, French, and Dutch voyages. The scarcity of Dutch translations in this series after the First World War is explained by the founding of the *Linschoten Vereeniging* in 1909. In contrast to the wide-ranging efforts of the English society, the *Linschoten Vereeniging* restricts its enquiries to the voyages of the Dutch nation. One further series deserves mention: the publications of the Navy Records Society, which, being chiefly concerned with naval and military matters, complement the Hakluyt Society's field of interest.

To conclude, the single most valuable source of information about music in Portuguese, Spanish, and French colonies is the missionary report. These survive in huge quantities. I have made particular use of the *Monumenta Historica Societatis Iesu* and its various sub-series such as the *Documenta Indica*.

Part I

MUSICAL LIFE ON SHIPS

THE MUSICIANS

The first musicians to take part in long-distance voyages were almost certainly trumpeters. Ships of the medieval navies of Europe traditionally carried trumpeters and other musicians for military and ceremonial purposes, and the practice was continued by the Portuguese in their early voyages down the coast of Africa. The first English ships to cross the Atlantic doubtless also carried trumpeters, but there is little firm evidence. The extant documentation for John Cabot's 1497 voyage to Newfoundland does not refer directly to trumpeters, yet the Letters Patent granted for the expedition empowered Cabot to sail under the King's "banners, flags and ensigns," a dispensation that implies the presence of military musicians in the colors of their sovereign.[1] In his brief report of Cabot's formal claim to territory in Newfoundland, John Day described how a small party of Englishmen went on shore with a crucifix and raised "banners with the arms of the Holy Father and the King of England."[2] If later English "acts of possession" in the New World are any guide, then this would have been the moment for a ceremonial fanfare.

The first firm evidence of trumpeters on long-distance English voyages comes from the reign of Henry VIII. In 1527, John Rut sailed

[1]D. B. Quinn, *New American World: A Documentary History of North America to 1612*: Vol. 1, *America from Concept to Discovery. Early Exploration of North America* (London, 1979), 94.

[2]Ibid., 98.

across the Atlantic with two ships, one of which, the *Mary Guildford*, was sighted near Santo Domingo. In a report of the incident, a Spaniard described how the English vessel set sail with someone "playing a bastard trumpet"("tocando una trompeta bastarda").[3] Legal depositions concerning the voyage of the *Barbara* to Brazil in 1540 show that one of the twelve Frenchmen on board was a trumpeter. A witness mentioned the desertion of four Frenchmen, "the pilotte, the pilottes boye, ther barber, ther trumpetor."[4] Others also referred in the singular to "oure trumpetor"and "ther trumpetor."[5] These early English voyages across the Atlantic were small in scale, and a single trumpeter may well have been deemed sufficient.

In the 1550s, with the Guinea voyages of Wyndham, Lok, and Towerson, English trade with West Africa began to expand rapidly. The larger scale of these voyages necessitated the recruitment of full bands of trumpeters as well as drum and fife players. The report of Towerson's second voyage to Guinea in 1556 is the first account to give detailed information about their duties. While stationed off the coast of Guinea, Towerson met up with three French ships, "verie finely appointed with their streamers, and pendants, and ensignes and noyse of trumpets."[6] The English and French captains agreed to trade together in defiance of the Portuguese. Towerson ordered five boats, "well appointed with men and ordinance, and with our noises of trumpets and drummes," to enter the river to barter.[7] Several days later they returned, the largest boat "with four trumpets, a drumme, and a fife."[8] One of Towerson's trumpeters was a Frenchman, whose dying moments brought forth the following comment: "We had aboord us a Frenchman, a trumpetter, who, being sicke and lying in his bed, tooke his trumpet notwithstanding, and sounded till he could sound no more, and so died."[9] The employment of French trumpeters on English ships was not uncommon at this period. The

[3]F. A. Kirkpatrick, "The First Recorded English Voyage to the West Indies," *EHR*, vol. 20 (1905), 117. See also Quinn (1979), 192–93.

[4]R. G. Marsden, "Voyage of the Barbara to Brazil, Anno 1540," in J. K. Laughton, ed., *The Naval Miscellany*, vol. 2 (*NRS*, vol. 40; London, 1912), 20.

[5]Ibid., 32 and 35.

[6]J. W. Blake, *Europeans in West Africa, 1450–1560*, vol. 2 (*HS*, 2nd series, vol. 87; London, 1942), 394.

[7]Ibid., 399.

[8]Ibid., 400.

[9]Ibid., 410.

greater experience of the French in transatlantic voyages to North America and Brazil led the English to make good use of their pilots, trumpeters and interpreters, just as, half a century later, Englishmen with professional skills (again pilots and musicians in particular) were hired by the Dutch for some of their early voyages to the East Indies.

The trumpeters of a mid-century Guinea ship feature in Robert Baker's poem, celebrating his 1563 voyage:[10]

> Our Trumpetter aloft
> now sounds the feats of war,
> The brasen pieces roving oft
> fling forth both chaine and bar.

In the heat of battle, the sound of the trumpets encourages the men:

> And still the trumpets sound
> with pleasant blast doth cheare
> Ech Mariner, so in that stound
> that they nothing did feare.

The regular recruitment of a full "noise" of trumpets for the Guinea voyages of the 1550s and the early 1560s gave a significant number of English musicians a taste of work on long-distance sailing ships.

[10]R. Hakluyt: *The Principall Navigations Voiages and Discoveries of the English Nation* (London, 1589). Facsimile edition with an introduction by D. B. Quinn (Cambridge, 1965), 136. Baker's poems were omitted from the enlarged edition of 1598.

CHAPTER 1

The Professional Consorts

The third slaving expedition of John Hawkins round the infamous triangle between England, West Africa, and the West Indies is the first long-distance voyage for which there is direct evidence of the employment of civilian musicians. They were mentioned by Miles Phillips in an account of the prisoners captured at San Juan de Ulúa in 1568. Among the men taken to face the Inquisition in Spain were the Master of the *Jesus*, Robert Barret: "and with him three or foure more of our men, of whom one was named Gregorie, and another John Browne, whom I knew, for they were of our Generall his Musitians."[1] The transportation of the musicians to Spain suggests that the Inquisition was keen to interrogate personal servants of Hawkins himself. The addition of a professional consort to the normal muster of a long-distance sailing fleet increased the number of musicians who were able to find employment at sea, and set a pattern of music-making on board English ships that was to persist until the Civil War.

In 1577 Drake hired a consort of musicians for his circumnavigation. The author of one account wrote: "neither had he omitted to make provision also for ornament and delight, carrying to this purpose, with him, expert musitians."[2] There are several clues to the instruments played by Drake's musicians. At Ternate in the Moluccas, the local ruler was received thus: at the approach of his canoe,

[1]R. Hakluyt, *The Principall Navigations Voiages and Discoveries of the English Nation* (London, 1589), 572. This statement was omitted from the enlarged edition of 1598.

[2]W. S. W. Vaux, *The World Encompassed by Sir Francis Drake* (*HS*, vol. 16; London, 1854), 7.

"our ordinance thundred, which wee mixed with great store of small shot, among which sounding our trumpets and other instruments of musick, both of still and loud noise."[3] No fewer than three independent sources testify to the fact that the "still" music on board the *Golden Hind* included string instruments, probably a viol consort. The best known of these is a letter dated 16 April 1579, written by Don Francisco de Zarate, a Spanish nobleman captured by Drake. Zarate's oft-quoted description of Drake included the observation that he dined and supped to the music of "vigolones."[4] A second Spanish reference to string instruments comes in a deposition made by the Factor of Guatulco in 1580. He described how, after reading the psalms, the Englishmen took out four "bihuelas de arco."[5] The only English eyewitness to mention string instruments was Edward Cliffe, who described an occasion on the shores of South America when a group of natives appeared "exceedingly delighted with the sound of the trumpet and vialles."[6]

The names of Drake's string players can be established with some certainty. Among the papers relating to the voyage in the Public Record Office is a document signed by 49 members of Drake's company.[7] Three of these men—Simon Wood, Thomas Meckes and Richard Clarke—were musicians, a fact established by their subsequent employment. A fourth name is recorded by Purchas, admittedly a late source[8]: "George a Musician" is listed among the men "noated to have compassed the world with Drake."

While Drake was still in the East, Sir Humphrey Gilbert began recruiting musicians for a voyage across the Atlantic. Details of the personnel of his fleet before departure on 19 November 1578 are given in a document entitled "The Names of all the shippes officers and gentlemen." In the flagship, the *Anne Aucher*, commanded by Gilbert himself, were six "musitians," one "trumpiter" and one "drume." Of the remaining six ships, the *Hope of Greenway* had one

[3]Ibid., 141.

[4]Z. Nuttall, *New Light on Drake* (*HS*, 2nd series, vol. 34; London, 1914), 207.

[5]Ibid., 355.

[6]Vaux (1854), 277.

[7]Nuttall (1914), 422–28.

[8]Purchas, 16:118.

"trumpiter," but the smaller vessels were not provided with musicians of any kind.[9]

Edward Fenton's unsuccessful attempt to reach China in 1582 is one of the few Elizabethan voyages for which the names of the musicians are known. The first list of the expedition's personnel is presented in a manuscript in the British Library, Cotton, Otho. E. VIII, fol. 151, which records the deliberations of the Council held on 20 March 1582: "Hereafter followeth the nomber of those that are appointed to goe in the shipps besyde the Marrinors." In the *Galleon*, to be commanded by Fenton himself, there were to be "iii mewsitiones" and in the *Edward Bonaventure*, to be commanded by Luke Ward, there were to be "ii mewsitiones." Between them the two ships were to carry 200 men.[10] A more detailed list appears in the diary of Richard Maddox, chaplain to the voyage. His muster lists the names of those who actually sailed.[11] In the *Galleon* were: Symon Wood, Thomas Meeke, Richard Clark, and John Kennar (musicians); two unnamed players (drum and fyf); Christofer Jacson, John Rawlyns, and Ambrose Harrison (trumpeters). In the *Edward Bonaventure* were: Tege Caroe, John Vobs, and Robert Wood (trumpeters); Davy Lake and Robert Pemberton (drum and fyfe). No musicians were carried in the two small vessels, the *Bark Francis* and the *Elizabeth*. On 5 May, while the fleet was riding out bad weather at Cowes off the Isle of Wight, Maddox assisted the four musicians during the allocation of storage space: "we fel a romeging chests and I for example was content to let the musicians have myne cause they were apoynted 4 to a chest, but cold se none do so els but my self."[12]

Several of Fenton's musicians had previous experience of life at sea. Simon Wood, Richard Clarke, and Thomas Meckes were all veterans of the circumnavigation. The diary of Maddox gives us an occasional glimpse of the musician Wood as the knowledgeable traveler. On one occasion, six whelps were cut out of the "belly" of a shark and thrown back in the sea. They swam away, reported Maddox, "as thogh they had been old knaves." An explanation of the

[9]D. B. Quinn, *The Voyages and Colonising Enterprises of Sir Humphrey Gilbert*, vol. 1 (*HS*, 2nd series, vol. 83; London, 1940), 211.

[10]E. G. R. Taylor, *The Troublesome Voyage of Captain Edward Fenton 1582–1583* (*HS*, 2nd series, vol. 113; Cambridge, 1959), 35–36.

[11]Ibid., 157–59.

[12]E. S. Donno, *An Elizabethan in 1582* (*HS*, 2nd series, vol. 147; London, 1976), 129.

phenomenon was then given by the musician: "Simon Wod sayeth 4 more fel owt of his mowth in haling fro the galery to the ship and that she wil let them yn and take them owt lyk an adder."[13] On another occasion, Wood was able to supply Maddox with a balme: "Having byn hytherto very yll and unable to brook any meat, Symon Wood gave me 3 drops of artificial oyl for 3 mornings which dryed up my rewme and did me much good and surely yt is a very exelant balme and cost a noble an ounce."[14]

One of the trumpeters, Christopher Jackson, was an equally experienced sailor, having accompanied Frobisher in 1577 and 1578.[15] He was also something of a raconteur. On Christmas Eve of 1582, a group of officers including the purser, the lieutenant, and the trumpeter were, in the absence of wind, entertaining each other by swapping yarns. Jackson contributed two tales of unusual betrothals.[16]

One of the musicians died during the voyage. A laconic entry in Fenton's own journal for 5 February simply states that "Ric Clarks arme being cutt of he dyed," presumably after amputation by the surgeon.[17]

In his account of Sir Humphrey Gilbert's 1583 voyage, Edward Hayes noted the presence of musicians: "we were provided of Musicke in good variety."[18] Later he described vividly the "swan-song" of the musicians aboard the *Delight*, the day before her wreck:

> The evening was faire and pleasant, yet not without token of storme to ensue, and most part of this Wednesday night, like the Swanne that singeth before her death, they in the Admiral, or Delight, continued in sounding of Trumpets, with Drummes, and Fifes: also winding the Cornets, Haughtboyes: and in the end of their jolitie, left with the battell and ringing of dolefull knels.[19]

[13]Ibid., 204.

[14]Ibid., 152.

[15]Payments to Jackson are recorded in the accounts in the Public Record Office: E 164/35, fols. 56v and 71v. He was employed on the *Ayde* during Frobisher's third voyage. See G. B. Parks, "Frobisher's Third Voyage, 1578," *HLB*, vol. 7 (1935), 190.

[16]Donno (1976), 271–72.

[17]Taylor (1959), 133.

[18]D. B. Quinn, *The Voyages and Colonising Enterprises of Sir Humphrey Gilbert*, vol. 2 (*HS*, 2nd series, vol. 84; London, 1940), 396.

[19]Ibid., 412.

A death at sea was traditionally marked by the sounding of a knell on the trumpets. The sounding of knells, as the Admiral took leave of his consorts, was seen by Hayes as an act of uncanny prescience. The following day, during a violent storm, the *Delight* was wrecked with the loss of nearly all on board, including, one must assume, the musicians. Gilbert himself had previously elected to travel on the *Squirrel*, a small frigate, for the purpose of searching "into every harbor or creeke, which a great ship could not doe."[20]

For his first voyage to discover a Northwest passage in 1585, John Davis employed four musicians. Two barks, the *Sunneshine* of London and the *Mooneshine* of Dartmouth, carried a total of 42 men. The 23 who sailed on the *Sunneshine* are named individually; the list includes: "James Cole, Francis Ridley, John Russell, Robert Cornish Musicians."[21] This is the smallest voyage for which a full consort of musicians is known to have been employed. They comprised nearly one tenth of the total muster.

Musicians are mentioned in Spanish depositions concerning Drake's capture of San Agostín in Florida in June 1586. Having described the preparations for the attack, the landing of men and artillery, one witness reported that: "it was understood that Francis Drake, corsair, was among them because where they set up the artillery in the afternoon there was music of cornets, sackbuts and fifes." The sound of the wind band was enough to convince him that the English commander was present, even though he did not actually sight him. Another man, who did see Drake, also reported that the English captain came ashore "with all his music."[22]

The 1585 expedition sent out to colonise Roanoke Island included musicians. The first reference to their presence on board Sir Richard Grenville's ships comes in a report by Hernado de Altamirano, a Spaniard captured in the West Indies. Writing of the English colonists, he commented: "they brought with them many musical instruments, 'chirimias' [shawms], organs and others, because, they said, the Indians liked music."[23] It is not known for certain

[20]Ibid., 409.

[21]Hakluyt, 7:382.

[22]I. A. Wright, *Further English Voyages to Spanish America* (*HS*, 2nd series, vol. 99; London, 1951), 199 and 182.

[23]D. B. Quinn, *The Roanoke Voyages 1584–1590*, vol. 2 (*HS*, 2nd series, vol. 105; London, 1955), 741.

whether there were musicians among the settlers themselves, because the Spaniard may well have been referring to Grenville's own consort. In June, Grenville put in at the port of Isabela on the northern coast of Hispaniola, where he was received with courtesy by the Spanish Governor. The Englishmen erected two banquetting houses and served a sumptuous feast "with the sound of trumpets and consort of musick, wherewith the spanyards were more than delighted."[24] The English colony was settled on Roanoke Island during the months of July and August, then Grenville set sail for England. Off Bermuda he captured another Spanish ship. On board was a Portuguese merchant, Enrique Lopez, who later made a statement in which he described Grenville as a man of quality for whom "many musical instruments" were played when he dined.[25]

The fate of the Roanoke colony is unknown. The men sent out in 1590 to find the settlers believed that they had located their countrymen when they saw the light of a great fire through the woods. They rowed close to the shore and "sounded with a trumpet a Call, and afterwardes many familiar English tunes of songs, and called to them friendly," but there was no reply.[26]

Little is known of the musicians who accompanied Thomas Cavendish on the second English circumnavigation. The death of "Ambrose the musitian," drowned during a skirmish with the Spanish off the Pacific coast of South America, is recorded in June 1587.[27] At least some of the musicians were still alive in March 1588 when, during a stay at Java, Cavendish arranged a reception in honor of a visitor: "Our Generall used him singularly well, banquetted him most royally, with the choyce of many and sundry conserves, wines both sweete and other, and caused his Musitians to make him music."[28] A few days later, Cavendish received two Portuguese men on board. Again, music was provided: "our Generall used and intreated them singularly well, with banquets and musicke."[29]

[24]D. B. Quinn, *The Roanoke Voyages 1584–1590*, vol. 1 (*HS*, 2nd series, vol. 104; London, 1955), 186.

[25]Wright (1951), 15.

[26]Quinn (1955), 2:13.

[27]Hakluyt, 11:318 .

[28]Ibid., 338.

[29]Ibid., 339.

A valuable document concerning the hire of musicians for Drake's expedition to Portugal in 1589 survives in the Norwich Court Book. The report is entitled thus: "The waytes to go to London to Sr Fraunceys Drake." Details are given of some of the instruments and sundry items provided by the city:

> This daye was redd in the court A letter sent to Mr Maior and his brethren from Sr Fraunceys Drake wherby he desyreth that the waytes of this Citie may bee sent to hym to go the new intendid voyage, whereunto the waytes beyng here called doe all assent; whereupon it is agreed that they shall have vj cloakes of Stamell cloath made them redy before they go; And that A wagon shalbe provided to carry them and their Instrumentes; And that they shall have iiij^{li} to buye them Three new howboyes and one treble recordr and x^{li} to beare their Chardgys; And that the Citie shall hyer the Wagon and paye for it; Also that the Chamberleyn shall paye Peter Spratt x^{s} for a Saquebutt Case; And the waytes to delyver to the Chamberlyn before they go the Cities cheanes.[30]

The use of city waits on a voyage is certainly unusual, but in the prevailing mood of nationalist fervor, one year after the defeat of the Armada, the decision of the Norwich Council to release their musicians for service with Drake, and indeed to equip them with replacement instruments and cloaks, was probably intended as a patriotic gesture. For most of the waits, the invitation was also their death warrant.

The details of the instruments provided by the Mayor (presumably to replace damaged or sub-standard instruments) show that in addition to the regular outdoor wind band (for which the new "howboyes" were provided) the waits proposed to take at least one other set of soft instruments—their recorders. The Norwich Waits are known to have possessed a case of five recorders, which was described in 1585 as "beeying a Whoall noyse."[31] It is possible that the treble recorder purchased for the voyage was an additional instrument for a sixth player. There seem to have been five regular waits at this period, but the purchase of six cloaks shows that Drake had requested six players.

[30]G. A. Stephen, "The Waits of the City of Norwich through Four Centuries to 1790," *NA*, vol. 25 (1933), 1.

[31]W. Edwards, "Consort" (*The New Grove*; London, 1980).

The return of the chains to the Chamberlain before the departure of the waits deserves some comment. When travelling locally to towns and cities near to the place of their employment, it was the custom for waits to retain their own liveries and insignia of office.[32] In this instance, however, it seems that the waits were in effect being discharged from service at Norwich. A new employer would require a new livery, which may account for the purchase of the stamell cloaks. Stamell, incidentally, was a coarse wollen material, usually dyed red, which was well suited to outdoor use. Several bands of waits are known to have worn it.[33]

A single reference betrays the presence of musicians on the disastrous last voyage of Cavendish in 1591. In his journal, Anthony Knivet paints a graphic picture of the undisciplined conduct of the English sailors when they landed on the coast of Brazil to look for food: "And as wee went, wee encountred with seven or eight of our companie that were together by the eares about a Hogge they had killed, and the strife was, who should have the best share." While everyone was brawling, Knivet and his companions stole a quarter of the beast and went inland to eat it. Returning with supplies the following day, they chanced upon the musicians in a house: "the next day wee came backe againe with good store of Potato rootes; and going into the house where the Generals musicians were, wee found them dressing of eight yong Whelpes for their dinner; wee giving them of our rootes they were contented that wee should dine with them."[34]

The departure of Sir Richard Hawkins from Plymouth on 12 June 1593 was marked first with his "noyse of trumpets," then with his "waytes" and finally with his "other musicke."[35] In addition to his "noise of trumpets," Hawkins may have had the luxury of two bands of musicians—waits, probably playing shawms, and other musicians, possibly playing string instruments, but in view of the circumstances, more probably playing cornets and sackbuts.

[32]W. L. Woodfill, *Musicians in English Society from Elizabeth to Charles I* (Princeton, 1953), 103–4.

[33]L. G. Langwill, "The Waits: a Short Historical Study," *HMYB*, vol. 7 (1952), 175.

[34]Purchas, 16:180.

[35]C. R. Drinkwater-Bethune, *The Observations of Sir Richard Hawkins, Knt, in his Voyage into the South Sea in the Year 1593* (*HS*, vol. 1; London, 1847), 30.

The fleet that set sail for the West Indies in 1595 under the command of Drake and John Hawkins was an unusually large one, comprising some 27 ships and about 2500 men. The detailed Exchequer Accounts of the voyage in the Public Record Office (E.351/2233) indicate that at least nineteen musicians and sixteen trumpeters were recruited:[36]

> Chardges concerninge xj musitions and vij Trumpettors at London and Plymouth viz for their Boordwages and Lodginge after the rate of vij^{s} the man by the weeke at lxxij^{li} iiij^{s}; And for apparell at xj^{li} x^{s}. In all iiijxx xiij^{s}.'
>
> Chardges of viij musitions and ix Trumpettors for Sr John Hawkyns Squadron for xj weeke being the time they were at London and Plymouth attendinge the said voyage—lx^{li} ix^{s}."[37]

The unusually large number of musicians is in part explained by the fact that the fleet was under joint command, but the eleven musicians taken by Drake comprised probably the largest single group employed on an Elizabethan voyage—enough to form, say, a five-part wind ensemble and a mixed consort of six. There is some evidence that this was indeed the disposition of Drake's musicians. After the return of the expedition, a legal dispute arose between Thomas Drake and Jonas Bodenham, the men who had assumed command of the *Defiance* after their leader's death. One of the documents concerning the case in the Public Record Office (C.2/33/96, Richard Drake v Jonas Bodenham, 1598) mentions "a chest of instrumentes of musicke" that had been removed from the *Defiance* which contained a lute, "hobboyes sagbutes cornettes and orpharions bandora and suche like."[38] This very much suggests a wind band and a mixed consort of the standard pattern: lute, bandora, cittern, treble and bass viols, and flute. Why these instruments were left in the ship is unclear. Either they belonged to Drake himself, perhaps supplementing his musicians' personal instruments, or they belonged to those musicians killed in the voyage. The Exchequer Accounts also

[36]This document, in an abbreviated form, is published as Document 14 in K. R. Andrews, *The Last Voyage of Drake and Hawkins* (*HS*, 2nd series, vol. 142; Cambridge, 1972).

[37]Other payments appear under "Diverse Persons for their Wages Rewardes and Necessaries": "To six musicions—xv^{li}"; "And to xviij Trumpettors and musitions—lxxi^{s}".

[38]Andrews (1972), 55.

include a single payment to the musicians of Hawkins's squadron: "Sondrie Instrumentes of musicke for viij musitions and ix trumpettors—xiiij^{li} xj^{s}." A payment of £14 11 shillings would not have equipped seventeen musicians with instruments. The sum must therefore have been intended to pay for any deficiencies—lost cases, broken instruments etc. Drums for the companies of foot soldiers were purchased: "Drumes viz ij at xxx^{s} the peece lx^{s} and xj boughte by agreement at xiiij^{li}. In all—xvii^{li}."

Immediately after the payment to Drake's musicians in the Exchequer Accounts comes the following entry: "Simon Wood for his entertaynment and chardges by the space of ciiijxx ix daies ended the xijth of June 1595 at xij^{d} per diem." A payment was also made to a man "to serve in his place at the Tower." If this Simon Wood was indeed the veteran of the circumnavigation, it suggests that Drake may have been using him as a recruiting agent. Presumably he was serving in some capacity at the Tower, perhaps as a wait—hence the payment for a temporary replacement.

From the evidence presented thus far it is possible to reconstruct with some confidence the normal pattern of employment of musicians engaged to serve on Elizabethan voyages. Recruitment seems to have taken place in London from the available "pool" of independent professionals. Once they had been engaged, musicians could expect to receive payment for the journey to the port of embarkation and during any delays caused by bad weather. The musicians were hired, in a formal sense, as part of the retinue of the leader of the expedition. Although their usual place was on the flagship, they were not attached to any one vessel as such. If the commander transferred to another ship or disembarked, the musicians would remain in attendance. Only in unusual circumstances (such as those that saved the life of Gilbert in 1583) would the musicians travel on another ship.

The number of musicians employed on voyages remained fairly constant throughout the reign of Elizabeth (the 1595 expedition being altogether exceptional). A basic consort of four to six players (excluding trumpeters) seems to have been the norm. The following is a summary of the known employment of musicians by Elizabethan commanders. A consort of an unspecified number is assumed to have consisted of a minimum of four—in those cases where exact figures are known, it is never less than this:

Table 1

Year	*Navigator*	*Number in Consort*
1567	Hawkins and Drake	4+
1577	Drake	4
1578	Gilbert	6
1582	Fenton	4
1583	Gilbert	4+
1585	Davis	4
1585	Grenville	4+
1585	Drake	4+
1586	Cavendish	4+
1589	Drake	6
1591	Cavendish	4+
1593	Hawkins	4+
1595	Hawkins and Drake	19

In assessing these figures, it should be remembered that a few musicians are known to have been reemployed. By 1585, however, it seems likely that there were at least three consorts of musicians with up to twenty musicians in all, serving on English ships across the Atlantic. Those Elizabethan commanders who are known to have employed musicians on one or more voyages—Drake, Gilbert, Fenton, Davis, Grenville, Cavendish, and John and Richard Hawkins—no doubt did so on all the ventures that they undertook, and it is a reasonable inference that others, such as Raleigh, did so as well. How far the practice extended to the privateering ventures, though, is debatable.

The single most important factor determining the recruitment of musicians was not the purpose of the expedition, nor the degree to which it was officially sanctioned, but quite simply the status of its commander. The Earl of Cumberland, one of England's leading privateers, may well have employed professional musicians on the flagships of his fleets. Even for a figure of his importance, however, the evidence is far from conclusive. Spanish depositions concerning an English raid in 1593 by ships of Cumberland's Seventh Voyage speak of "martial music" and the "trumpets and other instruments" played by the Englishmen as they attempted to land.[39] These "other instruments" were either drums and fifes or a wind band—probably the latter. But whether the host of lesser corsairs who sailed the waters of the Caribbean during the 1590s carried musicians other than trumpeters and drummers is doubtful. The employment of professional musicians on most of the major voyages of exploration and on at least some of the privateering ventures suggests that by the last two decades of Elizabeth's reign, at least a score of musicians (and a very much larger number of trumpeters and drummers) were in maritime employment at any one time.

The regular recruitment of a single consort of four to six musicians on the Elizabethan voyages points to the fact that versatility was at a premium. Woodfill argued convincingly, from limited evidence, that many of the important bands of city waits were able to play both wind and string instruments by the 1580s and 1590s.[40] It is clear that the independent professionals employed on the voyages were similarly talented. Indeed, the regular presence of musicians among these isolated communities at sea, away often for long periods, may actually have encouraged the general tendency of good professional bands to play a variety of instruments. The usual requirement at sea was for a wind band for ceremonial purposes with an additional consort of string instruments. The generally cramped conditions prevalent inside Elizabethan ships must have imposed some limitation on the number of instruments taken. Lack of storage space was certainly a problem in 1582 when Maddox felt obliged to give up a chest to the four musicians who apparently had but one chest between them. On the other hand, additional sets of small instruments, such as the recorders taken by the Norwich Waits, would have made valuable replacements for lost or damaged instruments. The action of the climate and sea air, together with the rough outdoor conditions in which instruments were often played during voyages, probably resulted in constant loss and breakage.

On the return of a fleet, the musicians, like most of the company, could expect to be discharged. The Exchequer Accounts concerning the refurbishment of ships in dock (Public Record Office E. 351/2193–

[39]K. R. Andrews, *English Privateering Voyages to the West Indies 1588–1595* (*HS*, 2nd series, vol. 111; Cambridge, 1959), 258 and 260.

[40]Woodfill (1953), 85–86 .

2333) indicate that while ships were being refitted, only a few gunners and watchmen were retained for security reasons. Unless they had a prior agreement, perhaps to accompany their commander while he made his report, surviving musicians probably returned to London to seek further engagements.

In the closing years of the 16th century, a significant new source of maritime employment became available to English musicians just across the Channel. The first Dutch voyage to the East Indies, under the command of Cornelis de Houtman, set sail in 1595. Its return in 1597 led directly to the rapid growth of Dutch interest in the East. In 1598, no fewer than four Dutch fleets were sent: eight ships under the command of Jacob van Neck and Wybrandt van Warwick and two ships under Cornelis de Houtman sailed for the Cape of Good Hope; five ships under the command of Jacob Mahu and four ships under Olivier van Noort sailed for the Straits of Magellan. Given the scale of the Dutch entry into the eastern hemisphere, it is hardly surprising that there were shortages of experienced men. The Dutch turned for assistance to their great ally. English pilots were recruited; John Davis, William Adams, and Captain Melis, all experienced men, were hired, respectively, for the fleets of Houtman, Mahu, and Noort.[41] Purchas considered their exploits "honours to the English."[42] The organizers of the 1598 ventures also recognized the value of experienced musicians and trumpeters. They therefore recruited musicians from London in significant numbers for the fleets of Mahu and Noort, and perhaps for the others as well.

The English musicians engaged to sail on the five ships commanded by Mahu are mentioned in records of the examination of the survivors from *De Blijde Boodschap* (the "Good News") which was taken by the Spaniards in Chile.[43] On the fourth ship, *De Trouw* ("The Fidelity"), there were apparently six English trumpeters, five of whom, according to one witness, were dead by the time that their ship passed through the Straits of Magellan. There were also a number of English string players. One of the Dutch captives de-

[41]William Adams mentions another English pilot in the fleet, "my good friend Timothy Shotten," Purchas, 2:330.

[42]Ibid., 187.

[43]F. C. Weider, *De Reis van Mahu en de Cordes door de Straat van Magalhaes naar Zuid-Amerika en Japan 1598–1600*, vol. 1 (*LV*, vol. 21; The Hague, 1923), 62–67.

scribed them as "musicos de biguela de arcos" ("viol players"), another as "musicos de ynstrumentos de cuerda de todo genero" ("players of string instruments of every kind") and a third as "musicos de cuerda" ("string players").[44] These comments suggest that Englishmen provided the Dutch fleet with a viol consort and perhaps with a mixed consort as well. The musicians almost certainly died during the course of the voyage, which was beset by a series of crippling disasters. The flagship of the fleet, on which they presumably sailed, was lost in a violent storm in the Pacific.

The Dutch fleet commanded by Noort employed one musician from London, John Caleway, who is described as "een speelman ende goed Musicien" ("a player and good musician").[45] His disappearance in the Philippines in 1600 was thought worthy of note: "Here they lost a Londoner, John Calewey, an excellent Musician surprized, as was suspected by some insidiarie Indians."[46] Several villages were destroyed in retaliation for the abduction and presumed murder of this man.

The English musicians employed on these fleets naturally worked alongside Dutch players. The smallest ship of Mahu's fleet, for example, had a trumpeter named Laurens, born of Dutch parents in Bergen, Norway,[47] and John Caleway, Noort's English musician, was accompanied by at least two Dutch trumpeters, David Davidsz and Pieter Jansz.[48] It is impossible to ascertain whether any of the English musicians who sailed with Mahu and Noort had any previous experience, but, collectively, these men came from a profession whose experience of long-distance voyages, successful and unsuccessful, went back several decades. There is some evidence of further Dutch recruitment of English trumpeters. In 1599, the muster rolls for the voyage of Jacob Wilkens and Jacob van Neck show that there were six Englishmen, of whom four were trumpeters from London.[49]

[44]J. W. IJzerman, *Dirck Gerritsz Pomp alias Dirck Gerritsz China de Eerste Nederlander die China en Japan Bezocht 1544–1604* (*LV*, vol. 9; The Hague, 1915), 66.

[45]J. W. IJzerman, *De Reis om de Wereld door Olivier van Noort 1598–1601*, vol. 1 (LV, vol. 27; The Hague, 1925), 99 and 183.

[46]Purchas, 2:199.

[47]Weider (1923), 62–67.

[48]J. W. IJzerman, *De Reis om de Wereld door Olivier van Noort 1598–1601*, vol. 2 (*LV*, vol. 28; The Hague, 1926), 67 and 69.

[49]J. H. A. van Foreest and A. de Booy, *De Vierde Schipvaart der Nederlanders naar Oost-Indië onder Jacob Wilkens en Jacob van Neck (1599–1604)*, vol. 2 (LV, vol. 83; The Hague, 1981), 196 .

The extent to which English musicians continued to serve on fleets of the Dutch East India Company in the early seventeenth century is uncertain. It seems likely, however, that English participation declined steadily after the high point of the years 1598 and 1599. With the rapid expansion of Dutch interests in the East, their own pilots and musicians quickly gained experience. Moreover, the cordiality which marked the early contacts between the two nations in the East soon gave way to a period of intense rivalry. Systematic recruitment of English musicians by the Dutch East India Company—as opposed to the hiring of freelance individuals, which continued unabated—probably declined during this period of deteriorating relations, even before the first arrival in Europe of reports of the "Massacre at Amboina"—a celebrated and hotly disputed incident in which a group of English factors on the Island of Amboina were accused of plotting against the Dutch factory and then executed after a cursory trial.

The emergence of the London East India Company as a major employer of professional musicians was the most significant factor in the growth in the number of English musicians serving on ships in the early seventeenth century. The Elizabethan companies, notably the Barbary Company, the Russia Company, and the Levant Company, all made periodic use of keyboard players and other musicians to accompany the instruments sent as diplomatic gifts, but it was not until the East India Company began its long series of annual sailings to the East that full professional consorts were employed in significant numbers by any trading organization. Hakluyt's advice to the Company in London on the necessity of hiring musicians for their fleets was unequivocal. In a memorandum entitled "Certain notes gathered of such as have had much familiaritie with the Portugales that trade in the East Indies," he wrote: "a jueller, a paynter, and certayne musisians are very necessarie for the voyage."[50] There is no independent confirmation, however, that professional musicians (as opposed to trumpeters and drummers) traveled on any of the early voyages of the Company. Not until the Sixth Voyage of 1610 is there firm evidence to show that the Company was following Hakluyt's advice.

[50]E. G. R. Taylor, *The Original Writings and Correspondence of the two Richard Hakluyts*, vol. 2 (*HS*, 2nd series, vol. 77; London, 1935), 482.

Four letters in the Original Correspondence of the Company relate to an incident during the Sixth Voyage when one of Sir Henry Middleton's musicians lost his instruments. The fleet had been instructed to call at Aden and Mocha, near the entrance to the Red Sea, with a view to establishing trade there. At first Sir Henry was well received, but, without warning, he and his companions were seized and held captive. In May 1611 the Englishmen contrived an escape. They had been moved from the "faire large house appointed us neere the Seaside" to a more closely guarded building in the town center, but after supplying their warders with drink, Middleton was able to slip away in an empty cask.[51] Most of the English party reached the safety of their ship, the *Trades Increase*, but Lawrence Femell and a few others were recaptured.

In the series of letters which then passed between Middleton and Femell are four that concern the loss of some musical instruments during the escape.[52] On 18 May 1611 Middleton wrote to Femell: "I pray yow send Mr Bownes his Bible Cornett Viall and what other Bookes and Instrumentes are heare." William Bownes, one of the party who escaped with Middleton, had evidently abandoned his belongings in the rush to leave. Femell replied from Mocha on 20 May that the instruments had been mislaid: "and for Mr Bownes thinges wth manie others is conveyed out of our howse, whereof noe tidinges cann bee heard; yoar Red prayer booke likewise is gonne; we have made inquiry for it, wth promise of recompence, to him that bringes newes of it, but as yet wee cannot understand what is become of it." As a postscript he added: "wee send yow all the Singinge Bookes that cann be fownd aboute the howse by this Bearer." Three days later, Femell, evidently in reply to a further request for information, confirmed that the instruments were no longer in the house: "Mr Boones Cornett, nor Treble voyall were left in the escape, as wee wrotte yow in our former, if we had fownd the same in the howse, it had bine sent wth the 3 singinge Bookes formerly sent, beinge all that wee could find Remayninge." On the same day, Middleton again wrote asking about the instruments: "If yow heere of the Cornute or treble vyall hereafter yow may send them; lay waite of them for the Consort

[51]Purchas, 3:154–59.

[52]India Office Library, East India Company, Original Correspondence, nos. 57, 61, 67, and 68. See F. C. Danvers, *Letters Received by the East India Company from its Servants in the East*, vol. 1 (London, 1896), 112, 115, 122, and 123.

is spoyled wthout them; the Cornute was left standinge in a Corner of the howse where J^{no} Cooke dyed."

From the evidence of these letters we may deduce with a fair degree of certainty two facts about the professional consort employed on the *Trades Increase*. Firstly, when Sir Henry Middleton originally disembarked at Mocha, he was accompanied by his musicians who remained with him during his captivity, apparently at liberty to perform. This is confirmed by Thomas Love's version of the Mocha incident: "This day att night, our Generall, with all our carpendoners and trompetters, our cornites, our master-surgane, our porser, with some of our marchantes, our chef marchant, and others of theme, with some of our sayleres to the nomber of 48, were all takene."[53] Secondly, William Bownes was the "treble" player of both a string and a wind consort, possibly also a singer. Middleton's musicians, then, were versatile professionals like the London and Norwich waits. The loss of both treble instruments, not surprisingly, spoiled the ship's consort. Bownes himself died a month after the loss of his instruments. He made a will on board the *Trades Increase* bequeathing money to his wife and, as was the custom at sea, requesting the sale of his effects on board.[54]

When Middleton reached Surat in the autumn of 1611, two of his musicians, obviously dissatisfied with their prospects, deserted to serve with the Portuguese. On 9 December, Downton wrote in his journal that "John Coverdale Trumpetter of the Admirall ran away to the Portugall Armie."[55] William Chambers, one of the musicians, also left, but he re-entered the Company's service one year later under Best.

An interesting postscript to the Mocha incident comes in the form of the possible reappearance of Bownes's treble viol. The evidence is in the journal of John Saris, Captain of the Eighth Voyage of the Company. In January 1613, Saris was at Bantam in Java, preparing for the second stage of his voyage on the *Clove*. On 14 January his journal states that he "sent Mr Cocks to buy a Treble voyall and a Tabor and pipe on board the Trade [the *Trades Increase*],

[53]C. R. Markham, *The Voyages of Sir James Lancaster, Kt., to the East Indies* (*HS*, vol. 56; London, 1877), 148.

[54]Guildhall Library, London, Commissary Court of London (London Division): Will Register 9171/22, fol. 343.

[55]Purchas, 3:266.

cost 7 rials 8."[56] The previous October, Sir Henry had left the *Trades Increase* and boarded the *Peppercorn*, instructing Captain Downton to bring the badly leaking flagship to Bantam for repairs. A possible explanation for the presence of an apparently redundant treble viol on the *Trades Increase* is that it was the instrument lost by Mr Bownes at Bantam (and then presumably recovered); its sale would have been in accordance with the musician's last wishes, to raise money for his wife. Another possibility is that the instrument belonged to the musician Chambers, and that it was left behind when he deserted to join the Portuguese. The purchase of the treble viol was no idle acquisition on the part of Saris. During the voyage to Japan, his consort was active in entertaining distinguished visitors.[57]

The Tenth Voyage of the Company sailed from London in 1612. Captain Thomas Best was accompanied by a consort of professional musicians and by a keyboard player who was to perform on a pair of virginals before the Great Mughal. Some time after his arrival at Surat, Best accepted the services of William Chambers, who had left Middleton the previous year. In a letter to Sir Thomas Smyth in London, he described how on 27 or 28 September three of his men, including "one of my musitioners" had been captured by the Portuguese as they were being rowed out to the English ships.[58] In his journal Standish confirms that "William Chamers (a musition)" was one of the three captives.[59] Two of the men, Chambers and Edward Christian, the purser of the *Dragon*, were held captive at Cambay. In reports of their subsequent escape, arranged by Chambers (who was allowed some freedom of movement), it was stated that the musician had deserted Middleton to join the Portuguese but had since changed his mind. Standish, for example, wrote how the purser had escaped "by meanes of one Chambers, who went away from Sir Henrie Midletton heere att Sualley and wentt to the Portingailles, who afterwards repented (as yt should seame) of that he had formerlie done, and to fre himselff of such slavery as he lyved in, did att Cambaia both convey himselff away and likewisse the pursser."[60]

[56]E. M. Satour, *The Voyage of Captain John Saris to Japan, 1613* (*HS*, 2nd series, vol. 5; London, 1900), 1.

[57]Ibid., 40, 80, 91, and 108.

[58]W. Foster, *The Voyage of Thomas Best to the East Indies 1612–14* (*HS*, 2nd series, vol. 75; London, 1934), 241.

[59]Ibid., 109.

[60]Ibid., 120.

The re-employment of Chambers may explain why on 2 November Best records without comment the discharge of another of his musicians, the cornetto player Robert Trully.

Provided that they kept enough musicians for their own needs, officials of the East India Company seem to have taken a reasonably pragmatic attitude to musicians, like Trully, who wished to seek their fortune abroad. There was little in any case that could be done to prevent the desertion of men with professional skills. If such men later wanted to re-enter the service of the Company, they might at least return with valuable information about the activities of commercial rivals.

The Twelfth Voyage of the Company set sail in 1613 under the command of Christopher Newport. On board was Sir Robert Sherley, ambassador to the Shah of Persia. Sherley's retinue of fourteen included a musician, John Herriot, and Newport also had his own musicians.[61] Having rounded the Cape of Good Hope, the *Expedition* entered the Gulf and crossed to the Persian Coast where it was hoped that Sir Robert's party could disembark. In his journal, Walter Peyton described how, the night before the ambassador's departure, a plot against the English had been uncovered and how, with the help of the musicians, it had been thwarted.[62] Sir Robert had sent his effects on shore with three musicians to watch over them. The same night, however, he received word about an ambush; it was planned to massacre all on board "except the Chirurgians, Musitians, Women and Boyes." An elaborate ploy was then devised to rescue the musicians on shore and the Ambassador's goods. A message was sent to say that Sir Robert was ill and wished to postpone his disembarkation until the following day. Using the plausible excuse that Lady Sherley needed her night-gowns, this man managed to smuggle the gold back on board in a trunk. That night, the English carpenters set to work to make a substitute trunk, "a great Chest, and a close-stoole, bound and maled up together with cords, very fast and handsomely." This was filled with rubbish and stones to make it heavy. The plan was that this trunk should be taken into the tent and that the three musicians should "come forth of the Tent, with each of them their instruments of musicke in their hands." If they were asked why the trunk was being brought back again, the reply was to be that it belonged to one of the merchants: "Likewise, if they demanded why

[61]Purchas, 4:180.

[62]Ibid., 196–97.

the men came aboord againe, answere should be made, that his Lordship did send for them, to accompany him ashoare with his musicke." Using this stratagem, the three musicians regained the safety of their ship without incident. The success of the plan depended on the fact that it was normal practice for an ambassador to be accompanied by musicians while being rowed ashore.

As it was clearly dangerous to attempt to land, Sir Robert Sherley remained on board the *Expedition* until she reached the Indian coast. After a series of setbacks, he arrived at Agra in the summer of 1614, but by this time Herriot the musician was dead. Thomas Kerridge, an employee of the Company, reported from Ajmer on 20 September that "The English that came with him since their landing are all dead, an apothecary only excepted."[63]

The musicians who sailed with Nicholas Downton in 1614 on the first "joint-stock" voyage of the Company are mentioned only once in journals of the voyage. During a stay at Socotra, an important staging point, their playing caught the attention of the local sultan, Amr-bin-Said, who "intreted to heare some of our musicke" which "he semed mutch to delight in."[64] The senior factor on this voyage was accompanied by an apprentice named Hutchinson. The Court of the East India Company made the appointment after hearing that the young man was "comended much for his partes, haveinge the Italian, French and Dutch tongues and writeth them all very faire, and is skilfull in accomptes and musique. . . ."[65]

In 1615 the East India Company felt the time was right for a major diplomatic mission to the Great Mughal. They hired as their representative Sir Thomas Roe. The musicians who accompanied the captain of this fleet, William Keeling, once again attracted the attention of Amr-bin-Said. He is reported to have asked about the "hoy-boyes" in Keeling's boat.[66]

By the time of Roe's embassy, the number of musicians working for the East India Company was a substantial one. As we have seen, a professional consort was hired for no fewer than six sailings between 1610 and 1615. Since a return voyage to the East could take up to two or

[63]Danvers, *Letters*, 2:107.

[64]W. Foster, *The Voyage of Nicholas Downton to the East Indies 1614–15* (*HS*, 2nd series, vol. 82; London, 1939), 77.

[65]India Office Library, East India Company, Court Book III, 22.

[66]Purchas, 4:322.

three years to complete, the six consorts who accompanied Middleton, Saris, Best, Newport, Downton, and Keeling, probably consisted of different groups of musicians. Taking into account a few musical servants accompanying ambassadors and senior factors, there may well have been up to 30 or so musicians in the Company's service at this period, making the organization one of the largest employers of professional instrumentalists after the Crown.

With a growing reputation as an employer of musicians, the Company began to attract applications from individuals anxious to find jobs. The Court Minutes for 14 October 1617 record an unsuccessful petition for employment by a "singing man."[67] The reasons given for the Court's refusal to entertain the request are instructive: "A peticion was red, preferd by Thomas Kinge, brought upp a singinge man, butt cannott playe upon any instrument, not able to labour, nor fitt for the Companies service. And therefore dismist." The musicians best suited to the Company's needs were instrumentalists; choirmen with no instrumental skills had little to offer as musicians in the East. Physical fitness and the ability to undertake manual labor were also prerequisites for employment.

In the same year, concern was expressed by the Company about the cost of maintaining so many musicians. The Court Minutes for November 1617 include two entries referring to the provision of musicians for the Company's forthcoming voyage, for which Captain Thomas Best, the successful commander of the Tenth Voyage was being considered. In the first extract, from the minutes of 11 November, Best's request for six or seven musicians is considered:

> Mr Offley acquaynted the courte that Captaine Best desireth to have 6 or 7 musitions (besides trumpetours), which cannott bee had but at deare rates, 40s. per month the least; which Captaine Best preremptorilie saith hee must and will have. But because of the greate charge to provide such persons and small use of their service, Mr. Offley desireth the opinion of this courte what they please to have done therein; who consideringe that formerlie he had some allowed, and therefore will nowe alsoe expect the like, they were contented to give him satisfaction in the same manner as formerlie, by allowing the some of 33s. 4d per month to each of them, butt noe more; which is as much as they can or will doe. And entreated Mr Offley to lett him knowe soe much when hee shall renew the said motions.[68]

[67]India Office Library, East India Company, Court Book IV, 35.

[68]Ibid., 58.

Best had personal experience of the value of musicians in India. Some of the officials in London, however, were clearly coming round to the view that a professional consort was an unneccessary expense. They seem to have accepted Best's demand with distinct reluctance. When Mr Offley returned to the Court, he made it known that he had "dealt with som Musitions for Captaine Best" but found that "none of them will proceede upon those tearmes."[69] The musicians would not agree to less than 40s a month (£24 per annum). The Company was probably right to regard this as "deare rates." Woodfill pointed out that even the London Waits were only paid £20 a year, though this basic rate would have been supplemented with gifts and rewards on special occasions.[70] In any event, Best was not chosen by the Company for the voyage, and so the dispute over his musicians was unresolved.

Mr. Offley's complaint that the East India Company had "small use" of the musicians' services was at least partially rectified by the practice of engaging musicians with additional skills. Musicians with linguistic ability were invaluable. The young musician in the service of the senior factor on Downton's voyage could speak three languages, his Dutch being especially useful in the East. One of the trumpeters on the same voyage could apparently speak Arabic; at Aden, "Jno Williams and Walter the trumpetter, linguists" were sent on shore with a present.[71] Edward Gault, another of the trumpeters on Downton's flagship, the *New Year's Gift*, had a more unusual, but no less valuable talent—as a maker of picture frames. Item 30 of Downton's commission drew his attention to this fact: "Edward Gault Trumpeter can give direction for making of the frames for the pictures: and can guild them also."[72] Whether or not they had special skills, all musicians overseas were expected to accept their share of general duties, such as foraging for food.

Despite occasional misgivings about the cost, the East India Company continued to employ consorts of musicians on flagships throughout the 1620s and 1630s. In 1627 the Company's factors at

[69]Ibid., 67.

[70]Woodfill (1953), 103.

[71]Markham (1877), 168. The trumpeter may have been Walter Stere who was punished by Keeling on the Third Voyage of the Company (see chapter 12).

[72]India Office Library, East India Company, Factory Records Miscellaneous XXV, 15.

Batavia in Java described in a letter to the council in London the arrival of an ambassador from Jambi in Sumatra. While being escorted off the *Dolphin,* he was accompanied by musicians on barges of the Company's Surat ships, playing "trumpets, sackbutts and still musicke."[73] Several consorts of musicians may have been involved in this performance, since the Surat fleet then included vessels from more than one sailing from London.

For his forthcoming voyage to Surat in 1629, Captain John Weddell requested the Company to provide him with musicians. In the Court Minutes for 6 February, it was agreed that Weddell should be allowed "to carry along with him to sea 'a noyse of cornetts' so as they do likewise their labours in the ship as hath been usual."[74] The implication that musicians had non-musical duties on board is of interest, but the important point to note is the phrase "as hath been usual." This strongly suggests that the East India Company was still making a regular practice of hiring a full consort for flagships. Weddell himself had previously undertaken voyages for the Company in 1621 and 1624.

It is significant that in 1636 Sir William Courteen's Association, a newly formed rival to the East India Company, hired a full complement of professional musicians for its first voyage. Peter Mundy, one of the most perceptive travel writers of the seventeenth century, describes a short trip down the Thames to Woolwich to view the ships in which Sir William was about to sail for Goa.[75] The transport used was a small vessel, appropriately named the *Pleasure Boate,* in which the great cabin was "furnished with a Table, Carpett, Benches, Cusheons, Windowes to open and shutt, painted within and without, with two prettie litle brasse peeces or carriages wherein Sir William and his friends often goe and disport themselves on the water from place to place." On this occasion the party was accompanied by the musicians engaged for the forthcoming voyage. Mundy was an amateur musician; he can be regarded as a reliable witness on the subject. In the following passage he paints a delightful picture of the start of the journey to Woolwich:

[73]India Office Library, East India Company, Original Correspondence, no.1255.

[74]India Office Library, East India Company, Court Book XI, 287–296.

[75]R. C. Temple, *The Travels of Peter Mundy, in Europe and Asia, 1608–1667*, vol. 3, part 1: *Travels in England, Western India, Achin, Macao, and the Canton River, 1634–1637* (*HS*, 2nd series, vol. 45; London, 1919), 14–15.

> Beinge well provided of meate and drinck for her voyage, away wee went one Morninge, Mr William [Courteen], Captane Molton, Mr Samuell Bunnell, myselfe and others, with the Musick entertained to goe on the shipps on the voyage. And settinge saile off Billingsgate, away shee seemingly flew downe the River of Thames, with a faire Wynde, Colours displayed, shooteing off our litle Gunns now and then, the Musick playinge all the way in a manner, sometymes the Lowd, as Consorts of Cornetts, as alsoe of Hautboys, sometymes againe on the still musick, as Vyolls, soe that, in my opinion, it would have animated the dullest spiritt to have forsaken all and followed the sea, had hee but seene or heard us.

In this passage, Mundy captures the sense of excitement and adventure that must have persuaded many musicians to volunteer for an overseas voyage, despite the very real uncertainty of return.

In considering how the East India Company voyages improved the employment prospects of musicians seeking work in London, several points should be noted. The very high mortality rate associated with eastern travel ensured a fast turn-over in this sector of the market. Since musicians were not normally dispersed throughout a fleet, a whole band could perish in a single accident. The length of time that each return voyage took also tended to increase the opportunities of those awaiting their chance in London. There were other factors limiting the size of the London market itself. Age, uncertain health, physical disability, timidity, or family responsibilities would have prevented many musicians from even applying for positions on long eastern voyages. The impact of an event like the Massacre at Amboina, widely reported in macabre detail at the time, gave even the boldest of spirits reason to reflect on the risks often taken by men working overseas.

Walter Woodfill's study *Musicians in English Society from the Reign of Elizabeth to Charles I* presented an account of the music profession in the hundred years or so after the upheavals of the Reformation, in which the traditional view of the period as something of a "Golden Age" was replaced by a sombre but more realistic assessment. His account was of an elite enjoying the luxury of secure employment while a substantial number of independent professionals led a hand-to-mouth existence that often left them little better off than vagabonds. In particular, Woodfill emphasized the fundamental insecurity of the independent musicians from whose ranks many of the consorts employed on ships must have been drawn. Their dependence on an unrelated succession of jobs—weddings, guild feasts, engagements at the town or suburban houses of merchants and gentlemen during Christmas week and at other festival times, and perhaps in the royal palaces or the inns of court—placed them in much the same situation as the seasonal laborer obliged to move from one low-paid engagement to another. These circumstances, he concluded, made it "difficult or impossible for many to earn a steady, adequate income."[76] The essential truth of this statement is not in doubt, yet the regular employment of consorts for overseas voyages suggests a modest revision. For the young, fit, adventurous musician, with a reasonable degree of technical competence, the prospect of a place on a voyage was good, at least by the early seventeenth century. Information about the wages offered to musicians for service at sea is scarce, but where exact figures are known, the rates of pay seem attractive, in line with the best of the city waits, though not on a level with members of the royal band. For Drake's last voyage of 1595 the musicians received 7s. a week a man for the period before embarkation, an annual rate of about 18 pounds. The documents from the East India Company in 1617 are even more conclusive. Unnamed musicians were offered 33s. 4d. a month (20 pounds per annum) but refused to accept less than 40s. a month (24 pounds per annum). The high rates of pay suggested by these figures points to the fact that on occasion the demand for suitably qualified musicians was actually greater than their availability, and that some felt in a position to hold out for "deare rates" of pay.

The growth in the recruitment of musicians for the long-distance voyages in the half century from ca. 1580 to ca. 1630 coincides exactly with a much better documented exodus: that of English viol players, lutenists, and other instrumentalists to Denmark, Germany, and the Low Countries. The list of English musicians who worked in Europe during the early seventeenth century is impressive: John Bull, John Dowland, Peter Philips, Thomas Simpson, William Brade, the Rowes (father and son), the Norcombes (father and son), John Price, and many others. The movement across the Channel was by no means confined to individuals; whole bands were recruited. The Acts of the Privy Council in London (22 June 1617) record the granting of a pass to George Vincent granting him permission "to carry over with him to the sayd Prince [of Poland] his master these

[76]Woodfill (1953), 30.

musitians: Richard Jones, Wm Corkine, Donatus O'Chaine, Thomas White, Wm Jackson, Tho. Sutton, Valentine Flood, John Wayd."[77] On 28 August the following year, another pass was granted to Vincent to enable him to take over to Poland a number of items including "such instrumentes of musicke as he shall have use of for his maister's service . . . and also five musitians."[78]

During his travels in Germany, John Taylor met up with a band of English musicians at Bückeburg. Of their performance in the Duke's chapel he wrote, no doubt with a degree of poetic license: "the Lutes, Viols, Bandoraes, Organs, Recorders, Sagbuts and other musicall instruments, all strike up together, with such a glorious delicious harmony, as if the Angelicall musicke of the Spheares were descended into that earthly Tabernacle." Upon leaving the town, Taylor was escorted by "certaine of my Countreymen my Lords Musicians."[79]

Not since the first half of the fifteenth century had such a wave of English musicians crossed the Channel. For a few decades at least, they enjoyed to the fullest the ascending bull market for their services.

Scholars have long recognized this migration as an unusually clear-cut and intense episode in the history of anglo-continental musical relations, and many suggestions have been made to account for the phenomenon. The apparently unassailable position of the Italian musical dynasties at the English court may well have inspired some Englishmen to look abroad. Religion, inevitably, played its part. The dangerous position of Catholics during the 1580s obliged a number of musicians to work overseas, while during the same period the involvement of English armies in the Dutch struggle against Spain opened the way for protestants. Dart suggested that some English musicians accompanied the itinerant acting companies that were so popular in Germany at this period.[80] Perhaps most important of all, many musicians gained a brief taste of what life on the Continent could be like, while serving in the retinue of ambassadors undertaking diplomatic missions of which there were an increasing

[77]J. V. Lyle, *Acts of the Privy Council of England 1616–1617* (London, 1927), 267.

[78]J. V. Lyle, *Acts of the Privy Council of England 1617–1619* (London, 1929), 247.

[79]J. Taylor, *All the Workes of John Taylor the Water Poet* (London, 1630), fol. Hhh3.

[80]R. T. Dart, "English musicians abroad," *Grove's Dictionary of Music and Musicians*, 5th ed. (London, 1954), 2:949.

number. In 1605, for instance, the Earl of Nottingham took eight musicians and seven trumpeters to Spain; and in the same year the Earl of Hartford traveled to Brussels with an identical number. From the details given by Price, it seems that the musicians accompanying the latter embassy included John Daniel, Robert Johnson, and John Bartlett.[81]

There seems to have been little interchange between the high-caliber instrumentalists who worked in Europe and lowly sea-going musicians, yet one thing the two groups did have in common—the need (or perhaps the desire) to travel to find employment suited to their musical skills. Naturally, the safer, more prestigious jobs in northern Europe were claimed by the more accomplished musicians, while the more arduous positions on ships eastward-bound were left to those who could get nothing else. In the overseas sector at least, it could be argued that, excluding those individuals for whom travel was a *preferred* mode of existence, there was an inverse correlation between the ability and status of musicians and the distance they had to travel to find work. This would not always be reflected in levels of pay. Such were the perceptions of hardship and physical danger associated with long-distance voyaging that it was by no means unusual for high wages to be offered to attract men of (presumably) quite modest abilities.

This view of overseas employment, whether in Europe or further afield, as a kind of safety-net to which those who relied on music for all or part of their income could periodically turn, must be seen against the wider background of employment policy. The Elizabethan advocates of a colonial policy often made precisely the point that overseas enterprise would provide work for the "idle," that is the unemployed. The author of "A true reporte" (1583) argued that "it will proove a generall benefite unto our Country, that through this occasion . . . a greate number of men which doo nowe live ydlely at home, and are burdenous, chargeable and unprofitable to this Realme, shall heereby be sette on worke. . . ."[82] Similarly in 1584, Richard Hakluyt advanced as an argument for American colonization the fact that "this enterprise will be for the manifolde imploy-

[81]D. Price, *Patrons and Musicians of the English Renaissance* (Cambridge, 1981), 127.

[82]D. B. Quinn, *New American World: A Documentary History of North America to 1612*: Vol. 3, *English Plans for North America. The Roanoke Voyages. New England Ventures.* (London, 1979), 50.

CHAPTER 2

The Trumpeters and Drummers

In almost all acounts of exploration, a clear distinction is made between musicians and trumpeters. The professional consorts were civilian musicians recruited as servants to the captain, but the trumpeters occupied an official naval rank. A trumpeter could be promoted up the chain of command—some, indeed, became pilots—or demoted to the rank of ordinary sailor from where the majority of them came. Trumpeters were carried on all armed men-of-war of the English navy and were thus employed in much larger numbers than civilian musicians who were usually recruited only for flagships. The wide range of ceremonial and military duties that they undertook made them indispensable members of the ship's crew.

Several sixteenth-century documents give us the recommended numbers of trumpeters for different classes of ship and their rates of pay. "The wages for the Officers of the Queen's Ships at Sea," compiled in 1582, will serve as an example[1]:

[1]J. S. Corbett, *The Spanish War 1585–1587* (*NRS*, vol.11; London, 1898), 258–62.

Table 2

Class I (800 tons and upwards)	Four Trumpeters 15s. 0d. A Drum and Fife 10s. 0d.
Class II (500–800 tons)	Two Trumpeters 15s. 0d. A Drum and Fife 10s. 0d. An Admiral—Three Trumpeters [i.e. if the ship is commissioned as an "admiral"]
Class III (300–500 tons)	A Trumpeter 15s. 0d. A Drum and Fife 10s. 0d. An Admiral—Two Trumpeters [i.e., if the ship is commissioned as an "admiral"]
Class IV (200–300 tons)	A Trumpeter 15s. 0d. A Drum and Fife 10s. 0d.
Class V (100–200 tons)	A Trumpeter 15s. 0d. A Drum and Fife 10s. 0d.
Class VI (Pinnaces)	A Trumpeter 15s. 0d. A Drum and Fife 10s. 0d.

The scheme of wages suggested in this document rewarded men with skills—pursers, surgeons, carpenters, gunners and trumpeters—with broadly comparable pay. The trumpeters were recommended for the same rate as the surgeons, the drummers for the same rate as the master gunners. The pay of trumpeters could sometimes be influenced by other factors such as the size of their ship. A distinction was also sometimes made between the master trumpeter and the trumpeter's mates.

Michael Lok's accounts for Frobisher's voyages of 1576 and 1577 include payments to trumpeters.[2] From these it is apparent that men engaged on voyages of exploration could expect much higher rewards than those on basic naval rates. In 1576 Frobisher sailed for the Northwest in a small bark of about 30 tons, the *Gabriell*. Richard Purdye, the single trumpeter required for a vessel of this size, was paid at the rate of 33s. 4d. a month, the sum received by the master gunner.[3] Rank-and-file sailors were paid 26s. 8d. a month. In 1577 Frobisher returned with a much larger ship, the *Ayde* of 200 tons, together with two small barks, the *Gabriell* and the *Michaell*. The number of trumpeters taken was commensurate with the larger size of this fleet.[4]

Table 3

The *Ayde* [admiral]	To Richard Coxe trompitor for 5 monthes and 1/2 at 40s.—£11. 0s. 0d.
	To Anthony Fysher[5] trompitor for 5 1/2 monthes at 40s.—£10. 15s. 0d.
	To Christopher Jacksone trumpiter for 4 monthes at 33s. 4d.—£6. 14s. 4d.
The *Gabriell* [vice-admiral]	To John Browne trumpiter For 6 monthes at 26s. 8d.—£7. 17s. 6d.
The *Michaell*	To Thomas Belle trompitor for 5 monthes and 1/2 at 23s. 4d.—£6. 8s. 11d.

Even the poorest rewarded trumpeter on board the *Michaell* received more than the suggested maximum for naval trumpeters in 1582. The wages paid to the musicians and trumpeters by Drake and Hawkins

[2]Public Record Office, E 164/35. A representative sample of the accounts for the 1576 voyage has been published in D. B. Quinn, *New American World: A Documentary History of North America to 1612*, Vol.4: *Newfoundland from Fishery to Colony. Northwest Passage Searches* (London, 1979), 193–200.

[3]E 164/35, fols. 9v and 14.

[4]Ibid., fols. 71v–72.

[5]Anthony Fysher and Christopher Jackson were also employed on the *Ayde* for Frobisher's third voyage. See G. B. Parks, "Frobisher's Third Voyage, 1578," *HLB*, no. 7 (1935), 190.

before their embarkation in 1595 (28s. a month) are equivalent to these higher figures.[6]

For long-distance ventures, trumpeters were evidently attracted by good rates of pay, but the recruitment of the large numbers of trumpeters and drummers needed by the English navy necessitated the use of impressment, to which musicians of this type were subject in the same way as soldiers or sailors. A blank warrant dated 22 September 1627 is typical:

> Whereas there is occasion for his Majesty's expresse service to employ certaine pilotts, trumpeters, drumes, fieffs, gunners, marriners, saylors and others to serve in his Majesty's shipp the [blank]; theise are therefore to will and require and withall to authorise your captaine [blank], captaine of his Majesty's said shipp, to imprest such and so many of the said pilotts, trumpets and others above mencioned as shalbe needfull for service in the said shipp, and make her fitt for his Majesty's present service, and in case any shall refuse, you are to require all mayors, sheriffs, justices of the peace, constables, headboroughs and all other his Majesty's officers and loveinge subjects, whom it may concerne, and every of them, if need shall require, to be ayding and assisting unto you; for which this shall be your warrant.[7]

The impressment of a full "noise" for their flagship was ordered by Popham and Blake in 1650: "We authorise you to impress for the service of the fleet now setting forth to sea such and so many able Trumpeters as shall from time to time be found necessary and particularly a complete noise for the ship appointed for us giving them conduct money for their repair to Chatham."[8]

Another way of recruiting trumpeters was to employ a single man and require him to train up volunteers from the ranks of common sailors. The East India Company, aware of the cost of recruiting a pre-formed "noise" of trumpets, sometimes adopted this approach. On 31 March 1626, the Court ordered "two Trumpetts for the Discovery, to trayne upp yonge men wth, for wch Trumpets the Master of the Shippe at his returne is to be accomptable."[9] Again, in

[6]K. R. Andrews, *The Last Voyage of Drake and Hawkins* (*HS*, 2nd series, vol. 142; Cambridge, 1972), 68.

[7]J. V. Lyle, *Acts of the Privy Council of England 1627 Sept.–1628 June* (London, 1940), 44.

[8]J. R. Powell, *The Letters of Robert Blake* (*NRS*, vol. 76; London, 1937), 53.

[9]India Office Library, East India Company, Court Book VIII, 347.

1645, the Court, having agreed to employ two principal trumpeters, one each for the *Mary* and the *Eagle,* ordered "four spare brass trumpets to be provided for the practitioners in the Mary, two for those in the Eagle."[10]

While the naval trumpeters functioned as the captain's principal military musicians, the drum and fife players were attached to companies of foot soldiers. This parallels the situation on land where a clear distinction between the trumpet as the instrument of the cavalry and the drum and fife as instruments of the infantry was observed. In his manual of military practice, *Five Decades of Epistles of Warre* (1622), Francis Markham wrote: "In Horse-Troupes . . . the Trumpet is the same which the *Drum* and *Phiph* is, onely differing in the tearmes and sounds of the Instrument." The wages received by the two groups—15s. for the trumpeters and 10s. or 12s. 8d. for the drum and fife players are typical figures for the late sixteenth century—indicate their relative status. On ceremonial occasions, drummers and fifers usually performed with the trumpeters, but during sea battles or marches on land they had duties of their own to perform, relating to the requirements of the foot soldiers to whom they were attached.

[10]Court Book XIX, 269 and 279.

THE MUSIC

Once a ship put to sea, those on board were subject to a carefully ordered routine of daily life in which music played a significant part. The form of music in religious worship and the signalling duties of the military musicians were specified in general orders, but other aspects of musical life on board, such as the extent to which the professional consorts were required to perform incidental music or the degree to which amateur music-making was encouraged, were matters for individual captains to determine. It is important to stress that musical practices did not change with embarkation. The psalms sung, the instruments played (with occasional limitations of size), and the dances danced at sea were the same as those on land. In fact, a long-distance sailing ship functioned rather like a time-capsule in which was preserved the musical culture of the country of origin at the time of embarkation. The following survey of ship-board musical life will tell us little that we do not already know about music in England, but, in the context of English exploration overseas, it is of relevance. We cannot fairly evaluate the part played by musicians during the long early process of colonization, from initial contact through to systematic settlement, without first examining the place of music on board ship—the exclusive representative (at least during the early years) of the incoming alien culture.

CHAPTER 3

Music For Public Worship

Great importance was attached to the regular observance of Divine Service on English ships, and the conduct of worship was invariably prescribed in a set of ordinances prepared for the captain. A set was prepared by Sebastian Cabot for the voyage undertaken in 1553 on behalf of the Merchant Adventurers of London by Sir Hugh Willoughby.[1] It states that:

> morning and evening prayer, with other common services appointed by the kings Majestie, and lawes of this Realme to be read and saide in every ship daily by the minister in the Admirall, and the marchant or some other person learned in other ships, and the Bible or paraphrases to be read devoutly and Christianly to Gods honour, and for his grace to be obtained, and had by humble and heartie praier of the Navigants accordingly.

In 1578 Frobisher received instructions that "a minister or twoo do go in this jorney to use ministration of devyne service and sacraments, accordyng to ye churche of England."[2] In his own orders, circulated in writing to the captains of the other four ships, Frobisher required them "to serve God twice a day, with the ordinarie service, usuall in churches of England."[3]

The pattern of religious observance on board ships of the East India Company in the early seventeenth century was developed in a series of ordinances which tell us a good deal about contemporary

[1]Hakluyt, 2:195–205.

[2]R. Collinson, *The Three Voyages of Martin Frobisher* (*HS*, vol.38; London, 1867), 217.

[3]Ibid., 229.

commercial attitudes to worship. The commission submitted to Sir Henry Middleton in 1604 before the departure of the Second Voyage of the Company charged him thus:

> And to thend that the wholle Companie Comitted to yor chardge may performe that due obedience and respect unto you wch is fitt to be yealded to their Gov^{r}no^{r} or Generall, we doe herein propound unto you the care of the due execution of that principall meane wch draweth all Christians to Conformitie and submission to such as are set over them wch is the dayly invocation . . . requiring you to take order that certaine houres and tymes in every day, may be sett aparte for publique prayer and calling upon the name of God.[4]

The commission given to Keeling and Hawkins for the Third Voyage in 1607 appeals in a similarly candid fashion to self-interest as a justification for religious observance.[5]

The link between godly behavior and commercial success was well understood in the mercantile community at large. The author of *The Marchants Avizo* (London, 1589) wrote of the importance of daily devotions for the young trader overseas.[6] Prayers were to be said "silentlie, reverently, and atentively," but not, the cynic will note, at too great a length "because of marchants lets and hinderance to continue in long prayer"! If his devotions were satisfactory the young merchant could expect that "all thinges" would go well, but if not, nothing to which he set his hand would "ever come to good passe or perfection." This line of argument was used again and again by the East India Company as it sought—vainly in many cases—to ensure that the behavior of its employees overseas did not adversely affect its commercial interests.

Not all commissions were phrased in the language of self-interest. The "Orders to be observed aboard the Royall Exchange" (1620) begin in an altogether loftier vein: "As it is our dutye first and principallye to serve God from whome we have not only our beinge, but our well beinge, soe in the first place I doe Charge and Command that no man whatsoever be absent from prayers at the tymes ap-

[4]G. Birdwood and W. Foster, *The First Letterbook of the East India Company 1600–1619* (London, 1893), 53.

[5]Ibid., 116.

[6]J. Browne, *The Marchants Avizo* (London, 1589): "A Generall remembrance for a servant at his first going to sea."

poynted but to come and attend reverentlie to devine service."[7] Failure to attend would result in a fine.

The Company's instructions concerning Divine Service were often accompanied by details of the provision of Bibles and psalters. In this respect they were following well-established practice. The accounts of Frobisher's 1576 voyage include a payment for "a Bible Englishe great volume."[8] The accounts for a much larger expedition, the last voyage of Drake and Hawkins (Public Record Office, E 351/2233), include payments for 1 Bible, 25 psalters and 2 service books. For the Fifth Voyage of the East India Company in 1609, David Middleton's purser was supplied with a Bible[9], and for the Seventh Voyage of 1611 Floris received "a faire Bible wth the booke of Comon Prayers."[10] Saris, commander of the Eighth Voyage, was also allowed "a Bible wherein is conteyned the booke of comon prayer" for each of his three ships.[11] Large-scale provision of psalters with music was made in 1627, when the Company in London ordered "50 Psalters for every ship with Singing Psalms in them."[12]

The most detailed of the early East India Company ordinances governing worship was that submitted to Downton in 1614.[13] It is worth citing this at length, since it sums up all the considerations so far discussed.

> For that religious goverm^{t} doth best binde men to performe ther duties as allso unto it the lord hath promised his blessinge: it is principally to be cared for: that prayers be saide beseemingly every morninge and Eaveninge in eavery of the saide shipps together wth readinge som portion of Gods word espetially and more amply upon the Lords day wth singinge of psalmes: for upone that day god hath commaunded his people to offer a dayly sacrifice that the whole comp^{an} of every ship be caled ther unto wth dilligence and reverence: both (to) hear the Lords counsaile in his word for ye better knowledge of his will: comfortinge of ther harts in faith and directinge of ther lives in

[7]India Office Library, East India Company, Marine Records, Miscellaneous, vol. 2:73.

[8]Public Record Office, E164/35.

[9]Birdwood and Foster (1893), 295.

[10]Ibid., 370.

[11]Ibid., 397.

[12]India Office Library, East India Company, Court Book IX, 386–409.

[13]Factory Records, Miscellaneous, vol. 25:5.

> obedience as allsoe to pray unto him fo^{r} his preservation through all the dangers of this longe and tedious voyadge his protextion against all ther enymies and his blessinges in all ther proseedinges: for the better performance whear of we have provided and delivered to the pussers of every ship: a bible: wth the forme of comon prayer togeather wth a booke of Searmones and other bookes of cronycles and navigacions for ther better passinge of the tyme.

These ordinances recommend specifically that psalms should be sung. Weddell's commission of 1620 similarly specified that services should include the "singing of psalmes."[14] Whether or not ordinances were drawn up in sufficient detail to include this requirement, psalms would have been sung as a matter of course. During the First Voyage of the Company, the following incident was recorded as Lancaster was about to leave Achin in Sumatra.

> And when the generall tooke his leave, the king said unto him: Have you the Psalmes of David extant among you? The generall answered: Yea, and wee sing them daily. Then said the king: I and the rest of these nobles about me will sing a psalme to God for your prosperitie; and so they did, very solemnly. And after it was ended, the king said: I would heare you sing another psalme, although in your owne language. So, there being in the company some twelve of us, we sung another psalme. And after the psalme ended, the generall tooke his leave of the king.[15]

As is evident from this little episode, psalm singing soon became part of the public profile of protestants working in the East.

It was also the custom on English ships to sing a psalm at the changing of the watch, especially at night. The instructions given by Essex and Howard to the 1596 Cadiz expedition included the following: "The watch shall be set every night by eight of the clock, either by drum and trumpet, and singing of the Lord's Prayer, some of the Psalms of David, or clearing the glass."[16] The orders signed by Raleigh before his ill-fated expedition to South America in 1617 required "the praising of God every night with the singing of a psalm at the setting

[14]Marine Records, Miscellaneous, vol.2:113.

[15]C. R. Markham, *The Voyages of Sir James Lancaster, Kt., to the East Indies* (*HS*, vol. 56; London, 1877), 97 .

[16]J. S. Corbett, "Relation of the Voyage to Cadiz, 1596; by Sir William Slyngisbie," *The Naval Miscellany*, vol. 1, ed. J. K. Laughton (*NRS*, vol. 20; London, 1902), 56.

of a watch[17]; those of Sir Edward Cecil in 1625 instructed commanders to "set and discharge every watch with the singing of a psalm and prayer usual at sea."[18] John Smith gave further details of how watches were to be set at night: "they may first go to prayer, then to supper, and a six a clock sing a Psalm, say a Prayer, and the Master with his side begins the watch, then all the rest may do what they will till midnight; and then his Mate with his Larboord men with a Psalm and a Prayer releeves them till four in the morning, and so from eight to twelve. . . ."[19]

The practice of singing at the change of a watch on a ship of the Dutch East India Company was observed by Cristoph Schweitzer in 1675. He noted down in his journal the words of the song:

> Here we sail with God most High,
> May God forgive us all our Sins,
> All our Sins and Mis-doings,
> May God preserve our good Ship,
> And all that Voyage in it,
> From Sea and the Sand,
> From Fire and Burning,
> From the hellish evil Fiend,
> And God protect us all from Ill.[20]

This was sung to waken the relief watch.

[17]J. S. Corbett, *Fighting Instructions, 1530–1816* (*NRS*, vol. 29; London, 1905), 36.

[18]Ibid., 52.

[19]J. Smith, *The Sea-Man's Grammar* (London, 1653), 38–39.

[20]The translation is from R. Raven-Hart, *Germans in Dutch Ceylon* (National Museum of Ceylon, Translation Series, vol. 1; Colombo, 1953), 39. The original text is:

Hier seglen wir mit Gott verheben,
Gott woll uns unsere Sünd vergeben,
All unsere Sünd und Missethat;
Gott wolle unser gutes Schiff bewahren,
Mit all den Leuthen die darinn fahren,
Vor See, vor Sand, vor Feuer und Brand,
Vor dem höllischen bösen Feyand,
For allem Quad uns Gott bewahr.

See S. P. L'H. Naber, *Christoph Schweitzer Reise nach Java und Ceylon 1675–1682* (Reisebeschreibungen von Deutschen Beamten und Kriegsleuten im Dienst der Niederländischen West-und Ost-Indischen Kompagnien 1602–1797, vol. 11 [The Hague, 1931], 9). For details of Spanish practice, see S. E. Morison, *Admiral of the Ocean Sea: A Life of Christopher Columbus* (Boston, 1942), 167–82.

At moments of great peril in battle or storm, psalms were sometimes sung to raise men's spirits, to appeal for divine intervention, or to offer thanks for deliverance. The English pilgrim, Sir Richard Guylforde, returning from the Holy Land in 1506, described how a violent storm almost wrecked his ships.[21] Two anchors had already pulled loose and the ship was close to the rocks. The pilgrims then "devoutly and ferefully, began to sing 'Salve Regina and other Antymes with versicles and colletis.' After the Reformation, psalms were invariably chosen in such circumstances. Journals of English voyages occasionally record the specific psalms sung at moments of crisis. The choice was usually apt. During an encounter between three English ships and a Spanish fleet in 1591[22], there was a lull in the action—a Spanish ship having retired to cope with a ball of fire "heaved into them" by the English; those on board the flagship "went to prayer and sang the first part of the 25. Psalme, praysing God for our safe deliverance." The opening words—"Unto thee, O Lord, do I lift up my soul. O my God, I trust in thee: let not mine enemies triumph over me."—seemed significant to the writer of Hakluyt's narrative who attributed the gale that enabled the English to escape to the intervention of God "which never faileth them that put their trust in him." Psalm 12 was sung at the very moment of shipwreck[23] when the *Tobie* ran aground off the coast of Barbary. As the ship split up, the men scaled the rigging to escape the waves, and, seeing nothing but imminent death, committed themselves to God and began "with dolefull tune and heavy hearts to sing the 12 Psalme. Helpe Lord for good and godly men." By the end of verse four, "the waves of the sea had stopped the breathes of most of our men." In 1609 after the *Ascension*, flagship of the Fourth Voyage of the East India Company, had run aground on a sandbank, the men loaded as much as they could on boats and then cast off "singinge of psalmes to the praise of God, leaving the shipp as yett standing, with her yards acrosse and the flagg atopp, to our greate greifes."[24]

[21]H. Ellis, *The Pylgrymage of Sir Richard Guylforde to the Holy Land* (*CS*, vol. 51; London, 1851), 65–66.

[22]Hakluyt, vol. 10, 178–83.

[23]Ibid., vol. 7, 124–29.

[24]W. Foster, *The Journal of John Jourdain, 1608–1617* (*HS*, 2nd series, vol. 16; Cambridge, 1905), 120.

Official documents such as sets of ordinances tell us little about the manner of psalm singing at sea. It is reasonable to assume that the musical skills of the professional musicians would have been put to some use, but their precise contribution is difficult to determine. The best evidence we have comes from a small number of Spanish reports which describe how Drake and other English captains conducted worship on board. In 1580 the Inquisition was preparing a case against Nuño da Silva, Drake's Portuguese pilot, who was accused of joining in, without compulsion, English "heretic" services. In order to strengthen the evidence, the Inquisition examined a number of Spanish prisoners. The witnesses were questioned about the English services and the attitude of the pilot towards them. Under oath, one eye-witness, Juan Pascual, claimed that every day before dinner and supper Drake had a table brought out on deck. He continued: "He took out a very large book and knelt down bareheaded, and read from the said book in the English language. All the other Englishmen whom he brought with him were also seated without their hats, and made responses. Some of them held books resembling Bibles in their hands and read in these."[25] In a later deposition, Pascual recalled further details, including the fact that Drake "chanted in a low voice" ("cantava en tono baxo") and that "everyone responded" ("y todos le respondian").[26]

The evidence of the Factor of Guatulco is of great interest. He described the Englishmen's service thus:[27]

> The said Francis Drake had a table placed on deck at the poop of the vessel, and, at its head, on the floor, a small box and an embroidered cushion. He then sent for a book of the size of the *Lives of the Saints* and when all this was in place he struck the table twice with the palm of his hand. Then, immediately nine Englishmen, with nine small books of the size of a breviary, joined him and seated themselves around him and the table. Then the said Francis Drake crossed his hands and, kneeling on the cushion and small box, lifted his eyes to heaven and remained in that attitude for about a quarter of an hour. He then said to this witness and to the other prisoners that if they wanted to recite the psalms according to his mode they could stay, but if not, that they could go to the prow. As they stood up to go towards the prow, he spoke again saying "that they were to keep quiet," and

[25]Nuttall (1914), 325.

[26]Ibid., 336.

[27]Ibid., 354–55.

> he began reading the psalms in the English language of which the witness understood nothing whatsoever. This act lasted about an hour and then they brought four viols ("bihuelas de arco") and made lamentations ("treneron") and sang "en canto de organo."[28] Witness does not know what they sang, as he could not understand it. Immediately afterwards he ordered a boy, whom he had brought as a page, to come and then made him dance in the English fashion, with which the service ended.

Other witnesses confirm many of these details. A man questioned by the Inquisition in the Canary Islands in 1592 reported that services on English ships were held twice daily, once in the morning before dinner, once in the evening before nightfall.[29] Like Pascual, he described how the company came up on deck and knelt down bareheaded to perform the act of worship. A Portuguese seaman picked up by Cavendish in 1588 told the authorities in the Philippines that those who did not wish to attend the "Lutheran" services on board the *Desire* had not been obliged to do so.[30] Pascual's description of what was probably the usual method of singing on board—the captain chanting solo, the responses or alternate verses being sung by all those present—is confirmed by the man interviewed in the Canary Islands. He stated that after praying for a while from a book, the officer in charge of his ship "sang" ("cantava") and "all the others then responded with singing" ("luego le respondian cantando los demas todos") what he took to be "psalms" ("salmos"). The musicians may simply have led the unison singing of the assembled company, but, as the Guatulco Factor's report suggests, instruments such as viols could have supported a version sung in harmony ("en canto d'organo") if required. In such performances the consort probably functioned like an organ, providing simple harmonic support.

Musicians employed on Portuguese ships were on the whole much more actively involved in the provision of music for services than their English counterparts. The high quality of the singing on

[28]Nuttall translated "y cantaron en canto de organo" as "and sang together with the accompaniment of the stringed instruments," but the phrase "en canto de organo" usually implied "measured" music—harmony or polyphony—as opposed to plainsong.

[29]L. de Alberti and A. B. Wallis, *English Merchants and the Spanish Inquisition in the Canaries* (*CS*, vol. 23; London, 1912), 38 and 113.

[30]W. L. Schurz, *The Manila Galleon* (New York, 1959), 311.

board ships of the East Indian fleet impressed many Jesuits. In 1566 one priest wrote of a service at sea that lamentations had been sung in harmony ("a canto de organo") with very good voices ("muy buenas bozes"), as though the ship were a cathedral church ("una iglesia cathedral").[31] Another reported in 1562 that vespers were sung in harmony ("de canto de organo") by those "who could do it well."[32] On important feast days, services usually incorporated a procession. During his voyage to India in 1578, Father Nicholas Spinola reported that on the Feast of Corpus Christi the men processed throughout the ship singing a Pange lingua.[33] The act of worship on feast days would often end with an orchestrated crescendo of celebration with firework displays, gunfire and musical instruments, usually bells ("campainhas"), trumpets ("trombetas"), shawms ("charamellas") and fifes ("pifanos").[34] According to Spinola, the Jesuits regarded these musical and ceremonial aspects of worship as useful in promoting good attendance. Daily services, he wrote, were sung "in musica di note" in order to prevent drunken brawling and other abuses. Every effort was made to provide attractive music, "the litanies being sung in two choirs, always with some novelty included" ("con le letanie cantate a duoi chori in musica, trovando sempre alcuna nova inventione").[35] Another example of the deliberate use of music in worship to improve discipline occurred during the voyage of Mendaña to the South Seas in 1595. In response to murmurings of discontent, Mendaña ordered vespers on feast days to be celebrated solemnly with flags and with the playing of "military instruments" ("los instrumentos de guerra").[36]

The value of daily religious observance was by no means universally acknowledged. On some French ships, if Pyrard de Laval is to be believed, a lax approach to worship led to a general breakdown in discipline. He attributed the appalling conduct of both officers and

[31]A. da Silva Rego, *Documentaçao para a História das Missões do Padroado Português do Oriente: India, vol. 10 (1566–1568)* (Lisbon, 1953), 42.

[32]Ibid., 9:8–9.

[33]J. Wicki, ed., *Documenta Indica,* vol. 11 (1577–1580) (*MHSI,* vol. 103; Rome, 1970), 311.

[34]Da Silva Rego (1953), 9:8–9.

[35]Wicki (1970), 310.

[36]D. J. Zaragoza, *Historia del descubrimiento de las regiones Austriales* (Madrid, 1876), 1:58.

sailors on board the *Corbin* during her voyage to the East Indies in 1601 to the fact that the French were less assiduous in their religious duties than the English, Portuguese or Dutch.[37] Drawing upon his own experience of Portuguese ships—he made the return journey in one—he observed that services on these ships were conducted in all respects as on land, save for the consecration of the elements. Evening prayers were said at nine o'clock: "the master with his whistle summons everyone to say a *Pater* and an *Ave*" ("le maistre avec un coup de siflet appelle tout le monde pour dire un *Pater* et *Ave*"); boy singers provided music for morning worship: "at day-break all the ship's boys chant an orison or sea-prayer" ("au poinct du jour tous les garçons du navire chantent une oraison ou prière de mer").[38] He concluded his "Advis pour aller aux Indes Orientales" with a plea to French captains to follow the example of other nations and insist upon correct religious observance. Pyrard may well have been fortunate in his experience of life on a ship of the East Indian fleet. We know from other sources that the conditions prevalent on these vessels were often atrocious, largely as a result of poor discipline. The drunkenness, the gambling, the debauchery, the violence of ill-disciplined soldiers, to say nothing of the horrible stench caused by squalid living conditions, conspired to make many and early passage to India a nightmare.[39]

[37] A. Gray, *The Voyage of François Pyrard of Laval to the East Indies, the Maldives, the Moluccas and Brazil*, vol. 2, part 2 (*HS*, vol. 80; London, 1890), 398.

[38] Ibid., vol. 2, part 1 (*HS*, vol. 77; London, 1888), 197.

[39] On conditions on board Portuguese East Indian ships, see C. R. Boxer, *The Tragic History of the Sea 1589–1622* (*HS*, 2nd series, vol. 112; Cambridge, 1959), 1–30.

CHAPTER 4

Signalling and Ceremonial Duties

The duties of the ships' trumpeters are summed up succinctly in two naval treatises of the seventeenth century. In the Naval Tracts of Sir William Monson, the trumpeters' responsibilities are outlined as follows:

> For the more reputation of this man's service in a ship of the King's, and under an Admiral, it is fit he should have a silver trumpet, and himself and his noise to have banners of silk of the Admiral's colours. His place is to keep the poop, to attend the General's going ashore and coming aboard, and all other strangers or boats, and to sound as an entertainment to them; as also when they hail a ship, or when they charge, board, or enter her. They set the watch at eight of the clock at night, and discharge it in the morning, and have a can of beer allowed for the same. This is not only incident to an Admiral, but to all captains that carry a noise of trumpets with them.[1]

John Smith wrote in a similar vein, recommending further that if a full "noise" of trumpets was unavailable, the trumpeter should teach some new recruits "to bear a part," for which service he should receive an extra reward.[2] Brief summaries like these do scant justice to the range of duties that trumpeters were required to undertake, but narratives of voyages are rich in information and give a better impression of the reality of life at sea for the trumpeter.

[1]G. E. Manwaring and W. G. Perrin, *The Life and Works of Sir Henry Mainwaring*, vol. 2 (*NRS*, vol. 56; London, 1922), 86.

[2]J. Smith, *An Accidence, or the path-way to experience necessary for all Young Seamen* (London, 1626). An enlarged edition was published in 1627, entitled *A Sea Grammar*. This was republished in 1653 as *The Sea-Man's Grammar*.

As trumpeters were required to accompany the captain at all times, they were allocated berths at the rear of the ship close to his cabin. In *The Seaman's Dictionary* Sir Henry Mainwaring commented on the traditional division of the ship's company into two parts: "the boatswain and all the common sailors under his command, to be before the main mast; the Captain, master, master's mate, gunners, quartermasters, trumpeters, etc., to be abaft the mainmast."[3] This arrangement was confirmed by Captain John Smith in *The Sea-Mans Grammar*: "And as the Captain and masters mates, Gunners, Carpenters, Quartermasters, Trumpeters, etc. are to be abaft the Mast, so the Boatswaine, and al the Yonkers or common sailors under his command is to be before the Mast."[4]

Plate 1. Trumpeters sounding on the poop deck. Joseph Furttenbach: *Architectura Navalis* (Ulm, 1629) plate 10. By permission of the British Library.

The usual station of trumpeters during daylight hours was on the poop deck at the rear of the ship above the captain's cabin and the officers' quarters (Plate 1). From here, they could command a clear view of the main deck below, the forecastle and the rigging of the ship, and sound signals upon the captain's orders. They could view clearly and hail any approaching vessel and would themselves be visible.

[3]M. Oppenheim, *The Naval Tracts of Sir William Monson*, vol. 4 (*NRS*, vol. 45; London, 1913), 57.

[4]Smith (1653), 35.

The sight and sound of a band of trumpeters sounding on the poop was in fact a recognized way of indicating that a ship was fully prepared for battle. The trumpeters of the *Susan* were placed on the poop for this purpose during William Harborne's embassy to the Sultan in 1583.[5] A party of Englishmen had landed on Majorca and been captured. As the English ship prepared to sail past the harbour in full view of the land guns to parley for their release, the company was placed in battle order: "our whole noise of trumpets were sounding on the poope with drumme and flute." A brief negotiation ensued: "all this while, our trumpets, drum and flute sounded, and so we passed out in face of them all."

A description of a skirmish fought by Robert Dudley while returning from the West Indies in 1595, shows that the trumpeters were required to occupy their dangerously exposed position on the poop even during exchanges of gunfire. Dudley, positioning his men for battle, ordered one of his captains "to take some few small shott upon the poope, placinge the trumpetts on topp of the masters cabbin."[6]

An unusual accident that befell a trumpeter on the poop is recorded in one of the accounts of Drake's circumnavigation. It occurred while the *Golden Hind* was passing through the Straits of Magellan:

> But before our going to land, wee had a strange and sodaine accident, for John Brewer, our trumpeter, standing upon the poope, sounding his trumpett, being now as great a calme as it had been a storme, without anny wind to moove or shake a silken thredd, most strangely a rope was so tossed and violently hurled against his body that it cast his body over into the sea, with that strength that tenn men with all their powers could not have don more to a block of his weight, for by estimation his body lighting in the water, was eight times his length distant from the direct point below to the place where hee fell, where labouring mightely for life (the boat being not redy) many ropes were cast round about him and upon him some, but he could not catch hold of anny one at all to help himselfe, till he called one by name to cast one to him, which no sooner was done, but he received it, and was saved at the last pinch, or, as it were, at the end of all hope.[7]

Brewer had been one of the accusers of Thomas Doughty, controversially executed by Drake. The author of this narrative commented pointedly on the trumpeter's mishap: "his judgement worth noting."

[5]Hakluyt, 5:248.

[6]G. F. Warner, *The Voyage of Robert Dudley to the West Indies 1594–1595* (*HS*, 2nd series, vol. 3; London, 1899), 60.

[7]W. S. W. Vaux, *The World Encompassed by Sir Francis Drake* (*HS*, vol. 16; London, 1854), 81.

The poop was the conventional place for the sounding of fanfares during the embarkation of visitors of rank. The forecastle could also be manned by musicians and trumpeters if an exceptionally elaborate welcome were required. In 1610 Phineas Pett received James I at the launching of the *Prince Royal* with "drums and trumpets placed on poop and forecastle and ther wind instruments by them, so that nothing was wanting to so great a royalty that could be desired."[8]

The position of the drum and fife players was usually on deck, close to the main mast where the companies of foot soldiers were stationed. Dutch marine artists frequently depict the drummers here (Plate 2).

Plate 2. Heemskerk's defeat of the Spaniards off Gibraltar on 25 April 1607: a drummer standing by the mainmast of a Dutch ship. Cornelis Hendrickszoon Vroom, c. 1607. Rijksmuseum, Amsterdam.

[8]W. G. Perrin, *The Autobiography of Phineas Pett* (*NRS*, vol. 51; London, 1918), 81.

Spare drums are sometimes shown slung over the side (Plate 3).

Plate 3. Heemskerk's defeat of the Spaniards off Gibraltar on 25 April 1607: a drummer leaning against the side of a boat; a drum tied over the side. Cornelis Claeszoon van Wieringen, 1619. National Maritime Museum, London.

When a ship set sail from port, the first duty of her trumpeters was to salute those remaining on land. There are many references to trumpeters sounding their instruments as their ship left harbor for the open sea. Thomas Stevens, leaving Lisbon in 1579 on a Portuguese fleet bound for Goa, commented on the great solemnity of their departure "with trumpets and shooting of ordinance."[9] The best description of a musical farewell is an evocative passage in Sir Richard Hawkins's account of his departure from Plymouth in 1593:[10]

[9]Hakluyt, 6:378.

[10]C. R. Drinkwater-Bethune, *The Observations of Sir Richard Hawkins, Knt, in his Voyage into the South Sea in the Year 1593* (*HS*, vol. 1; London, 1847), 30.

> The greater part of my companie gathered aboord, I set sayle the 12th of June 1593, about three of the clocke in the afternoon, and made a bourd or two off and in, wayting the returne of my boat, which I had sent a-shore, for dispatch of some businesse: which being come aboord, and all put in order, I looft [plyed] near the shore, to give my farewell to all the inhabitants of the towne, whereof the most part were gathered together upon the Howe, to shew their gratefull correspondency, to the love and zeale which I, my father, and predecessors, have ever borne to that place, as to our naturall and mother towne. And first with my noyse of trumpets, after with my waytes, and then with my other musicke, and lastly, with the artillery of my shippes, I made the best signification I could of a kinde farewell. This they answered with the waytes of the towne, and the ordinance on shore, and with shouting of voyces; which with the fayre evening and silence of the night, were heard a great distance off.

The solemnity of formal leave-taking was increased by the sure knowledge that many on board would never return.

Once at sea, trumpeters were required to hail passing ships. Sir Henry Mainwaring defined "hailing" a ship as "calling to her to know whence she is, or whither she is bound."[11] The phrase "hailing with trumpets or whistles" indicated the usual manner of this act. It was the custom for ships in a large fleet to disperse a certain distance during the day, the better to watch for enemy ships, and to gather again in the evening to report to the Admiral. The trumpeters would always hail each other at these meetings. The practice is well described in a report of the voyage of Essex and Howard to Cadiz in 1596:

> All which squadrons, albeit they did every day separate themselves of purpose, by the distance of certaine leagues, as well to looke out for such shippes as were happily under sayle, as also for the better procuring of sea-roome: yet alwayes commonly eyther that day, or the next day, towarde evening, they came all together, with friendly salutations and gratulations one to another: which they terme by the name of Hayling: a ceremonie done solemnly, and in verie good order, with sound of Trumpets and noyse of cheerefull voyces: and in such sort performed as was no small encouragement one to the other, beside a true report of all such accidents, as had happened in their squadrons.[12]

[11]Manwaring and Perrin (1922) 159–60.

[12]Hakluyt, 4:242. See also J. K. Laughton, "Book of War by Sea and Land," *Naval Miscellany*, vol. 1, ed. J. K. Laughton (*NRS*, vol. 20; London, 1902),14.

Unfamiliar ships could be hailed to find out their purpose and destination. While off the Isle of Wight in 1594, Robert Dudley observed two large ships coming down the Channel. He approached to investigate, "halinge them with his noyse of trumpetts."[13] Failure to reply to a salute from trumpeters was certain to raise suspicions about the identity and purpose of the silent vessel. In a letter to the East India Company in London, Cocks, their chief merchant in Japan, wrote of an incident during which some English ships had hailed a Dutch ship with a "noes of trumpetes," but had received no answer which made them "stand in dowbt whether they were frendes or noe."[14]

During the course of a voyage, trumpeters were expected to set and discharge the night watch. They were also apparently expected to take their turn with other seamen as watchmen or lookouts. John Brewer, the trumpeter on the *Golden Hind*, witnessed the loss of the *Marigold* in the Straits of Magellan during a night watch:

> The storme being so outragious and furious, the bark Marigold, wherein Edward Bright, one of the accusers of Thomas Doubty, was captayne, with 28 soules, were swallowed up with the horrible and unmercifull waves, or rather mountanes of the sea, which chanced in the second watch of the night, wherein myself and John Brewer, our trumpeter, being in watch, did heare their fearfull cryes, when the hand of God came upon them.[15]

Trumpeters sometimes manned lookout posts on the rigging of their ship. Christopher Jackson, one of the trumpeters with Frobisher in 1578, was sent up into the top on one occasion to help set a correct course[16], and in 1587 one of Cavendish's trumpeters reported sighting a Spanish ship from his position aloft.[17] A trumpeter on the *Darling*, one of the ships under the command of Middleton in 1610, was killed while asleep in the lookout position. Downton described how the enemy came on board, and "seeing no man stirring, thought themselves surelye possest of her, murthering the trumpeter, whom they found aloft asleep."[18]

[13]Warner (1899), 4.

[14]E. M. Thompson, *Diary of Richard Cocks*, vol. 2 (*HS*, vol. 67; London, 1883), 332.

[15]Vaux (1854), 79.

[16]R. Collinson, *The Three Voyages of Martin Frobisher* (*HS*, vol. 38; London, 1867), 300–1.

[17]Hakluyt, 11:324.

[18]C. R. Markham, *The Voyage of Sir James Lancaster, Kt., to the East Indies* (*HS*, vol. 56; London, 1877), 174.

In periods of poor visibility, trumpeters and drummers sounded their instruments to help avoid collisions. The "Instructions given to the Masters" by Anthony Jenkinson in 1557 includes the following: "It is constituted that if any ship shalbe severed by mist or darke weather, in such sort as the one cannot have sight of the other, then and in such case the Admiral shall make sound and noise by drumme, trumpet, horne, gunne or otherwise or meanes, that the ships may come nigh together, as by safetie and good order they may."[19] Fogs were a major hazard for ships sailing to Newfoundland and other areas of North America, and this was one reason why all fifteen ships in the fleet commanded by Frobisher in 1578 were required to carry audible means of signalling: "Every ship in the fleete in the time of fogges, whiche continually happen with little winds and most parte calmes, shall keepe a reasonable noyse with trumpet, drumme or otherwise to keepe themselves cleere one of another."[20] According to the journal of Thomas Ellis, Frobisher was indeed troubled by fogs. On one occasion "there fell such a fogge and hideous mist that we could not see one another; whereupon we stroke our drums, and sounded our trumpets, to the ende we might keepe together; and so continued all that day and night, till the next day that the mist brake up."[21] The requirement for trumpeters to be available during periods of fog became a standard one in later naval ordinances. A typical example comes in the instructions for the expedition to Cadiz in 1596: "In fogs (if any happen) when your ships are becalmed, you shall cause some noise to be made by drum, by trumpet, by shooting off a musket or calliver, now and then, or by some other like means, that hearing you to be near, one may take heed, lest he fall foul of another."[22] Other sounds suggested were the shouting of men[23] and the ringing of the ship's bell.[24]

During the course of a voyage, trumpeters could expect many duties of a ceremonial nature: welcoming the captain or distinguished visitors aboard; escorting them back on shore; sounding death-knells at funerals. A detailed description of the ceremonies appropriate to the reception of a visitor of high rank, such as a Prince

[19]Hakluyt, 2:376.

[20]Collinson (1867), 228.

[21]Hakluyt, 7:233.

[22]J. S. Corbett, "Relation of the Voyage to Cadiz, 1596; by Sir William Slyngisbie," *The Naval Miscellany*, vol. 1, ed. J. K. Laughton (*NRS*, vol. 20; London, 1902), 27.

[23]J. S. Corbett, *Fighting Instructions 1530–1816* (*NRS*, vol. 29; London, 1905), 57.

[24]Oppenheim (1913), 10.

or High Admiral, appears in Boteler's *Dialogues*. The duties of the trumpeters are stated clearly:

> By the break of that day, the ship is in every part to be made neat and clean, and to be trimmed with all her ensigns and pendants; the ship's barge is early in the morning to be sent from the ship to the shore, perfectly furnished with carpets, cushions, tilt, and the like; the Coxswain with his whistle and best clothes being to attend in the stern, and the barge's gang in their liveries to row. And as soon as the Prince hath set his foot within the barge, the Standard Royal, or at least the flag, is to be let fly and to be fixed in the head of the barge; the which flag or standard is afterwards, at his coming aboard the ship, to be let fly, or heaved out in her main-top; and upon the first ken of the barge from the shore, the ship's decks, tops, yards, and shrouds, are all to be thoroughly manned; and the shrouds to be (as it were) hung with men. Upon the more near approach of the barge, the ship's noise of trumpets are to sound; and so to hold on until the barge come within less than musket shot of the ship. And then the trumpets are to cease; and all such as carry whistles are to whistle a welcome three several times; and in every interim the ship's whole company are to hail the barge with a joint shout, after the custom of the sea. As soon as the whistles and shouts of salute and welcome are stilled, the trumpets are again to sound a welcome to the ship's side. And that side which is the port, or entering side, is to be very well manned with the primest and best fashioned men of the ship's company ready on both sides of the ladder. The Captain of the ship is upon the deck to present himself, just as the Prince enters, upon his knee; and so to receive him into the ship, and from thence to conduct him into all the principal rooms and offices of the ship; and at last into the great cabin, which is to be royally furnished, that there he may make his retirement and take his repast. And being ready for his meat, the trumpets are to sound at the carrying of it up, and the music to be at hand to play when he is at it; all the guns of the ship being to be ready laden and primed, that so he may command what he pleaseth of that nature.
>
> And thus having been entertained, and fully informed by the Captain in all his demands, he is in the like manner to be waited upon at his departure, as he was at his coming in. And being returned into his barge, after the trumpets have sounded a loath-to-depart, and that the barge is fallen off a fit and fair berth and distance from the ship, he is to have his farewell given him with so many guns as the ship is able to give; provided that they be always of an odd number.[25]

[25]W. G. Perrin, *Boteler's Dialogues* (*NRS*, vol. 65; London, 1929), 265–66. See also *The most royall and honourable Entertainement of the famous and renowmed King Christiern the Fourth, King of Denmarke* (London, 1606): "And presently, at the command of the

The division of musical duties on such occasions followed the conventional pattern for the reception of guests on land with the "noise" of trumpets sounding for arrivals, departures and meal times, and the professional musicians performing incidental music during the reception itself. In *Some Rules and Orders for the Government of the Household of an Earl* (1621), Richard Braithwaite observed: "At great feastes, when the Earle's service is going to the table, they are to play upon shagbuttes, Cornetts, Shalmes, and other instruments going with winde. In meale times to play upon Violls, Violins or other broken musicke."[26] On small ships, individual gentlemen could sometimes hire their own trumpeters. Marmaduke Rawdon employed one for a voyage "whosse dewtie was to sound when his dinner and supper was brought up, att aney time when he was disposd to be mery or drinke healths abord, also when he understood he was arisinge or goinge to bed, also when soever he went ashore or came abord."[27] The Loath-to-depart mentioned by Boteler was a traditional tune, sounded when guests were about to depart. In later naval parlance, a loath-to-depart was a signal for wives and sweethearts to leave the ship.[28] The term came to include all tunes played at the moment of departure. Teonge mentions the title of one tune played as a loath-to-depart by the trumpeters of his ships—"Maids, where are your hearts?"[29]

The embarkation of royalty at Channel ports was a genre much favored by the patrons of seventeenth-century marine artists. Many

---

lord-admiral of the fleet, the company was by the boatswains' whistles called up, and in all gallant manner that might be, each man in his livery, making a gallant show, and noise of trumpets after the sea manner, and meeting of friends; the tacklings, tops and every part of the ship was so replenished with men, that hardly might you discern the ropes, or see the ship's sides."

[26]D. Price, *Patrons and Musicians of the English Renaissance* (Cambridge, 1981).

[27]R. Davies, *The Life of Marmaduke Rawdon of York* (*CS*, vol. 85; London, 1863), 30.

[28]The *OED* definition of a Loath-to-depart is: "Originally the tune of a song (probably containing those words) expressive of regret for departure," *transferred sense*, "any tune played as a farewell."

[29]G. E. Manwaring, *The Diary of Henry Teonge* (London, 1927), 91. References to specific tunes played by trumpeters occur from the mid-seventeenth century. In *A Narrative or Journal of the Proceedings of their Excellencies, the Right Honourable the Lord Holles, and the Lord Coventry* (London, 1667), 5, it was reported that: "The Yachts lowred their Topsails, their Trumpets sounded, and the first salute of their Trumpets we observed to be the Tune of *The King shall enjoy his own again.*"

Plate 4. The embarkation of the Elector Palatine and Princess Elizabeth at Margate in 1613: a "noise" of trumpets salutes on the quay. Adam Willaerts, 1623, St. James Palace, London. The Royal Collection©1994. Her Majesty The Queen.

pictures were commissioned of important historical journeys such as that of the Elector Palatine in 1613 (Plate 4), Charles II in 1660 and William of Orange in 1688 (Plate 5). Typically, in the middle distance, the fleet is depicted riding at anchor with flags and pendants flying and the crews assembled on deck, while in the foreground on the quay the royal personnage is welcommed or bad farewell. The trumpeters are usually shown waiting in a boat or on the quay.

Sounding death-knells was an all-too-common occurrence for trumpeters at sea. As the body of a deceased person was lowered over the side of a ship, the trumpeters would sound a knell. When Drake died in 1595, his body was put down into the sea in a coffin of lead, "the Trumpets in dolefull manner echoing out this lamentation for so greate a losse."[30]

Teonge, who conducted the funeral of a boatswain while his ship was anchored off Scanderoon, describes the manner of a

[30]Andrews (1972), 102.

Plate 5. The departure of William of Orange from Hellevoetsluis on 19 October 1688: a "noise" of trumpets waits in the royal boat. Anon. National Maritime Museum, London.

trumpeter's knell.[31] The man's body was placed in a coffin covered with a flag, with his silver whistle and chain of office between two crossed pistols on the lid. The officers and half the ship's company disembarked and followed the coffin to a nearby churchyard, with "eight trumpeters sounding dolefully, whereof the four in the first rank began, and the next four answered, so that there was a continued doleful tone from the ship to the shore, and from thence to the grave." As soon as the party left the churchyard, the trumpeters sounded "merry levitts." A trumpeter's knell, then, consisted of repeated tones, like the tolling of a bell. Teonge, indeed, uses this comparison himself when describing the commemoration of the execution of Charles I; the ceremony concluded with the trumpeters "ringing the bells on the trumpets very dolefully, and also the guns firing at half a minute distance."[32] The trumpeters then sounded "Well-a-day" (a lament) as an appropriately sombre finale.

As a mark of respect, English trumpeters sometimes played at the funerals of other Europeans. On 17 June 1613, Best attended the burial of a Dutch captain at Achin, the English trumpeters "sounding his knell."[33] Drummers at a funeral would muffle their instruments with cloth and beat in a slow tempo as a mark of respect to the deceased. The practice is well described in an account of the funeral of Alvaro de Mendaña in 1595 in the New Hebrides. His coffin was carried by eight men and the soldiers stood with their guns reversed; "two drums covered in mourning cloth" ("dos atambores cubiertos de luto") were played with "slow and muffled beats" ("unos golpes tardos y rancos") and the "pifano" echoed a similar sentiment.[34]

On festive occasions such as Christmas Day, the trumpeters visited the cabins of officers. According to Teonge: "At 4 in the morning our trumpeters all do flat their trumpets, and begin at our Captain's cabin, and thence to all the officers' and gentlemen's cabins, playing a levite at each cabin-door, and bidding Good morrow, Wishing a merry Christmas."[35] After this they would go up to their station on the poop

[31]Manwaring (1927), 97–98.

[32]Ibid., 125.

[33]W. Foster, *The Voyage of Thomas Best to the East Indies 1612–1614* (*HS*, 2nd series, vol. 75; London, 1934), 165.

[34]D. J. Zaragoza, *Historia del descubrimiento de las regiones Austriales* (Madrid, 1876), vol. 1:123.

[35]Manwaring (1927), 117.

and sound three more "levites" in honor of the morning. In his diary for 22 December 1617, Cocks, the English merchant in charge of the Japan factory, received an early call from the Dutch trumpeters in honor of the New Year: "The Hollandes generall sent his nois of trompets to geve me a salve this mornyng before day. . . ."[36]

The military duties of naval trumpeters included both actions at sea and skirmishes on land. A sea-battle would commence with the trumpeters hailing the enemy ships, usually when they were within range of the guns. Richard Hawkins described the beginning of a fight with a Spanish fleet in the Pacific thus: "being within musket shott, we hayled first with our noise of trumpets, then with our waytes, and after with our artilery; which they answered with artilery, two for one."[37] The use of "waytes" or shawm players to reinforce the trumpeters' call to battle was not unusual. The hailing of enemy ships was intended to encourage the men to fight bravely. When a small English ship was surrounded by a Turkish fleet in the Mediterranean in 1563, the master decided to offer resistance, and the trumpeters and the drum and fife players inspired the company to valiant deeds: "Nowe likewise sounded up the drums, trumpets and flutes, which would have encouraged any man, had he never so litle heart or courage in him."[38] The English boatswain fought with memorable courage until a shot smashed his whistle and killed him. During the heat of battle, the trumpeters would remain at their station on the poop and sound again at every new assault. In 1587 during the course of his fight with the *Santa Anna*, Cavendish encouraged his men afresh "with the whole noyse of trumpets."[39] A Spanish survivor later reported hearing the English musicians play "los clarines y trompetas."[40]

The sight and sound of trumpet players on the poop deck was intended to terrify the enemy, and it often had that effect. The trumpeters on the *Hector* in 1599 were used to excellent effect to scare off a potentially hostile fleet of galleys near the Island of Samos. In order to escape, the *Hector* ventured down a narrow channel between Samos and the mainland. As she passed the enemy fleet, the English ship put on a show of bravado. In the words of Dallam, "our master caused all of our company to stand up and make as great a show as we coulde, and when we weare

[36]E. M. Thompson, *Diary of Richard Cocks*, vol. 1 (*HS*, vol. 66; London, 1883), 343.

[37]Drinkwater-Bethune (1847), 184.

[38]Hakluyt, 5:154.

[39]Hakluyt, 11:325.

[40]W. M. Mathes, *Documentos para la Historia de la Demarcacion Comercial de California 1583–1632*, vol. 1 (Madrid, 1965), 68.

ryghte over againste them, our five trumpets sounded sodonly, which made them wonder, loukinge earnestly upon us, but gave us not a worde, so we Dashte them oute of countenance who mente to have feared us."[41]

Spanish and Portuguese ships did not always carry trumpeters and when hailed by the English would sometimes reply with whistles or other instruments. An account of the *Centurian*'s fight with a Spanish fleet off Gibraltar in 1591 mentions the silver whistles blown by the Spaniards:

> During which time there was a sore and deadly fight on both sides, in which the Trumpet of the Centurian sounded foorth the deadly points of warre, and encouraged them to fight manfully against their adversaries: on the contrary part, there was no warlike Musicke in the Spanish Gallies, but onely their whistles of silver, which they sounded foorth to their owne contentment."[42]

Before an engagement with a Portuguese ship in 1616, Edward Terry reported that: "we saluted her with our Trumpets, shee us with her wind Instruments."[43] Furttenbach illustrates a galley in his *Architectura Navalis* with "Trommetter, Zincken und Posaunenblaser" sounding on deck (Plate 6).

Plate 6. "Trommetter, Zincken und Posaunenblaser" sounding on a galley deck. Joseph Furttenbach: *Architectura Navalis* (Ulm, 1629) plate 1. By permission of the British Library

[41]J. T. Bent, *Early Voyages and Travels in the Levant* (*HS*, vol. 87; London, 1893), 42.

[42]Hakluyt, 7:36.

[43]Purchas, 9:6.

Few details survive of the precise nature of the "deadly points of warre" sounded by naval trumpeters, but some sixteenth- and seventeenth-century treatises do give information about the military calls used by army trumpeters to signal to the cavalry.[44] The *Rules and Ordynaunces for the Warre* published in 1544 required that: "Every horseman at the fyrst blaste of the trumpette shall sadle or cause to be sadled his horse, at the seconde to brydell, at the thirde to leape on his horse backe, to wait on the kyng, or his lorde or capitayne." Naval trumpeters no doubt used a similarly detailed code. During the Earl of Cumberland's voyage to the Azores in 1589, a command was sent to the trumpets to sound, but the shooting of any gun was forbidden until a further order. This was misunderstood: "some of the companie, either not well perceiving or regarding what he sayd, immediatly upon the sound of the Trumpets discharged their pieces at the Islanders."[45] Either through disobedience or ignorance, the gunners misconstrued a precise trumpet signal.

English military treatises outline the basic signals given by drum and fife players. Ralph Smith, writing in c. 1557, suggested that fifers should "teach the companye the soundes of the marche, allarum, approache, assaulte, battaile, retreate, skirmishe, or any other challenge that of necessetie should be knowen." Markham, writing "of Drummes and Phiphes," gave similar details of drum signals:

> First in the morning the discharge or breaking up of the *Watch*, then a preparation or Summons to make them repaire to their colours; then a beating away before they begin to march; after that a *March* according to the nature and custom of the country (for divers countries have divers Marches), then a *Charge*, then a *Retrait*, then a *Troupe*, and lastly a *Battalion* or a Battery, besides other sounds which depending on the phantasttikenes of forain nations are not so useful.

There is no reason to suppose that naval drum and fife players used a different set of signals. Indeed, the characteristically English terminology of drum signals—"watch"; "alarum"; "march"—often appears in reports of voyages or overseas settlements.

The detailed code of signalling used by trumpeters and drummers in effect enabled a commander to do two things: he could

[44]P. Downey, "The Trumpet and its Role in Music of the Renaissance and Early Baroque" (diss., Queen's University of Belfast, 1983).

[45]Hakluyt, 7:16.

convey information to his own men, or he could convey information, either true or false, to the enemy. From the point of view of his own side, the sounds of the trumpets and drums enabled a captain to relay commands quickly in situations of great confusion and panic and thus coordinate an action much more easily than would be possible by visual means. The necessity for audible musical signals during the noise and confusion of battle is clear from Edward Terry's colorful evocation of an early seventeenth-century sea fight:

> I want words to express the extreme horror that is to be observed in these sea fights, where fire like lightning darts into mens eyes, and the over-loud cracks of great ordance like thunder roars in their ears, besides the noise made by muskets, drums and fifes, with men hurrying up and down the ship in a confused tumult, wrapt about in a thick cloud of suffocating smoak made by the powder. . . ."[46] In these situations the drum-beat provided the discipline necessary for orderly movements by the foot soldiers.

A drum beat was regarded as the best method of coordinating the flotilla of small craft used to disembark a force on a beach held by the enemy. The orders given by Essex and Howard for the landing of their army during the 1596 expedition to Cadiz specified that the boats were to be drawn up in ranks, the leader carrying the flag of St George or a white pennant in the prow: "That when the drum that beateth the first rank shall beat a march, they shall all row forward such a pace, as the first leadeth, who shall be appointed to row no faster than the slowest boat may conveniently keep company. And if the leading boat stay and the drums cease beating, then shall they all stay."[47] In Sir Francis Vere's report of this landing, the drummer is said to have provided a beat specifically for the oarsmen: "at a signall given with the drum from his boat, the rest were to follow according to the measure and the time of the sound of the said drum, which they were to observe in the deeping of their oars."[48] A general silence was ordered "as well of warlike instruments as otherwise" in order that the drum beat could be heard clearly.

A drum beat could be a message to assemble for a public announcement, as when an offender was "drummed out" of the armed forces. Before the expedition to Cadiz sailed from Plymouth in 1596,

[46]E. Terry, *A Voyage to East-India* (London, 1655), 48.

[47]Corbett (1902), 63.

[48]*The Commentaries of Sir Francis Vere* (London, 1657).

an unnamed lieutenant was "by sound of Drumme publickly in all the streetes disgraced, or rather after a sort disgraded, and cashierd."[49] The sound of the drum ensured maximum publicity. A list of abuses supposedly committed by the Dutch against the English in the East Indies between 1616 and 1620 included the complaint that Englishmen had been stripped naked and whipped in public and that the Dutch had "beaten up their Drumme and called the Blackes together to see it done."[50]

To the enemy, trumpets and drums could convey a sense of disorder. Especially at night, trumpet signals could keep enemy forces in a state of constant confusion by sounding false alarms. At the Azores in 1597, the Earl of Essex, hoping to disembark an army in secret, deployed his trumpeters thus: "[we] did all the night give them perpetuall Alarums, with Shot, Drummes, and Trumpets, in such Boats as were left, sometimes in one place, sometimes in another, alongst the Shoare, where the Spaniards kept their Corps de Guards, and fiers, who were often in great amazements, calling, and running to and fro, thinking verily that wee were landing in that place or about it."[51] In other situations, a commander could prevent an attack by ordering his trumpeters and drummers to provide audible evidence of his state of readiness. The Englishmen involved in the sige of Ormuz in 1622 set their watch at night "with a vollie of small Shot, Drumme and Trumpets, which the Portugals might easily heare and see."[52]

An alternative tactic was to silence the drums and trumpets in order to lull the enemy into a false sense of security. Dudley marched through Trinidad in 1595 to the sound of "trumpetts and drome" and "the continuall noyse of shootinge."[53] This was done partly as a matter of simple bravado "to maugre the Spaniards berd," but it later enabled him to surprise an Indian, who, "beinge accostomed unto our sounde of trumpetts and shootinge of our peeces at the settinge and dischardging of everie watch, never mistrusted us untell wee weare come upon him."[54] In 1589 an English regiment in Portugal

[49]Hakluyt, 4:237.

[50]Purchas, 5:170.

[51]Purchas, 20:111.

[52]Purchas, 10:339.

[53]Warner (1899), 46.

[54]Ibid., 45

"marched without sound of Drum, and somewhat faster then ordinary," the aim being to approach the enemy without being observed.[55]

The carrying of messages to and from the enemy was usually entrusted to trumpeters or drummers.[56] In theory, under a flag of truce, they were immune from direct attack; in practice, some were killed while engaged on this kind of mission. In 1590 one of Frobisher's trumpeters was shot dead after landing on one of the Azores to ask for supplies.[57] The execution of a messenger was regarded as an extremely hostile act which would be avenged if possible. A man who had killed an English drummer sent as a messenger during Drake's 1589 expedition to Portugal was hanged in full view of the English army, the defenders indicating by this action that they wished to have "faire warres."[58] The most effective protection a commander could offer one of his messengers was to threaten reprisals against enemy prisoners. One of Drake's trumpeters in 1589 was sent with a message to Lisbon; on his passport was written an explicit threat to execute the highest ranking Portuguese prisoners if any violence were done to him.[59]

Additional rewards were usually given to trumpeters in return for the delivery of a message in hazardous circumstances. A Spanish trumpeter with a perfectly innocent message caused great alarm by sounding his trumpet unexpectedly outside an English camp: "About two houres in the night, a Trumpet sounded a parley neere the Campe, which so amazed them, that they were greatly in doubt of the Spaniards treacherie."[60] The English commander sent first a single trumpeter to summon the man, then his "whole noise," and finally a company of men, who discovered the trumpeter with two others bearing gifts of wine and food. The trumpeter was given a large reward for his pains.

[55]Purchas, 19:536.

[56]See, for example, J. X. Evans, *The Works of Sir Roger Williams* (Oxford, 1972), 13, 79, 110.

[57]P. A. Tiele, *The Voyage of John Huyghen van Linschoten to the East Indies*, vol. 2 (*HS*, vol. 71; London, 1885), 302–3.

[58]Hakluyt, 6:488.

[59]Ibid., 509.

[60]*The Honourable Actions of that most Famous and Valiant Englishman, Edward Glemham Esquire, Latelie obtained against the Spaniards, and the Holy League* (London, 1591).

A recognized way of confirming one's identity in the hazardous areas between two forces was to play a popular tune of the day. A French fifer who deserted the Spanish in Florida in 1586 to join Drake played a tune which he knew the English sentries would recognize: "forthwith [out of the fort] came a French man being a Phipher (who had bene prisoner with them) in a litle boate, playing on his phiph the tune of the Prince of Orenge his song, and being called unto by the gard, he tolde them before he put foote out of the boate, what he was him selfe, and howe the Spaniards were gone from the fort."[61] Hakluyt identified the fifer as Nicholas Borgoignon. It is interesting that according to the English report the fifer claimed to be an escaped prisoner, while a Spanish witness described him as a foreign deserter.[62] The transition between one army and another always required some duplicity on the part of the deserter.

The profession of naval trumpeter was a dangerous one with a high mortality rate. During battles at sea, trumpeters were exposed to enemy fire with little protection. Dutch marine artists such as Cornelis Hendrickszoon Vroom and Cornelis Claeszoon van Wieringen often depict trumpeters in their battle scenes in positions on the poop deck (Plate 7) or standing in boats (Plate 8). They seem especially to have delighted in depicting the gory fate of young drummers during battle. Vroom's study of the Battle of Gibraltar (25 April 1607) shows two halves of a drummer and his drum being blasted many hundreds of feet into the air. Another favorite detail is the drum floating in the water with its owner being pulled into a rescue boat (Plates 9 and 10). John Taylor gives a graphic description of the deaths of two trumpeters during a battle fought between a small English ship, the *Dolphin* of London, and five Turkish vessels in 1616. Despite her small size—she was manned by 36 men and two boys—the *Dolphin* carried a full noise of trumpeters. Two of them survived, but their colleagues were less fortunate: "William Sweat,

[61] D. B. Quinn, *The Roanoke Voyages 1584–1590*, vol. 1 (*HS*, 2nd series, vol. 104; London, 1955), 197. The Prince of Orange's Song was the unofficial "anthem" of Protestant Europe. At Patani twelve trumpeters employed on the voyage of Jacob Wilkens and Jacob van Neck performed the "liedt van Wilhelmus van Nassouwe" in ceremonial fashion with their "nieuwe oraenje-vlagghe." See J. H. A. van Foreest and A. de Booy, *De Vierde Schipvaart der Nederlanders naar Oost Indië onder Jacob Wilkens en Jacob van Neck (1599–1604)*, vol. 1 (*LV*, vol. 82; The Hague, 1980), 258.

[62] I. A. Wright, *Further English Voyages to Spanish America 1583–1594* (*HS*, 2nd series, vol. 99; London, 1951), 186.

Trumpetter, as hee sounded in the fight had one arme shott off, yet hee sounded till another great shot stroke off his other arme, with his Trumpet and all, then after hee was kild with a shot thorow the body"; "William James, Trumpetter, burn'd with wild fire, that he flamed like a fierie man all over, then *John Ross* Purser cast water on him, he lived 5 dayes in great paine; in the fight an arrow came betwixt the Maisters legs at the helme and ran into the said *Iames* his leg which the Maister puld out."[63] Their importance as signallers made trumpeters prime targets for sharpshooters. Eliminating an enemy's means of communication has always been an effective tactic of war. The account of Barker's 1576 expedition to the West Indies speaks of an English trumpeter "trecherously slain" as an act of sabotage.[64] During hand-to-hand fighting, trumpeters probably carried arms for their own protection. Linschoten described the last exploit of a valiant Dutch trumpeter who served with the Portuguese in India. When he saw a Portuguese ensign-bearer desert his colors during battle, "casting his Trumpet at his backe, he ranne in great furie, and with his rapier killed the Arabian that held it."[65] Paradoxically, after surrender, trumpeters and musicians had a better chance of survival than ordinary soldiers or sailors because they had a skill to offer.[66]

Their usefulness in so many situations made the trumpeters indispensible in warfare. As signallers, their contribution could change the course of a battle and thus of history itself. As we shall see, a single mistimed trumpet call probably saved the life of the greatest naval hero of the Elizabethan Age.

[63]*All the Workes of Iohn Taylor the Water-Poet* (London, 1630), fol. Ccc5v.

[64]Hakluyt, 10:83.

[65]Tiele (1885), 186. This is yet another example of a trumpeter, through capture, desertion or free choice, serving in a ship of another nation. We have already noted examples of French trumpeters serving on English ships, English trumpeters serving on Dutch ships and an English trumpeter serving on a Portuguese ship. There was apparently a Dutch trumpeter, one "Artyur", serving under Drake in 1577. See Z. Nuttall, *New Light on Drake* (*HS*, 2nd series, vol. 34; London, 1914), 42.

[66]Purchas, 4:180.

Plate 7 (opposite, top). A skirmish between Dutch and English fleets in 1605: a trumpeter at his station by the flag on the poop deck. Cornelis Hendrickszoon Vroom, 1614. Nederlandsch Historisch Scheepvaart Museum, Amsterdam.

Plate 8 (opposite, bottom). A skirmish between Dutch and English fleets in 1605: a trumpeter signals at the rear of a boat while a drummer stands close to the soldiers by the mast. Cornelis Hendrickszoon Vroom, 1614. Nederlandsch Historisch Scheepvaart Museum, Amsterdam.

Plate 9 (above). Heemskerk's defeat of the Spaniards off Gibraltar on 25 April 1607: a drum floats in the sea after an explosion on a Spanish ship. Cornelis Hendrickszoon Vroom, c. 1607. Rijksmuseum, Amsterdam.

Plate 10. Heemskerk's defeat of the Spaniards off Gibraltar on 25 April 1607: a drummer struggles for survival in the sea as his boat sinks. Cornelis Claeszoon van Wieringen, c. 1607. Nederlandsch Historisch Scheepvaart Museum, Amsterdam.

CHAPTER 5

Amateur Music-Making

It is only to be expected that while the public, formal elements of musical life on board are frequently described in journals, much less is known about the informal music-making that went on among amateur musicians. The major figures of Elizabethan exploration, Drake, Frobisher, Grenville and Gilbert, came from a generation for whom playing the lute, cittern or orpharion was an increasingly common accomplishment. Ward has estimated from the London Port Book for 1567–1568 that 86 lutes, 14 gitterns, 18 citterns and 13,848 lute strings were imported into London during a period of only ten months.[1] Woodfill's documentary evidence of instrument ownership during the reign of Elizabeth confirms that plucked instruments were favored by most gentlemen amateurs at this period, the viol becoming popular only towards the end of the century.[2] In his plan for "The erection of an Achademy in London for educacion of her Maiesties Wardes, and others of the youth of nobility and gentlemen," Sir Humphrey Gilbert (whose own musical accomplishments, if any, are not known) stipulated that provision be made for "one Teacher of Musick . . . to play on the Lute, the Bandora and Cytterne. . . ."[3] Against this background, it comes as no surprise that Elizabethan captains with musical interests usually played plucked instruments. The Earl of Cumberland, England's leading privateer, purchased a "gittern lute" for ten shillings while a student at Trinity

[1]J. M. Ward, "A Dowland Miscellany," *JLSA*, vol.10 (1977), 116.

[2]W. L. Woodfill, *Musicians in English Society: from Elizabeth to Charles I* (Princeton, 1953).

[3]Ward (1977), 116.

College.[4] A setting of one of his poems in Robert Dowland's *A Musicall Banquet* (1610) suggests continuing musical interests. Sir Carew Raleigh, Sir Walter's elder brother, was a keen player of the orpharion. John Aubrey recalled: "I have heard my grandfather say that Sir Carew had a delicate cleare voice, and played singularly well on the olpharion (which was the instrument in fashion in those days) to which he did sing."[5]

Several young men who served as volunteers on Elizabethan ships are known to have been amateur lutenists. Philip Gawdy, a student at Clifford's Inn, wrote to his father on 6 February 1581 about a lute that he had bought: "I have heare a lute wch I have bestowed some cost uppon, wch dothe not alltogether ffall out so well as I cold have wyshed, and therefore if yow culd any waye devise to send upp the same [another lute] safe and sounde I shold thynke myself every kynd of waye much better furnished and provyded to learne to playe of the lute then I am now at this present."[6] In 1591 Gawdy was one of the few Englishmen to survive the most celebrated naval defeat of the Elizabethan Age, the loss of the *Defiance* and the heroic death of Sir Richard Grenville at Flores in the Azores. After his ransom had been paid, Gawdy returned to England, where his correspondence contains evidence of his continuing interest in music: a reference in 1594 to a colleague who "wanteth nothing but a good cyterne to his voyce"[7], and in 1602 a promise to send Lady Dorothy Gawdy "two songes for the viall" given to him by a musician at court.[8]

Another amateur lutenist, Arthur Throckmorton, took part in the attack on Cadiz. During a tour of Italy in 1581, he studied the lute in several cities. After his arrival in Padua, he noted in his diary: "I writ to Thomas Leigh for my luting book."[9] One "Bergamasco" was engaged to teach him. In Venice he took lute lessons with "Romano,"[10] and in Florence he was instructed in singing by no less a figure than Vincenzo Galilei.[11] Back in England in 1585, he began

[4]G. C. Williamson, *George, Third Earl of Cumberland (1558–1605)* (Cambridge, 1920), 9.

[5]A. L. Rowse, *Ralegh and the Throckmortons* (London, 1962), 131.

[6]I. H. Jeayes, *Letters of Philip Gawdy* (London, 1906), 4–5.

[7]*HMC: Seventh Report* (London, 1879), 522.

[8]Ibid., 525.

[9]Rowse (1962), 89.

[10]Ibid., 90.

[11]Ibid., 92.

buying musical instruments—a pair of virginals and a bandora. He took up another instrument: "Spryn came to teach me of the cithern, to whom I gave 7s by the month."[12] In 1596 Throckmorton sailed with his brother-in-law, Sir Walter Raleigh, receiving a knighthood for his part in the action at Cadiz.

Whether young gentlemen like Gawdy and Throckmorton would have been permitted to take musical instruments on board during their relatively short periods of active service at sea is not at all clear. Employees of the trading companies, however, traveling to take up longer-term postings overseas, were undoubtedly allowed, perhaps even encouraged, to take musical instruments. John Sanderson, a servant of the Levant Company, seems to have taken his lute with him on all four of his voyages to the East. Educated at St. Paul's in London, he served an apprenticeship as a draper and then entered the service of a group of merchants trading in the Levant. In 1584 he sailed for Constantinople with Harborne. After several years in Egypt, he went to Tripoli in Syria, where he was suddenly taken ill and collapsed, smashing his lute:

> When I came backe in my chamber some hower after, standing at a table, sowinge a little gould in my doblett (for the next day I should have gone for Aleppo, my horse hire paid for and apparrell sent), I sonke downe uppon a lute, that stode at the corner of my bourd, and broke it all in peces. At last, a littell recouveringe, I crept to the dore and cauled for aqua-vitae; which was brought, and I threwe myselfe thawart the bed.[13]

Sanderson returned to England, but after a period in Europe and an unsuccessful attempt to reach the East Indies in 1590, he returned to Constantinople. In 1599 he was again sent to the Levant and traveled on the *Hector*, the ship transporting Dallam and his mechanical organ. In 1600 he wrote from Constantinople to a friend in Venice asking him to supply "40 to 50 knotts of the best lut strings"—clear evidence of his continuing interest.[14] Sanderson may not have been the only English lutentist at Constantinople. After his final return to London in 1606, he wrote to a colleague in Constantinople, Robert Barton, that he had "a very good lute" with him "whiche I wishe with

[12]Ibid., 107.

[13]W. Foster, *The Travels of John Sanderson in the Levant, 1584–1602* (*HS*, 2nd series, vol. 67; London, 1931), 5.

[14]Ibid., xxxii.

you," and that Sir Thomas Glover, the new ambassador, was carrying "all sorts of instruments and exelent men in musique; so that I doubt not but your felicitie in particular wilbe increased."[15] Sanderson owned or had access to a collection of lute songs. On folio 77v of Lansdowne 241 he copied out two verses under his own name and that of his sweetheart: "Sleepe, waward thoughts" from Dowland's *First Booke of Songs or Ayres* (1597); and "Change thy mind," Richard Martin's setting of a poem by the Earl of Essex, published in Robert Dowland's *A Musicall Banquet* (1610).[16]

The emergence of the East India Company as a major employer of men from a range of middle-class occupations led to a substantial increase in the number of gentlemen amateurs traveling on English ships in the early years of the seventeenth century. The relatively spacious conditions prevalent on Company flagships now enabled music-making to flourish on a scale impossible on the smaller Elizabethan vessels.

A fascinating glimpse into musical life on board the ships of an early East India Company sailing is given by Captain William Keeling in his journal of the voyage of 1615. The fleet consisted of four ships: the *Dragon*; the *Expedition*; the *Peppercorn*; and the *Lyon*. On 8 March Keeling's ship (the *Dragon*) had already passed the Lizzard on her voyage down the Channel. He wrote: "I sent my Lord Emb*assador* a live sheepe, some silke stringes for the violl, and 100 oysters had at Weymth very good."[17] Sir Thomas Roe, the urbane and successful diplomat employed by the East India Company as their ambassador to the Great Mughal, is known from another source to have had his viol with him on board the *Lyon*. A manuscript in the British Library (Additional 6115, fol. 280) contains a short list of payments to Roe under the heading: "Disbursed for my provision to Sea against my goinge into India." Included among the petty expenses are payments for: "Bookes for the househould as service bookes—cost £4. A Viole, case, and provision for yt—cost £5. 10s." The provision, at the Company's expense, of a musical instrument for the personal use of one of its servants was unusual but not perhaps surprising in view of Roe's eminence. The strings sent by Keeling would either have been

[15]Ibid., 233.

[16]Ibid., 24.

[17]M. Strachan and B. Penrose, *The East India Company Journals of Captain William Keeling and Master Thomas Bonner 1615–1617* (Minneapolis, 1971), 64.

supplied by his professional musicians (who doubtless doubled on wind and string instruments in the usual way) or else came from his own personal stock. The use of silk strings on a viol is interesting; it suggests the possibility that gut had been found an unreliable material in the humid and hot conditions experienced on previous voyages. Three weeks later on March 30, Keeling recorded a musical gift sent to him by one of the passengers on the *Peppercorn*: "Mr Boughton sent me a sett of 6 Italian madrigalls, I sent my L*ord* a quarter and Mr Boughton a loyne of mutton."[18] Humphrey Boughton was a freelance traveller who had expressed a wish to see something of India and had been granted passage on one of the Company's ships.[19] These exchanges of musical gifts between ships of the fleet give some indication of the seriousness with which amateur musicians pursued their hobby on board. Gentlemen, their servants and the professional musicians together formed a small musical community which would have been well able to perform viol consorts or madrigals. Given the popularity of Italian madrigals among English viol players, it is tempting to suggest that the set of six books sent to Keeling were for the use of a viol consort.

The focal point of amateur music-making was invariably the captain's "great cabin" which was probably the only place on board where a vocal or an instrumental consort could play in comfort. Pepys records with typical enthusiasm the musical sessions he enjoyed during a voyage across the Channel in 1660 while employed as secretary to Edward Mountagu. Mountagu was himself a keen musician, and his servant, William Howe, was a proficient violinist. Once on board, Pepys and Howe lost no time in getting together to make music, usually after supper, but sometimes, if they had no pressing business, in the afternoon. On 6 April Pepys wrote: "In the afternoon, W. How and I to our Viallins, the first time since we came on board."[20] On the night of 10 April, Pepys was alone in his cabin "in a melancholy fit," playing his "Viallin."[21] Mountagu would sometimes join in to form a three-part consort. On 23 April, Pepys wrote: "W. Howe and I went to play two Trebles in the great Cabbin below;

[18]Ibid., 68.

[19]Ibid., 60.

[20]R. Latham and W. Matthews, *The Diary of Samuel Pepys*, vol. 1 (London, 1970), 104.

[21]Ibid., 106.

which my Lord hearing, after supper he called for our instruments and played a set of Lock's two trebles and a bass."[22] (Locke's *Little Consort of Three Parts: containing Pavans, Ayres, Corants and Sarabands* was published in 1656.) The arrival on board of Charles North enabled a consort of four to be formed. On 2 May Pepys commented that North seemed a fine gentleman and that he did "play his part exceeding well at first sight."[23] Three days later, the four men enjoyed "good Musique" together.[24] Music-making continued during the short trip across the Channel and during the return journey. On June 5, perhaps to celebrate the successful conclusion of his mission (the return of Charles II), Mountagu arranged an evening of light-hearted barber's-shop music: "After supper my Lord called for the Lieutenant's Gitterne, and with two Candlesticks with money in them for Symballs we made some barber's Musique."[25]

In his journal of the Voyage to Tangier in 1683, Pepys paints a similar picture of music-making among the gentlemen on board. On most evenings there was music in the Great Cabin after dinner. On the afternoon of 7 September, the sea was calm enough to allow Pepys and three others to cross in a boat to another ship, where they were entertained by two gentlemen playing violins.[26] On another occasion, Pepys was asked into the Captain's cabin for a glass of wine, which was followed by "mighty pretty music upon the flutes in the night."[27] A rough list of Pepys's personal effects for the voyage includes "Musiq" and "Flute-bookes."[28]

The instruments taken on board by gentlemen amateurs—violins, bass viols,[29] theorbos, guitars and recorders—were of course those that they played on land. Mountagu, a keen musician, made a regular practice of taking his instruments on board. On 17 November 1665, after visiting him on board the *Royall James*, Pepys wrote that

[22]Ibid., 114.

[23]Ibid., 123.

[24]Ibid., 129.

[25]Ibid., 169.

[26]E. Chappell, *The Tangier Papers of Samuel Pepys* (*NRS*, vol. 73; London, 1935), 12.

[27]Ibid., 14.

[28]Ibid., 251.

[29]Henry Teonge, chaplain to the *Assistance*, was a bass viol player. In his diary for 24 May 1678, he describes an evening spent playing a lesson or two on his "vyall" in the great cabin. See G. E. Manwaring, *The Diary of Henry Teonge* (London, 1927), 208.

he had heard "my Lord playing upon the Guittarr, which he now commends above all Musique in the world."[30] In 1666 a list of effects taken on board by Mountagu for his voyage to Madrid included a "theorbo-lute,"[31] and there were presumably other of his instruments on the ship, perhaps the violin and the bass viol that he played in Madrid during an afternoon of informal music-making with a member of the Spanish royal family.[32] Marine archaeologists have found the physical remains of just this kind of string ensemble on the wreck of a Swedish flagship, the *Kronan*, which exploded in 1676 during a battle in the Baltic. Parts of two violins and a bass viol were recovered from a site near the officers' quarters.[33]

Unlike officers and gentlemen, ordinary sailors were permitted to bring on board only what could be fitted into their chest of personal belongings. Gunners, surgeons, boatswains and rank-and-file soldiers and sailors tended, therefore, to favor small instruments such as fiddles, citterns, guitars and pipes. Some of the instruments recovered from the wreck of the *Mary Rose* illustrate the musical tastes of English sailors in the mid-sixteenth century.[34] In a storage area, divers found two pipes, a fragment of a tabor and the remains of two fiddles. A further pipe was found close to a cabin occupied by an archer and a carpenter. The pipe-and-tabor players would have provided dance music for the crew, but they might also have been required to join the military musicians on ceremonial occasions. In a description of the Elizabethan navy, Horsey mentioned "dromes, trompetts, taber, pipe and other instruments of warlicke designes" as though the pipe-and-tabor was part of the usual military band.[35]

[30]R. Latham and W. Matthews, *The Diary of Samuel Pepys*, vol. 6 (London, 1972), 301.

[31]F. R. Harris, *The Life of Edward Mountagu, K. G., First Earl of Sandwich 1625–1672*, vol. 2 (London, 1912), 50.

[32]I. Woodfield, "The First Earl of Sandwich, a Performance of William Lawes in Spain and the Origins of the Pardessus de Viole," *Chelys*, vol. 14 (1985), 40–42.

[33]C. Karp, "Musical Instruments recovered from the Royal Swedish Flagship Kronan (1676)," Second Conference of the ICTM Study Group on Music Archaeology, Stockholm, November 19–23, 1984, vol. 1: *General Studies*, C. Lund, ed. (*PRSAM*, vol. 53; Stockholm, 1986), 94–104.

[34]F. Palmer, "Musical Instruments from the *Mary Rose*: a Report of Work in Progress," *EM*, vol. 11 (1983), 53–59.

[35]E. A. Bond, *Russia at the Close of the Sixteenth Century* (*HS*, vol. 20; London, 1856), 186.

Similarly in 1583, Luke Ward reported that he had escorted visitors in a skiff with "trumpets, drum and fife, and tabor and pipe."[36]

The guitar was the preferred instrument of Portuguese and Spanish sailors at this period.[37] Guitars are known to have been taken on two Spanish expeditions to the South Seas. The author of an account of Mendaña's voyage in 1568 described how the Spaniards entertained the inhabitants of the Solomon Islands: the trumpet, drum and fife were first sounded on Mendaña's orders; then the soldiers sang and danced to a guitar to the evident pleasure of the islanders.[38] One of the sailors who accompanied Quiros in 1605 is reported to have played the "vihuela."[39] Goods taken off the wreck of the *San Felipe*, the Acapulco Galleon lost off the coast of Japan in 1596, included a number of "bigüelas" and "guitarras."[40] The Japanese official investigating the wreck was intrigued by the instruments and asked if any of the survivors could play and sing to them.

The recovery of artifacts from a ship of the Spanish Armada, the *Trinidad Valencera*, wrecked off County Donegal in 1588, has brought to light the crudely made fingerboard of a plucked instrument that has the characteristics of a late sixteenth-century cittern[41], with twelve chromatic frets for the first octave, six additional frets on the treble side only, and scallop-shaped carving on the lower end of the bass side of the fingerboard (Plate 11). The *Trinidad Valencera* was part of the Levant Squadron of the Armada[42] and carried many Italians—a list of some 25 survivors includes a Venetian captain, a Venetian

[36]Hakluyt, 11:191.

[37]The recreations popular with sailors on board Portuguese ships are discussed in J. D. Spence, *The Memory Palace of Matteo Ricci* (London, 1984), 76–78. See also the introduction to C. R. Boxer, *The Tragic History of the Sea 1589–1622* (*HS*, 2nd series, vol. 112; Cambridge, 1959).

[38]W. A. Amherst and B. Thomson, *The Discovery of the Solomon Islands by Alvaro de Mendaña in 1568*, vol. 2 (*HS*, 2nd series, vol. 8; London, 1901), 233.

[39]D. J. Zaragoza, *Historia del descubrimiento de las regiones Austriales*, vol. 1 (Madrid, 1876), 328.

[40]C. R. Boxer, *The Christian Century in Japan, 1549–1650* (Berkeley, 1951), 422. For the original text of the relevant passage, see L. Pérez, "Fray Juan Pobre de Zamora su relación sobre la pérdida del Galeón San Felipe y martyrio de San Pedro Bautista y compañeros," *EIU*, vol. 2 (1931), 217–35.

[41]C. Martin, "La Trinidad Valencera: an Armada Invasion Transport Lost off Donegal. Interim site report," *IJNA*, vol. 8 (1987), 13–38.

[42]J. K. Laughton, *State Papers Relating to the Defeat of the Spanish Armada*, vol. 2 (*NRS*, vol. 2; London, 1895), 379.

Plate 11. The fingerboard of a late 16th-century cittern recovered from the wreck of the Trinidad Valencera in County Donegal, Republic of Ireland. Ulster Museum, Belfast.

gunner, and two Italian drummers.[43] The cittern, a popular instrument in late sixteenth-century Italy, probably belonged to one of these men.

Guitars and citterns would have been particularly useful for song accompaniment, and it is hardly surprising that books of songs are occasionally recorded among the effects of Iberian sailors. In 1595 the master of a small Spanish ship that ran aground off the coast of Carmarthenshire stated that there were no books or letters on board "except for a few Spanish songs, which were destroyed by water."[44] Nuño da Silva, the Portuguese pilot captured by Drake in 1579, had with him on the *Golden Hind*, according to a list of possessions compiled for the Inquisition, "a popular music book written in the Portuguese tongue."[45]

Not until the early seventeeth century is there firm documentary evidence concerning the instruments played by English sailors on long distance sailing ships. In the Testamentary Records of the Commissary Court of London (London Division) are a large number of wills made by boatswains, gunners, trumpeters and ordinary seamen who died on ships of the East India Company.[46] A sailor who died in service could dispose of his goods in the usual way, or he

[43]H. C. Hamilton, *CSP, Ireland, Elizabeth,1588, August–1592, September* (London, 1885), 59.

[44] M. A. E. Green, *CSP, Domestic, Elizabeth, 1595–1597* (London, 1869), 139.

[45]Z. Nuttall, *New Light on Drake* (*HS*, 2nd series, vol. 34; London, 1914), 361.

[46]M. Fitch, *Index to Testamentary Records in the Commissary Court of London (London Division), now preserved in Guildhall Library, London, Volume III, 1571–1625* (*BRS*, vol. 97; London, 1985).

could request the purser to sell off his belongings "at the mast" and then bequeath the proceeds of the sale. The most interesting wills are those that list individual bequests. From these it is immediately evident that the books most commonly owned by sailors were Bibles, collections of sermons and navigational works. Musical instruments are mentioned in the following wills from registers (in the 9171 series) up to 1620: Thomas Gaytes (trumpeter) of the *Hector* (died 1606): "my Trumpet"; "my banner that is belonginge to the trumpit" (9171/20/fol.185); Thomas Juett (boatswain) of the *Peppercorn* (died 1611): "my whistle, my rapier and cittrone [cittern]" (9171/22/fol.228v); Henry Springall of the *Charles* (died 1617): "my whistle and chaine thereto belonging" (9171/23/fol.196v); David Brown of the *Charles* (died 1618): "one new trumpett" (9171/23/fol.200v); William Lucas (boatswain) of the *Unicorn* (died 1618): "a silver whistle" (9171/23/fol.344v); Richard Bleanen of the *Dragon* (died 1619): "a sitterne" (9171/24/fol.342v); William Dawson of the *Diamond* (died 1620): "my Trumpett" (9171/24/fol.304v); Howell Jones of the *Globe* (died 1620): "my trumpett" (9171/24/fol.129v). These specific bequests obviously represent but a small proportion of the total number of instruments taken on board by sailors. Only one of the seven deceased trumpeters, for instance, made a will with a specific bequest of his instrument.[47] One interesting point to emerge from this small sample is the number of trumpets in the possession of ordinary sailors. It seems that many men took trumpets on board in the hope of filling a vacancy after the death of one of the official trumpeters, little musical ability being required for the position of naval trumpeter. With the high mortality rate prevalent at sea, this type of promotion must often have been made.

As the seventeenth century progressed, sailors with musical talent began to play an increasingly significant part in the provision of music on board English ships. The status of these sailor-musicians may best be described as semi-professional. They were recruited as ordinary sailors but could expect some small additional rewards for their musical ability. Popular instruments of the day—fiddles, citterns, bagpipes and harps—were favored by these men. Above all, it

[47]The wills of the other trumpeters are: Ralph Geoyles of the *Hector* (9171/23/fol.51v); Richard Russell of the *Hector* (9171/23/fol.52); Anthony Blare of the *Hector* (9171/23/fol.209v); John Collins of the *Newyear's Gift* (9171/23/fol.570); John Dolton of the *James Royall* (9171/24/fol.16v); Hugh Larman of the *Ruby* (9171/24/fol.591).

was the fiddler who came to occupy something akin to an official position on English ships of the Restoration period. Even in a very limited sample of seamen's wills from the second half of the seventeenth century, the fiddle predominates to a marked extent. Two small collections of wills made aboard ships of the East India Company show this. Only three musical instruments are mentioned: "one old violend" was bequeathed by a man on board the *Restoration* between July 1660 and March 1661[48]; two of the deceased on board the *London* during her voyage to Surat in 1663 owned a fiddle and a trumpet.[49]

By far the most important duty of sea-going fiddlers was the playing of jigs and other popular dance tunes for members of the crew. A passage in John Baltharpe's curious journal in verse, "The Straights Voyage," is devoted to the fiddler as dance musician:

> One thing of note I told yea not,
> I had it almost quite forgot,
> Our Fidlar did in Triumph fetch,
> His Fiddle from Aboard a Ketch
> Call'd the *Portsmouth*, and did play,
> Oft times to pass the time away;
> Sometimes to passe sad Cares away,
> on Fore-castle we dance the Hay;
> Sometimes Dance nothing, only hop about,
> It for good Dancing passes mongst the rout;
> Yet on my word, I have seen Sailors,
> More nimbler Dance then any Taylors.[50]

Dance fiddlers of this sort were usually illiterate. Dampier, at the Island of Mindanao in the Philippines in 1686, sent for his "violins" and some that could dance "English Dances." One of the men who performed was described as "a Seaman bred," who could neither read nor write, but who had formerly "learnt to dance in the Musick-houses" around Wapping.[51] The lowly status of fiddlers is made clear enough by Captain Woodes Rogers who in 1712 described with some contempt the "Tinkers, Taylors, Hay-makers, Pedlers, Fidlers, etc." in

[48]India Office Library, East India Company, Marine Records, Miscellaneous, vol. 11.

[49]Ibid., vol. 12.

[50]J. S. Bromley, *The Straights Voyage* (*LSR*, no. 20; Oxford, 1959), 21.

[51]A. Gray, *A New Voyage round the World by William Dampier* (London, 1937), 246.

his crew.[52] Yet enlightened captains fully recognized the entertainment value of fiddlers. William Bligh, for one, was at great pains to employ one on the *Bounty*. He wrote: "Some time for relaxation and mirth is absolutely necessary, and I have considered it so much so that after 4 o'clock the evening is laid aside for their amusement and dancing. I had great difficulty before I left England to get a man to play the violin and I preferred at last to take one two-thirds blind than come without one." Michael Byrne, the Irish fiddler eventually recruited for the *Bounty*, was among the mutineers, but escaped the death penalty because he was considered to have had little choice but to remain on board. In a list of mutineers compiled in his log shortly after he had been cast adrift, Bligh observed that Byrne was "worthy of mercy."[53]

On slave ships, fiddlers and other musicians had the specific duty of performing dance music for the purpose of exercising slaves. In his journal of a slaving voyage in 1693, Thomas Phillips wrote: "We often at sea in the evenings would let the slaves come up into the sun to air themselves, and make them jump and dance for an hour or two to our bag-pipes, harp and fiddle, by which exercise to preserve them in health."[54]

Another passage in Baltharpe describes the early-morning Christmas greeting traditionally given by musicians on ships:

> The Five and Twentieth as some say,
> Of this Month called *Christmas-day*:
> Our Fidler then did Play and Sing,
> At Cabin door, made Steerage ring.
> With cheerful Voice, bid them good morrow,
> I think that he did Verses borrow
> From some fam'd Poet, for he'd sing
> Brave merry Songs, made all to ring.[55]

The perks offered for this service were money and wine.

[52]W. Rogers, *A Cruising Voyage round the World* (London, 1712), 8.

[53]G. Mackaness, *The Life of Vice-Admiral William Bligh* (Sydney, 1931), vol. 1:70 and 135.

[54]A. and J. Churchill, *A Collection of Voyages and Travels*, vol. 6 (London, 1732), 246. See also D. J. Epstein, "African Music in British and French America," *MQ*, vol. 59 (1973), 61–69.

[55]Bromley (1959), 38.

CHAPTER 6

Music for Entertainments

Important though it undoubtedly was in the maintenance of good discipline, daily routine could not alleviate all the frustrations of life at sea. Sheer boredom was correctly diagnosed as a primary cause of inefficiency, disaffection, and even outright mutiny. Enlightened captains therefore made a practice of encouraging their men to take part in special events such as amateur theatrical entertainments. Plays were often performed on English, Portuguese, and Spanish ships during the early seventeenth century. They seem to have been rehearsed seriously and staged with as much spectacle as possible. On special occasions of this kind, the musical resources of the whole ship, professional and amateur, were brought together.

Performances of Shakespeare, given on board the *Dragon* when she called at Sierra Leone in 1607, are recorded in the journal of Captain Keeling. The relevant pages of the manuscript were cut out in the nineteenth century, undoubtedly because of their reference to the early performance of Hamlet in Africa, but extracts had already been published in an early issue of the Hakluyt Society.[1] On 5 September, Keeling wrote: "I sent the interpreter, according to his desier, abord the Hector, whear he brooke fast, and after came abord mee, wher we gave the tragedie of Hamlett." Later that month, Keeling invited Hawkins for dinner on two consecutive evenings: "September 30. Captain Hawkins dined with me, wher my companions acted Richard the Second. September 31 (sic). I envited Captain Hawkins to a ffishe dinner, and had Hamlet acted abord me, w[ch] I

[1]C. R. Markham, *The Voyages of Sir James Lancaster, Kt., to the East Indies* (*HS*, vol. 56; London, 1877), ix.

p'mitt to keepe my people from idlenes and unlawfull games, or sleepe." Captains of subsequent voyages of the East India Company continued this enlightened practice. On 18 June 1610 Sir Henry Middleton invited Captain Downton on board the *Trades Increase* "to dinner and to play."[2] Thomas Love wrote in his journal: "we had a great feast and a play play'd."[3] On 28 December 1612 Saris wrote in his journal during a stop at Bantam: "Our cheife China marchant causde a playe to be made and invitde Sr Henrie myselfe and all the marchants to dynner wheare it was thought fitt to bestowe upone the players som monye."[4] The range of musicians on these early fleets of the East India Company was probably equal to that of any theatre on land.

Plays were often performed on board ships of the Portuguese Indian fleet. In 1610 a comedy was enacted on a ship returning from Goa, as part of the celebrations following the rounding of the Cape. Pyrard de Laval's brief description shows the preparation and rehearsal of this entertainment to have been anything but casual: "On the Sunday following was represented a very pretty comedy that had been got ready and rehearsed during the voyage from Gôa to the Cape, to be played when we passed it; thus we had good entertainment for the three days after passing the Cape."[5] Two comedies were enacted during the return journey of a Portuguese ship from Goa in 1617. According to the narrative of one of the passengers, on the feast day of St. Anthony of Padua "a comedy was played, very well done, which afforded much amusement."[6] A second comedy was performed on 16 June, again to mark a saint's day. In 1578 Spinola witnessed a play in honor of St. Anthony, enacted in costume, during which, he wrote, there were "many songs and much fine music" ("molti canti e suoni honesti").[7]

The full pageantry of a feast day celebrated with music, fireworks, processions, and plays is best captured by Thomas Gage in his fine description of the festivities arranged on two Spanish ships

[2]Ibid., 153.

[3]Ibid., 147.

[4]India Office Library, East India Company, Marine Records, XIV, 28 December 1612.

[5]A. Gray, *The Voyage of François Pyrard of Laval to the East Indies, the Maldives, the Moluccas and Brazil*, vol. 2, part 2 (*HS*, vol. 80; London, 1890), 295.

[6]*A Chronicle of the Carmelites in Persia* (London, 1939), 222.

[7]J. Wicki, ed., *Documenta Indica*, vol. 11 (1577–1580) (*MHSI*, vol. 103; Rome, 1970), 318.

sailing for the West Indies in 1625. While there is no reason to doubt the veracity of this man-for-all-seasons, the following passage from *The English-American* (London, 1646) should be read in the light of his religious sympathies—he trained as a Jesuit at Omer and Valladolid, deserted to the rival Dominican Order and ultimately renounced Catholicism altogether:[8]

> The last day of *July* (being according to the Jesuites Order, and *Romes* appointment, the day of Ignatius their Patron and founder of their Religion) the gallant ship called Sta *Gertrudis* (wherein went 30 Jesuites) for theirs and their Saints sake made to all the rest of the Fleet a most gallant shew, shee being trimmed round about with white linnen, her flags and top gallants representing some the Jesuites arms, others the picture of *Ignatius* himself, and this from the evening before, shooting off that night at least fifty shot of Ordinance, besides four or five hundred squibs (the weather being very calme) and all her masts and tacklings hung with paper Lanthornes having burning lights within them; the waits ceased not from sounding, nor the Spaniards from singing all night. The daies solemne sport was likewise great, the Jesuites increasing the *Spaniards* joy with an open procession in the ship; singing their superstitious Hymnes and Anthemes to their supposed Saint, and all this seconded with roaring Ordnance, no powder being spared for the compleating of that daies joy and triumph. The fourth of *August* following, being the day which *Rome* doth dedicate to *Dominick*, the first the founder of the Dominicans or Preachers Order, the ship wherein I was, named *St. Anthony*, strived to exceed Sta *Gertrudia*, by the assistance of 27 Dominicans that were in her. All was performed both by night and day, as formerly in Sta *Gertrudis*, both with powder, squibs, lights, Waits and musick. And further did the Dominicans joy and triumph exceed the Jesuites, in that they invited all the Jesuites, with *Don John Nino de Toledo* the President of *Manila*, with the Captaine of the ship of Sta *Gertrudis*, to a stately dinner both of Fish and Flesh; which dinner being ended, for the afternoones sport they had prepared a Comedy out of famous *Lope de Vega*, to be acted by some Souldiers, Passengers and some of the younger sort of Fryers; which I confesse was as stately acted and set forth both in shewes and good apparell, in that narrow compasse of our ship, as might have been upon the best stage in the Court of *Madrid*. The Comedy being ended, and a banquet of sweet meates prepared for the closing up of that daies mirth, both ours, and Sta *Gertrudis* Cock-boat carried backe our invited friends, bidding each other adieu with our Waits and chiefest Ordnance.

[8]T. Gage, *The English-American* (London, 1646), 16.

The element of competition could be an important motivation in the provision of theatrical and musical entertainments, either, as in the scenes described by Gage, between sister ships of a fleet, or, in a spirit of friendly rivalry, between ships of different nations. Pyrard de Laval, whose ship the *Corbin* kept company with a Dutch fleet for three or four days during her outward voyage round Africa, described it as a matter of honor between the French and Dutch captains who should provide the best cheer "with the sound of trumpets, several kinds of instruments and volleys of cannon" ("avec son de trompettes, plusieurs sortes d'instrumens, et volees de canon").[9]

A composite picture of musical life on board long-distance sailing ships points to a remarkable range of musical activity. When, at special moments such as at the taking of leave, all the various types of musicians played, the result was a striking symphony of sound, all the more intense because of the confined space from which it emanated. More than any other writer, the great Portuguese historian João de Barros captured this feeling in his poetic description of the departure of Cabral's fleet for India in 1500. The sound of the "trombetas," "atabaques," "sestros," "tambores," "pandeiros," and "gaitos," he wrote, raised the spirits of men and enabled them "to obtain relief from the wearisomeness of the sea" ("pera tirar a tristeza do mar").[10]

The other point worth making is the regularity with which musical sounds—trumpet calls, drum beats, whistles, psalm singing, incidental music—punctuated the day. It is hardly any wonder then that as a ship approached the shoreline of an unfamiliar country, these sounds should have attracted so much attention. From the point of view of the musicians, a "land-ahoy" heralded a notable change in the pattern of their lives and also in the significance of their contribution to the undertaking at hand. For as long as their ship remained at sea, they performed their regular duties at meals, services and watches—an important contribution, but not one essential to the success of the enterprise. Once their ship reached inshore waters and ports, however, they could expect a major change in the pattern of their lives, as the tedium of life at sea gave way to the challenges of diplomacy on land. The musicians were now required to perform a much greater variety of duties. Whether acting as

[9]Gray (1890), 397–98.

[10]João de Barros, *Da Asia* (Lisbon, 1552), Decade 1, Book 5, Chapter 1.

ambassadors to potentially hostile tribes, playing at receptions, escorting distinguished guests on ship and back ashore, or traveling inland with gifts, the musicians were now in constant demand, and, as we shall see, their performances were sometimes crucial to the successful outcome of a voyage.

PART II

THE ROLE OF MUSICIANS OVERSEAS

EXPLORATION AND COLONIZATION IN THE NEW WORLD

CHAPTER 7

Initial Contact

The history of the part played by musicians during early encounters between Europeans and the native peoples of Africa and the New World is a fascinating one. It was easy enough, approaching an unknown race on an unfamiliar shoreline, to demonstrate hostile intent, but to establish friendly relations was something of an art. By performing music in boats or on the shore, professional musicians and trumpeters were often able to reassure an otherwise cautious people and attract some of them close enough to enable the distribution of bells and other trinkets, the conventional tokens of friendship. The music performed at these first moments of contact was one of the most significant contributions made by musicians to overseas exploration.

The value of musicians in this type of situation became evident at an early date. Few detailed accounts survive of the Portuguese–African voyages which inaugurated the age of Renaissance exploration, but by the second half of the fifteenth century there is ample evidence to show that Portuguese captains were beginning to make very effective use of their musicians on the shores of Africa. A report of the reaction of the Senegalese to a bagpipe played by one of Alvise da Cadamosto's sailors in 1455 is typical:

> The sound of one of our country pipes ["una di queste nostre pive della villa"], which I had played by one of my sailors, also caused wonderment. Seeing that it was decked out with trappings and ribbons at the head, they concluded that it was a living animal that sung thus in different voices, and were much pleased with it. Perceiving that they were misled, I told them that it was an instrument, and placed it, deflated, in their hands. Whereupon, recognising that it was

made by hand, they said that it was a divine instrument, made by God with his own hands, for it sounded so sweetly with so many different voices. They said they had never heard anything sweeter.[1]

The pleasing effect of European instruments on African auditors encouraged the Portuguese to take their musicians on shore every time that their ships put in to land. They were often greeted in return by African performers. Accounts of Vacso da Gama's epic voyage to India in 1497 describe one such encounter at the Cape of Good Hope.[2] The Portuguese were met by a band of natives playing four or five flutes ("frautas"), some high, others low in pitch, that "sounded very well together" ("comçertavam mujto bem").[3] In return, Vasco da Gama ordered his trumpets to sound, and his men danced with the Africans. Perhaps because of its association with dancing, bagpipes seem to have been especially favored by the Portuguese on such occasions. During Cabral's brief stay on the coast of Brazil in 1500, one of his officers "took with him one of our bagpipe players, and began to dance among the Indians, taking them by the hands, and they were delighted and laughed, and accompanied him very well to the sound of the pipe."[4]

The simple but efficacious techniques of musical diplomacy pioneered by the Portuguese on the shores of West Africa were taken up by the Spaniards in the New World. The importance of published accounts in spreading knowledge of what musicians could achieve can hardly be underestimated. The organizers of the English voyages to West Africa in the mid-sixteenth century doubtless learned much from Richard Eden's books, the first accounts published in English of the exploits of Columbus, Magellan and the other great pioneers of exploration. The report of Columbus's third voyage, for instance, published in *A Treatise of the Newe India* (1553), described how a wind

[1]G. B. Ramusio, *Delle Navigazione e Viaggi* (Venice, 1550), 114v. G. R. Crone, *The Voyages of Cadamosto* (*HS*, 2nd series, vol.80; London, 1937), 50.

[2]The references to musicians during the African part of Vasco da Gama's voyages are discussed in R. Stevenson, "The Afro-American Musical Legacy to 1800," *MQ*, vol. 54 (1968), 475.

[3]E. G. Ravenstein, *A Journal of the First Voyage of Vasco da Gama, 1497–1499* (*HS*, vol. 99; London, 1898). In the facsimile edition of the *Roteiro*, edited by D. Peres, A. Baião and A. de Magalhães Basto, *Diário da Viagem de Vasco da Gama* (Oporto, n.d.), the passage referring to the flute players is on page 8.

[4]W. B. Greenlee, *The Voyage of Pedro Alvares Cabral to Brazil and India* (*HS*, 2nd series, vol. 81; London, 1938), 22 .

band was deployed in an attempt to pacify a group of seemingly hostile Indians: "The Admirall perceaving that he could nought prevayle, by signes and tokens, he determined with musicall instrumentes to appease their wildnesse. As the minstrelles therefore blewe theyr shaulmes, the barbarous people drew neare, suspecting that noyse to bee a token of warre, whereupon they made ready theyr bowes and arrowes."[5] Another report of this incident appeared in *The Decades of the Newe Worlde or West India* (1555), as well as several descriptions of musical encounters managed more successfully, of which the following is typical[6]: "And when they yet drewe nerer to the shippe, and harde the noyse of the fluites, shalmes, and drummes, they were wonderfully astonyed at the sweete harmony therof."[7]

The use of small musical trinkets as gifts was an integral part of the strategy adopted by Columbus and other Spanish explorers in their attempts to "allure to courtesy" the native peoples they encountered. Favorable reactions to bells, jews harps, or whistles are possibly the most frequently reported musical "events" in the history of Renaissance exploration. The evident fascination of so many of the indigenous peoples of Africa and America with these "instruments"—alluring shining objects that could be rung or blown—made them ideal objects, not only as gifts, but also, once initial caution had been overcome, as merchandise for barter. In economic terms, an artifact like a small bell could hardly be bettered; it cost very little and yet was often highly prized by the recipient. Better still, small musical trinkets remained popular even when increased expectations led to demands for a wider range of goods.[8] The disparity between the worth placed upon such objects by Europeans and native peoples was the subject of frequent comment, and once again Eden's translations contain many examples. Readers of *The Decades* were informed of the fabulous wealth bartered for practically nothing after the discovery of pearl fisheries in the Gulf of Paria. In 1499 Peralonso Niño discovered men and women "laden with cheynes, garlandes, and braselettes of pearles."[9] The Spaniards were well stocked with "haukes

[5]E. Arber, *The First Three English Books on America* (London, 1895), 35.

[6]Ibid., 88.

[7]Ibid., 86 and 164.

[8]See, for example, the lists of goods traded by Harcourt. C. A. Harris, *A Relation of a Voyage to Guiana by Robert Harcourt, 1613* (*HS*, 2nd series, vol. 60; London, 1928), 76 and 106.

belles, pynnes, nedels, braselettes, cheynes, garlandes, and rynges with counterfet stones and glasses, and such other tryfelles," all of which were bartered for pearls within the space of an hour. The Spaniards discovered that they could purchase fowl for next to nothing: a peacock for four pins, a pheasant for two pins, a turtle dove or a stock dove for one pin, a goose for a small looking-glass. Of all the trinkets bartered by the Spaniards, bells were the most sought after: "but above al thynges haukes belles were most esteemed amonge them, for theyr sounde and faire coloure." The ship returned to Spain so laden with pearls that they were with every seaman "in maner as common as chaffe."[10] Tales of the value of bells in the New World, range from the fantastic—the five hundred pearls for one bell claimed for Vespucci[11]—to the realistic—the "haukes belles and other great belles" presented by Magellan to a Patagonian.[12]

The influence of published accounts on the conduct of English transatlantic expeditions was no doubt real enough, but it is hard to establish a direct link. A much more tangible piece of evidence survives in an articulate statement of the strategy to be adopted during early encounters with native peoples, drawn up for the Merchant Adventurers of London by Sebastian Cabot, a man with long personal experience of overseas exploration, including four years in Brazil. He posed the question: "for as much as our people and shippes may appeare unto them strange and wonderous, and theirs also to ours: it is to be considered, how they may be used." On the use of musical instruments he wrote:

> If people shal appeare gathering of stones, gold, mettall, or other like, on the sand, your pinnesses may drawe nigh, marking what things they gather, using or playing upon the drumme, or such other instruments, as may allure them to harkening, to fantasie, or desire to see, and heare your instruments and voyces, but keepe you out of danger, and shewe to them no poynt or signe of rigour and hostilitie."[13]

The suggested method of approach was thus to anchor large ships a little offshore and to send a small party with some musicians closer to the shore in a boat, from which the general demeanour of

[9] Arber (1895), 94.

[10] Ibid., 96.

[11] Ibid., 38.

[12] Ibid., 251.

[13] Hakluyt, 2: 202–3.

any people could be observed at close quarters. The musicians, while not at this stage risking their own safety, could attempt to "allure" them closer still. Cabot insisted that natives should not be provoked by any "distaine, laughing, contempt or such like," but used "with al gentlenes and curtesie." Especially on small-scale voyages, respect for natives was a matter of obvious self-interest. Faced with inevitable deaths through disease, a prudent commander would not risk further losses in a series of pointless skirmishes on shore. The smaller the force, the more important was this consideration. In his "Instructions for the North-East Passage" of 1580, the elder Hakluyt advised the organizers of a very small party of less than twenty men "to have great care to preserve your people, since your number is so small."[14]

The first English voyage for which there is detailed evidence of the use of musicians as shoreline ambassadors is Drake's circumnavigation. Accounts suggest that Drake was keenly aware of the potential value of music as a diplomatic "language." During the three years of the voyage, all the musicians on board the *Golden Hind* played a full part in Drake's attempts to make contact with the peoples that he encountered. Three narratives contain descriptions of the activities of the musicians on shore: the printed account *The World Encompassed* (London, 1628); a manuscript in the British Library (Sloane 61) which describes the first part of the voyage; and Edward Cliffe's brief report in Hakluyt.[15]

A clear statement of Drake's policy comes in a passage near the beginning of *The World Encompassed*. The author, no doubt with a degree of hindsight, commented on Drake's reasons for taking musicians:

> Neither had he omitted to make provision also for ornament and delight, carrying to this purpose with him, expert musitians, rich furniture (all the vessels for his table, yea, many belonging even to the Cooke-roome being of pure silver), and divers shewes of all sorts of curious workmanship, whereby the civilitie and magnificence of his native contrie might, amongst all nations withersoever he should come, be the more admired.[16]

[14]E. G. R. Taylor, *The Original Writings and Correspondence of the two Richard Hakluyts*, vol. 1 (*HS*, 2nd series, vol. 76; London, 1935), 150.

[15]W. S. W. Vaux, *The World Encompassed by Sir Francis Drake* (*HS*, vol. 16; London, 1854). The various sources for the circumnavigation are assessed in the introduction to this volume.

[16]Ibid., 7.

Subsequent events showed that of all the trappings of "civilitie and magnificence" the musicians were the most consistently effective.

Drake's ships reached the coast of Brazil during April 1578. He set sail southwards, anchoring, from time to time, in suitable bays. On 13 May, in the manner earlier suggested by Cabot, he and a few others set out in a small boat and rowed into a bay to observe: "and being now very nigh the shore, one of the men of the countrey shewed himselfe unto him, seeming very pleasant, singing and dancing, after the noise of a rattle which he shooke in his hand, expecting earnestly his landing."[17]

The singing or dancing of men on shore at the approach of a boat was usually considered a good sign, but on this occasion a sudden change for the worse in the weather prevented a landing. On 17 May the Englishmen located another bay, "faire, safe and beneficiall to us," where they anchored and remained for two weeks. The first meeting between the natives and the Englishmen is described in some detail:

> While we were thus employed, after certaine dayes of our stay in this place, being on shore, in an Iland nigh unto the maine, where at lowe water was free passage on foot from the one to the other, the people of the country did shew themselves unto us with leaping, dancing, and holding up their hands, and making outcries after their manner; but being then high water, we could not go over to them on foot. Wherefore the General caused immediatly a boat to bee in readinesse, and sent unto them such things as he thought would delight them, as knives, bells, bugles, etc. Whereupon they beeing assembled together upon a hill, half an English mile from the water side, sent downe two of their company, running one after the other with a great grace, traversing their ground as it seemed after the manner of their warres, by degrees descending towards the waters side very swiftly. Notwithstanding drawing nigh unto it, they made a stay, refusing to come neere our men; which our men perceiving, sent such things as they had, tyed with a string upon a rod, and stucke the same up a reasonable distance from them, where they might see it. And as soone as our men were departed from the place, they came and tooke those things, leaving instead of them, as in recompence, such feathers as they use to weare about their heads, with a bone made in a manner of a toothpick, carved round about the top, and in length about six inches, being very smoothly burnished. Whereupon our Generall, with divers of his gentlemen and companie, at low water, went over to them to the maine.[18]

[17]Ibid., 43.

[18]Ibid., 47–48.

It was certainly not unusual to experience difficulty in attracting natives close enough to make contact. By leaving presents and then retiring, however, a measure of confidence was often established. Once the trinkets had been examined, the Indians approached closer, whereupon Drake ordered his musicians to play. Cliffe describes this moment. Having taken the gifts the "countrey people" approached the Englishmen, and Mr. Winter danced with them. They appeared to be "exceedingly delighted with the sound of the trumpet and vialles."[19] Leaving nothing to chance, Drake had both his trumpeters and his professional musicians on hand. As a further sign of friendship, one of the Englishmen danced with them. Everything about this encounter was well managed: the initial choice of location was ideal, the selection of presents apt, and the musical performance well received.

Drake's men soon found that anything musical was regarded with keen interest:

> Theire men being delighted much with danceing, make instruments of musick, which being made of barkes of trees, and sewed together with thredds of guttes of ostriges, like lute strings, and little stones put in them and painted over, are like our children's rattles in England, these they hang by stringes at their girdles, when they are disposed to sport themselves; which no sooner begin to make a noise but they beginn to dance, and the more they stirr their stumps the greater noyse or sound they give and the more their spirits are ravished with mellodye; inso much that they dance like maddmen, and cannot stay themselves unto death if som friend pluck not away the bables, which being taken away, they stand as not knowing what has become of themselves for a long tyme. In the great stormes, whereof we have spoken before, myselfe having some loss of good things spoiled in my trunck, of provision of physick for the voyage, among other things glass vialls, bottles, went to wreck, among the which, som being covered with wicker roddes, the broken glass remained within the cases, whereof one being in my hand and make-ing noyse, one of the giants supposeing it to be an instrument of musick, must of necessity have it; which when he had received, he and his companions were so overcom with the sweetness of the musick, that he shakeing the glass and danceing, they all followed and danced after his pipe, over mountaines and vallies, hills and dales, day and night, till all the strings were consumed; for the glass being continual-ly laboured did becom small powder, and wasted by little and little,

[19]Ibid., 277.

> quite away, and, the musick ended, the next day they came againe, but all-a-mort that their sweet instrument had lost its sound, and made great moanes to have another. They did admire at our still musick, but the sound of our trumpett, noise of the drum, and especially the blow of a gunn was terrible to them.[20]

Ad hoc instruments such as rattles or aqua-vitae bottles were often just as effective as more conventional instruments in these situations.

As Drake continued round the coast of South America, he maintained a conciliatory posture. On two occasions, however, he met with a show of friendship, only to be surprised by an unexpected attack. No matter how friendly an initial contact might be, it was considered prudent to maintain constant vigilance. Cabot, one of many writers to urge caution, suggested that it would be unwise "to credit the faire words of the strange people, which be many times tried subtile, and false."

In June 1579, Drake reached a bay on the coast of California, the northernmost point of his journey up the west coast of America. The Englishmen disembarked, and within a few days a great assembly had gathered. A representative of the people delivered a "long and tedious oration,"[21] after which the Englishmen were horrified to observe the women "crying and shrieking piteously, tearing their flesh with their nailes from their cheekes in a monstrous manner." Drake sought to attract their attention by praying and singing psalms. During the service the Indians sat very attentively. They took such pleasure in the psalm-singing that at later encounters their first request was always for singing.[22]

Reassured by their manner of singing and dancing, Drake allowed them into his encampment and was able to observe at close quarters the wounds of the women, parts of whose bodies were indeed "bespotted with bloud."[23] Their delight in the psalm-singing of the Englishmen was once again put to the test when, shortly before Drake's departure, a sacrifice was burned. Having tried all other means to dissuade them, the Englishmen started to pray and sing psalms "whereby they were allured immediatly to forget their folly." The Indians imitated the actions of the Englishmen, "lifting of

[20]Ibid., 50–51.

[21]Ibid., 122.

[22]Ibid., 124.

[23]Ibid., 127–28.

their eyes and hands to heaven."[24] In a situation like this, Drake seems to have regarded music as his most powerful means of communication.

From California, Drake sailed across the Pacific to the Moluccas. At the Island of Ternate he established excellent relations with the local ruler, once again using his musicians to good effect at the first meeting. As the King's boat approached the *Golden Hind*, the Englishmen observed with interest the skill of the rowers. Two men sat in the front of each canoe, one holding a "tabret," the other a piece of brass, upon which they beat simultaneously, "observing a due time and reasonable space betweene each stroake." At the end of each stroke, the rowers gave out a "song," warning the others to strike again.[25] The King was received by Drake with volleys of shot and all the music available on the *Golden Hind*. The report in Hakluyt stated that he "seemed to be much delighted with the sound of our musicke."[26] The more detailed narrative in *The World Encompassed* gives a better impression of the real impact of Drake's musicians:

> He was received in the best manner we could, answerable unto his state; our ordinance thundred, which wee mixed with great store of small shot, among which sounding our trumpets and other instruments of musicke, both of still and loud noise; wherewith he was so much delighted, that requesting our musick to come unto the boate, hee ioyned his Canow to the same, and was towed at least a whole houre together, with the boate at the sterne of our ship. Besides this, our Generall sent him such presents, as he thought might both requite his courtesy already received, and worke a farther confirmation of that good liking and friendship already begunne.[27]

The King, "being thus in musicall paradise," sent for his brother to hear the performance.

Drake's final port-of-call in the Far East was the Island of Java, where he stayed for two weeks in March 1580. His musicians were in greater demand than ever before. After an initial meeting on shore during which Drake presented his "musicke," the *Golden Hind* received frequent visits from Javanese, anxious to view the curiosities

[24]Ibid., 133.

[25]Ibid., 140.

[26]Ibid., 246.

[27]Ibid., 141.

on board the English ship:[28] "Few were the dayes that one or more of these kings did misse to visit us." Drake showed the commodities on board and demonstrated the weaponry, "his musicke also, and all things else whereby he might do them pleasure, wherein they tooke exceedingly great delight with admiration." On 21 March one of the local chiefs came aboard and "in requitall of our musick which was made to him, presented our Generall with his country musick, which though it were of a very strange kind, yet the sound was pleasant and delightfull."[29]

Three voyages were undertaken by Frobisher in 1576, 1577, and 1578 in search of a passage through the Northwest. He did not employ a consort of professional musicians, but with the assistance of his trumpeters and a large stock of musical trinkets, he was able to adopt comparable methods of musical diplomacy.

Accounts and inventories relating to these voyages include details of the stock of bells taken. These give fascinating insights into the range of artifacts taken and the care which went into their choice. Before his ship set sail in 1576, the following were purchased (Public Record Office E 164/35): from an ironmonger [fols. 23v–24]: "2 bells; 4 bells for coues; 3 dossen rounde bells brasse for horses; 1 dossen rounde bells brasse for horses"; from a haberdasher [fols. 24–24v]: "16 dossen of belles; 8 dossen belles." These items formed but a tiny part of the stock of goods purchased for the voyage which also included many rings, stones, beads, plates, combs and looking-glasses. After Frobisher's return, the remaining stock was offered for sale to any of the crew who wished to make purchases. Some "horse bells" were sold off in this way (fol. 28). In 1577 bells were again purchased: from an ironmonger [fol. 61]: "Horse bells iij dossen; Horse bells i dossen; Sackeringe bells [sacring-bell: *OED*, "a small bell rung at the elevation of the host"] ij dossen." The cargo also included some goods from the first voyage which had not been sold off: "lases bells" (fol. 62), probably the costume bells supplied by a haberdasher in 1576, and "horse bells" (fol. 62v). The goods sold off after the return of the second voyage included a job-lot in which were: "hawkes belles, 3 dossen; Beles littelle; saunts bells [i.e., saunce-bells or sanctus-bells]; horse bells 12."

[28]Ibid., 160.

[29]Ibid., 161.

The goods disposed of after the return of the 1578 voyage included a still larger selection (Public Record Office E 164/36): "belles great hawkes vi dossen; belles small hawkes xiiij dossen; sacringe belles xi; cowe belles ix; horse bells v dossen; 10 horse belles, rounde; 6 hawkes belles, whyte; 4 sacringe belles." These accounts show that many kinds of bells were used in voyages of exploration. There were two sources of supply: ironmongers provided larger bells such as cowbells, horsebells, and bells of the kind used in church; haberdashers supplied the smaller bells used in costumes for morris dancing and in falconry.[30]

The first meeting of Frobisher's men with a group of Eskimos in 1576 seemed friendly enough, and "belles, looking glasses and other toyes" were exchanged for seal and bear skins.[31] The pleasure that these items gave was duly noted. However, five of his crew, foolishly ignoring advice, went off in a boat out of sight of the *Gabriell* and were not seen again.[32] Their loss was a serious blow, and Frobisher tried hard to recover them. The next day he sailed as close to the shore as he dared, ordered his trumpeter Richard Purdye to sound, and shot off a gun. There was no response. Unable to land—he had no other boat—Frobisher despaired of ever seeing his men again, but soon a number of boats were observed in the distance approaching with caution. The only remaining chance of bargaining for his men lay in taking a hostage. As the Eskimos were obviously terrified of the guns, the Englishmen kept them out of sight and then attempted to lure one of them closer. The knowledge that Eskimos were "greatly delighted with any thinge that is brighte or giveth a sounde"[33] and that they "delight in musicke above measure, and will keep time and stroke to any tune which you shall sing, both wyth their voyces, hande, and feete, and wyll sing the same tune aptly after you"[34] suggested an obvious course of action. Frobisher called for a selection of bells and began to ring them:

[30]"Certen Morys bells" were part of the merchandise taken by Gilbert in 1578. See D. B. Quinn, *New American World*, vol. 3: *English Plans for North America. The Roanoke Voyages. New England Ventures* (London, 1979), 206.

[31] R. Collinson, *The Three Voyages of Martin Frobisher* (HS, vol. 38; London, 1867), 73.

[32]Ibid., 73.

[33]Hakluyt, 11:227.

[34]Collinson (1867), 283.

> And therefore to deceive the deceivers he wrought a prettie pollicie, for knowing well how they greatly delighted in our toyes, and specially in belles, he rang a pretie lowbel, making wise that he would give him the same that would come and fetch it. And bycause they would not come within his daunger for feare, he flung one bell unto them, which of purpose he threw short that it might fal into the sea and be lost. And to make them more greedie of the matter he rang a lowder bell, so that in the ende one of them came neare the ship side to receive the bell, which, when he thought to take at the captaine's hand he was thereby taken himself; for the captain being redily provided, let the bel fal and caught the man fast, and plucked him with maine force boate and al into his bark out of the sea.[35]

Another account of this incident (British Library, ms. Otho E VIII) reinforces the impression that extreme caution was needed to take the man and that the bells were crucial to the deception:

> Wherat the capitayn likewise made him signes of freendship as though that he would so doo, and thus entertayned him with signes of freendship, and placed him self at the waste of the ship at the syde alone having at his fete in secret his weapons, and caused all his men to wthdraw from him, whereby he might appere to them open as though without any malice. And made offer of small things to geve him at the ship's syde, but the man a while stood in susspition and wolde not approche. Wheropon the captain cast into the sea a shirt and other things that would swym which the streame caryed from the ship, and he toke them up. And likewise made offer of a bell in his hand, which he toke of him hard at the ships syde.
>
> Wherwithall one of the mariners mynded with a botehoke to have taken holde of his bote, which the man espyed and so suddenly put of his bote far from the ship, and in a long tyme would no more approche, which was no small grief to the capitayn and the rest. Yet at the last with the fayr offers and entisements with gifts of the capitayn he approached agayn with his bote to the ships syde, but stood upon garde with his ore in one hand next to the ship ready to put of his bote agayn suddenly yf nede should have byn through any cause of suspition that he might have perceived. And in this order of dealing in the presence of the rest of all his company he toke on bell more at the cap[itayn's] hands .... But the capi[tayn] ... offred him . . . freendly countenance and made a short arme [and let the] bell fall into the sea to move the man ... to approche more nere within him. Whereat the [man seemed] to be greatly sory for the los thereof and thereupon sudde[nly the] capitayn called for an other bell which allso

[35]Ibid., 74.

> he [rea]ched to him with a short arme, and in that reach [he] caught holde on the man's hand, and with his other hand [he] caught holde on his wrest; and suddenly by mayn force of strength plucked both the man and his light bote owt of the sea into the ship in a tryse and so kept him withowt any shew of enmity, and made signes to him presently that yf he would bring his v men he should go againe at liberty, but he would not seem to understand his meaning, and therefore he was still kept in the ship with sure garde.[36]

It soon became apparent that his men would not be returned, and Frobisher decided to set sail for England.

In 1577 he returned with a larger force. His instructions now urged caution in any dealings with the Eskimos: "you shall mistrust rather to muche than any thinge to litle towching the matter of yor salftie."[37] Expeditions inland were accordingly restricted to large groups. On one occasion, a party of 40 gentlemen and soldiers, returning from a ceremony to name a hill "Mount Warwick," observed some men "wafting us backe againe, and making great noise, with cries like the mowing of bulls."[38] Frobisher, wishing to establish contact, "answered them again with the like cries, whereat, and with the noise of our trumpets, they seemed greatly to rejoice." Two men from each side met to exchange presents, but "neyther parte (as it semed) admitted or trusted the others curtesie." In this atmosphere of mutual mistrust—neither side could produce the men taken the previous year—the singing and dancing of the Eskimos, which in happier circumstances might have been seen as a friendly gesture, took on an atmosphere of menace:

> They mustered themselves in our sight uppon the toppe of a hill, to the number of twentie in a ranke, all holdyng handes over theyr heads, and dauncing, with greate noyse and songs togither, wee supposed they made thys daunce and shew for us to understand, that we might take vew of theyr whole companyes and force, meaninge belike, that we should doe the same. And thus they continued uppon the hyll toppes untyll nighte, when hearinge a peece of oure greate ordinance, whiche thundered in the hollownesse of the hygh hylles, made unto them so fearfull a noyse, that they hadde no greate wyll to tarrie long after. And this was done, more to make them knowe oure force, than to do them anye hurte at all.[39]

[36]Ibid., 85–86.

[37]Ibid., 120.

[38]Ibid., 129.

[39]Ibid., 149.

Little progress was made during the third voyage of 1578. Attempts were still being made to reassure the Eskimos with gifts. Shortly before his final departure, Frobisher, in one final effort to "allure those brutish and uncivill people to courtesie against other times of our comming," left a selection of goods in a house: "we left divers of our countrey toyes, as belles and knives, wherein they specially delight, one for the necessry use, and the other for the great pleasure thereof. Also pictures of men and women in lead, men on horsebacke, looking glasses, whistles and pipes."[40]

I have looked in detail at the voyages of Drake and Frobisher because it is evident that the techniques of musical diplomacy pioneered (with varying degrees of success) during these epic undertakings were widely emulated during the following years. On their return, the veteran musicians of the circumnavigation (who were employed in at least one later voyage) were undoubtedly able to pass on details of the various musical stratagems that they had employed. The dual policy of using musicians and small gifts soon became a standard one. It was openly avowed by Sir Humphrey Gilbert before his ships set sail in 1583: "Besides, for solace of our people, and allurement of the Savages, we were provided of Musicke in good variety: not omitting the least toyes, as Morris dancers, Hobby horsse, and Maylike conceits to delight the Savage people, whom we intended to winne by all faire meanes possible. And to that end we were indifferently furnished of all petty haberdasherie wares to barter with those simple people."[41]

With experience, landing parties of soldiers and musicians were able to manage with growing confidence the highly delicate balance that had to be struck between presenting an image that was strong enough to deter any thoughts of aggression and yet friendly enough to establish a working relationship. This balance comes out very clearly in the excellent description of John Davis's first encounter with inhabitants of North America in 1585:

> Then we went upon another Island on the other side of our shippes: and the Captaine, the Master, and I, being got up to the top of an high rocke, the people of the countrey having espied us, made a lamentable noise, as we thought, with great outcries and skreechings: we hearing

[40]Ibid., 272.

[41]D. B. Quinn, *The Voyages and Colonising Enterprises of Sir Humphrey Gilbert*, vol. 2 (*HS*, 2nd series, vol. 84; London, 1940), 396.

> them, thought it had bene the howling of wolves. At last I hallowed againe, and they likewise cried. Then we perceiving where they stood, some on the shoare, and one rowing in a Canoa about a small Island fast by them, we made a great noise, partly to allure them to us, and partly to warne our company of them. Whereupon M. Bruton and the Master of his shippe, with others of their company, made great haste towards us, and brought our Musicians with them from our shippe, purposing either by force to rescue us, if need should so require, or with courtesie to allure the people. When they came unto us, we caused our Musicians to play, our selves dancing, and making many signes of friendship. At length there came tenne Canoas from the other Islands, and two of them came so neere the shoare where we were, that they talked with us, the other being in their boats a prety way off. Their pronounciation was very hollow thorow the throat, and their speech such as we could not understand: onely we allured them by friendly imbracings and signes of curtesie. At length one of them pointing up to the Sunne with his hand, would presently strike his brest so hard that we might heare the blow. This hee did many times before he would any way trust us. Then John Ellis the Master of the Mooneshine was appointed to use his best policie to gaine their friendship; who strooke his breast, and pointed to the Sunne after their order: which when he had divers times done, they beganne to trust him, and one of them came on shoare, to whom we threw our cappes, stockings and gloves, and such other things as then we had about us, playing with our musicke, and making signes of joy, and dauncing. So the night comming, we bade them farewell, and went aboord our barks.[42]

With only 42 men, a hostile approach was out of the question. Davis therefore followed the well-tried path of conciliation. As often happened, the Eskimos brought a musical instrument of their own to play in return: "another thing made like a timbrell, which he did beat upon with a sticke, making a noise like a small drumme."

Perhaps the key quality needed to manage a shoreline encounter successfully was flexibility. Any one of the four initial gambits—playing music, leaving gifts, dancing, imitating gestures—could cause offence, and it was necessary to observe carefully every nuance of the situation, encouraging those overtures that met with a friendly response and withdrawing quickly or changing tack at the first signs of unease. There is also a strong sense in many accounts of the importance of the correct management of the physi-

[42]Hakluyt, 7:386–87.

cal arena of the shoreline. The distance between the forward party, which usually included the musicians, and the main force had to be just right: close enough to effect a rescue if necessary; not so close as to intimidate. A fine description of how a group of Englishmen, exploring in the Trinity Bay region of Newfoundland in 1612, gained the confidence of a group of Indians gives a good idea of the fluidity of the situation and the manner in which a rapprochement was achieved:

> The 6 day they returned to the barke from the high hill, and about two of the clocke in the afternoone, about two houres after the return, theare was peceived a fire in the sownd a mile of, wheareupon all the companie repayred aboorde, because yt could be noe other then the doeing of savages. Presentlie two canoas appeared, and one man alone comming towardes us with a flag in his hand of a wolfe skinne, shaking yt, and making a lowde noice, which we tooke to be for a parlie, wheareupon a white flag was put out and the barke and shallope rowed towardes them: which the savages did not like of, and soe tooke them to theire canoaes againe, and weare goeinge away. Wheareupon the barke whearyed onto them and flourished the flag of truce, and came to anker, which pleased them, and then they stayed. Presentlie after the shalloppe landed master Whittington with the flag of truce, who went towardes them. Then they rowed into the shoare with one canoa, th'other standing aloofe of, and landed two men, one of them having the white skinne in his hand, and comming towardes master Whittington, the savage made a loude speeche, and shaked the skinne, which was awnsweared by master Whittington in the like manner and as the savage drew neere he threw downe the white skinne into the grownde. The like was done by master Whittington. Wheareupon both the savages passed over a little water streame towardes master Whittington daunsing leaping, and singing, and comming togeather the foremoste of them, presented unto him a chaine of leather full of small perwincle shelles, a spilting knife, and a feather that stucke in his heare. The other gave him ane arrow without a head, and the former was requited with a linnen cap, and a hand towell, who put presentlie the linnen cap upon his head, and to the other he gave a knife. And after hand in hand they all three did sing, and daunce. Upon this one of our companie called Fraunces Tipton went a shoare, unto whom one of the savages came running: and gave him a chaine such as is before spoaken of, who was gratefied by Fraunces Tipton with a knife, and a small peece of brasse. Then all fower togeather daunced, laughing, and makeing signes of ioy, and gladnes, sometimes strikeing the breastes of our companie and sometymes theyr owne. When signes was made unto them that they should

> be willing to suffer two of our companie more to come one shoare, for two of theires more to be landed, and that bread, and drinke should be brought ashoare, they made likewise signes that they had in their canoaes meate also to eate. Upon this the shalloppe rowed aboorde and broughte Iohn Guy, and master Teage a shoare, who presented them with a shirte, two table napkins and a hand towell, giving them bread, butter and reasons of the sun to eate, and beere, and aquavitae to drinke. And one of them blowing in the aquavitae bottle, yt made a sound, which they fell all into a laughture at.[43]

The accidental success of this bottle is reminiscent of the incident during Drake's circumnavigation when a broken glass gave pleasure as a makeshift rattle.

Once the period of initial contact was over, music continued to provide one of the main focal points of communication. During this phase, the musicians were expected to promote continuing friendship. They would perform for and, if possible, with Indians. As Drake had discovered, it was almost impossible to predict what would attract attention in any given place, but this was precisely the point at which the *range* of musical activities on board ship proved to be of most value. If, as in California, psalm-singing seemed of particular interest, Indians would be encouraged to attend. On Roanoke in 1585 the English settlers aroused the curiosity of the Indians of North Carolina in this way: "The Wiroans with whom we dwelt called Wingina and many of his people would be glad many times to be at praiers, and many times call upon us both in his owne towne, as also in others wither he sometimes accompanied us, to pray and sing Psalmes; hoping thereby to bee partaker of the same effects which wee by that meanes also expected."[44] If, on the other hand, a particular musical instrument caught the general fancy, it could be featured prominently. There is a rather charming account of an incident during Martin Pring's voyage to North Virginia in 1603, in which a young man (who may not have been a professional musician) made a great hit with his cittern:

> We had a youth in our company that could play upon a Gitterne, in whose homely Musicke they tooke great delight, and would give him many things, as Tobaco, Tobacco-pipes, Snakes skinnes of sixe foot

[43]G. T. Cell, *Newfoundland Discovered: English Attempts at Colonization, 1610–1630* (*HS*, 2nd series, vol. 160; London, 1982), 73–74.

[44]D. B. Quinn, *The Roanoke Voyages 1584–1590*, vol. 1 (*HS*, 2nd series, vol. 104; London, 1955), 377.

> long, which they use for Girdles, Fawnes skinnes, and such like, and danced twenty in a Ring, and the Gitterne in the middest of them, using many Savage gestures, singing Jo, Ja, Jo, Ja, Ja, Jo: him that first brake the ring, the rest would knocke and cry out upon.[45]

Another potentially useful ploy was to allow Indians to "have a go" on an instrument, although there was always the risk of inadvertent damage. This kind of gesture is not often reported, perhaps for the reason just mentioned, but on one occasion in the early years of the New England Colony, Captain Standish, meeting an Indian chief, asked his trumpeter to let him try the instrument.[46]

When the time came to leave, music, which had signalled the arrival of a ship, would also herald its departure. Bartholomew Gosnold took leave of some Indians in New England in the following fashion: "Being in their canowes a little from the shore, they made huge cries and shouts of joy unto us, and we with our trumpet and cornet, and casting up of our cappes into the aire, made them the best farewell we could."[47]

Although there were some failures, the strategy of using musicians as shoreline ambassadors seems on the whole to have been a highly effective one. Far from being mere extras in the pageantry of diplomacy, musicians were cast in the leading role, their music expressing the immediate intentions of the visitors more effectively than attempts at verbal communication.

There remains to be considered the later history of this kind of musical diplomacy. In general, the part played by professional musicians became less and less significant during the seventeenth century as European ships became an ever more familiar sight round the coasts of the world. There was one large area still to be explored—Australia and the South Sea Islands. The traditional techniques of musical diplomacy proved as valuable here as elsewhere. Increasingly, it was left to *ad hoc* groups of sailor musicians to serenade islanders. During Abel Tasman's celebrated voyage of 1642, two ordinary seamen ("matroosen") with two trumpeters provided a musical entertainment for some islanders. The curious, but apparently effective ensemble, consisted of a trumpeter and a sailor

[45]D. B. Quinn and A. M. Quinn, *The English New England Voyages 1602–1608* (*HS*, 2nd series, vol. 161; London, 1983), 220.

[46]Purchas, 19:334–35.

[47]Quinn and Quinn (1983), 157.

with a fiddle ("violons") from one ship, with a trumpeter and a sailor with a German flute ("duijtsche ffluijt") from the other.[48]

The copious documentation concerning the preparations for Cook's expeditions includes several orders for the recruitment of musicians. On 25 January 1772 a recruit "who plays bagpipes" and a "drummer who plays violin"—clear evidence, this, of semi-professional status—were ordered to be ready for embarkation.[49] On 5 May, Cook was told to take on board "two marines with bagpipes" and discharge two others to make room for them.[50] Cook describes in his journal how he entertained the "King" of Tahiti with the music of bagpipes and the dancing of sailors: "When the King thought proper to depart I carried him again to Oparre [Pare] in my Boat and entertained him with the Bag-pipes of which musicke he was very fond, and dancing by the Seamen; he in return ordered some of his people to dance also which dancing consisted chiefly in strange contortions of the Body; there were some of them that could imitate the Seamen tollerable well both in Country dances and Horn pipes."[51] The musical scenes enacted on the shores of South Sea Islands like Tahiti in the late eighteenth century differ little in essence from those described in accounts of Portuguese–African voyages some three centuries earlier.

[48]R. P. Meyjes, *De Reizen van Abel Janszoon Tasman en Franchoys Jacobszoon Visscher in 1642/3 en 1644* (*LV*, vol. 17; The Hague, 1919), 40 and 61.

[49]J. C. Beaglehole, *The Journals of Captain Cook on his Voyages of Discovery*, vol. 2: *The Voyage of the Resolution and Adventure 1772–1775* (Cambridge,) 912.

[50]Ibid., 928.

[51]Ibid., 208.

CHAPTER 8

The Formal Act of Conquest

Informal shoreline encounters with the peoples of America did not, even in their own terms, confer on Europeans the right to settle. To lay formal claim to land, it was necessary to perform an "act of conquest." Deliberately theatrical in conception, this was a ceremony in which the leader of an expedition claimed possession of a newly discovered land on behalf of his sovereign. Musicians played an important symbolic role in these bizarre rituals, the unfamiliar sounds of their instruments being an audible sign of the incoming alien culture.

The history of the act of conquest can be traced back to the fifteenth-century voyages of Diogo Cão and Bartholomew Dias and the Portuguese custom of leaving stone pillars on land to mark the extent of their progress down the coast of Africa. In the New World, the first Spanish acts of conquest derived their authority from the celebrated Papal Bull of 1493 which authorized the Spanish to explore and settle all newly discovered lands to the west of a line of demarcation that was set, after negotiation, at the meridian of 46° west. (This left Brazil in the Portuguese sphere of influence.) Spanish acts of possession are described in several sixteenth-century accounts. The best known took place on a peak in Darien, when on 25 September 1513, Vasco Nuñez de Balboa became the first European to sight the Pacific Ocean. According to Peter Martyr's account as translated by Eden—another instance of the probable part played by translations in spreading knowledge of the techniques of colonization throughout Europe—Balboa halted his force of men just below the summit, advanced alone the last few yards and, seeing the great ocean, flung himself dramatically to the ground to pray. He ordered his men "to raise certaine heapes of stones in the steede of alters for a token of possession."[1] In his *Historia general y natural de las Indias,* Fernandez de Oviedo y Valdes described how the Spaniards then sang the Te Deum "with tears of great devotion" ("con lagrimas de muy alegre devoción").[2] During the march down the mountain, Balboa's soldiers raised further piles of stones at intervals and carved the King of Castile's name on the bark of trees as further proof of their "conquest". On the shores of the Pacific, in another act of dramatic ritual, Balboa waded out into the sea in full armour, a sword held aloft in one hand and a Castilian banner in the other, to seal the Spanish claim to the area. The deliberate theatricality of these demonstrations was for once justified by the momentous nature of the event.

Alexander VI's tidy division of the world into Spanish and Portuguese spheres of influence was not accepted by the other maritime nations of Europe. France and England had territorial ambitions in the New World and both nations made use of the act of possession to validate their claims. Two early French ceremonies are described in the published accounts of Cartier's voyages of 1534 and 1535. An English translation of the account in Ramusio's *Delle Navigazioni e Viaggi* was published in 1580 under the title *A shorte and briefe narration of the two navigations and discoveries to the northwest partes called Newe France.* The first ceremony took place on 24 July 1534 in the Gulf of St. Lawrence:

> Upon the 24 of the moneth, wee caused a faire high Crosse to be made of the height of thirty foote, which was made in the presence of many of them [the local inhabitants], upon the point of the entrance of the sayd haven, in the middest whereof we hanged up a shield with three Floure de Luces in it, and in the top was carved in the wood with Anticke letters this posie, Vive le Roy de France. Then before them all we set it upon the sayd point. They with great heed beheld both the making and setting of it up. So soone as it was up, we altogether kneeled downe before them, with our hands toward Heaven, yeelding God thankes: and we made signes unto them, shewing them the Heavens, and that all our salvation dependeth onely on him which in

[1]R. Eden, *The Decades of the Newe Worlde or West India* (London, 1555). See E. Arber, *The First Three English Books on America* (London, 1895), 139.

[2]G. Fernández de Oviedo, *Historia general y natural de las Indias,* Book 29, Chapter 4. I have used the edition published as volumes 117–121 of *Biblioteca de Autores Españoles* (Madrid, 1959). The reference is from vol. 119, p. 212.

> them dwelleth: whereat they shewed a great admiration, looking first one at another and then upon the Crosse.[3]

Lacking the authority of the Pope, the French Captain made his claim on behalf of the supreme secular authority of his country, the King, while at the same time invoking the blessing of God. A similar monument was erected towards the end of Cartier's second visit.

Stone pillars, rather than wooden crosses, were chosen by Jean Ribault in 1562 to mark the first French colony in Florida. In *The whole and true discoverie of Terra Florida* (London, 1563), Ribault described the "planting" of two such columns:

> The next day in the morning we retourned to land agayne, accompaned with the captayns, gentilmen, souldiers, and others of our smale troup, carring with us a piller or columne of hard stone, our Kinges armes graven therin, to plaint and sett at the entrye of the porte in some high place wher yt might be easelly sene.[4]

Later, a second "colme graven with the Kinges armes" was taken on land.[5] Both columns are also described in René de Laudonnière's *A notable history containing foure voyages made by certaine French captaines unto Florida* (London, 1587).[6] The arrival of the French in Florida posed a direct threat to Spanish interests in the area, and it was not long before a punitive expedition was sent out under Hernando Manrique de Rojas. The Spanish commander was specifically charged with the task of locating the stone columns and destroying them, or, if they could be moved, of bringing them back.[7] One of the French pillars was discovered close to the fort which was by now abandoned. It was described by Manrique de Rojas as a white stone, about the size of a man, inscribed with a shield containing three

[3]J. Cartier, *Brief récit de la navigation faict es isles de Canada* (Paris, 1545). The English translation is from *A shorte and briefe narration of the two navigations and discoveries to the northwest partes called Newe France* (London, 1580).

[4]J. Ribault, *The whole and true discoverye of Terra Florida* (London, 1563), reprinted in D. B. Quinn, *New American World: A Documentary History of North America to 1612*, vol. 2: *Major Spanish Searches in Eastern North America. Franco-Spanish Clash in Florida. The Beginnings of Spanish Florida* (London, 1979), 290.

[5]Ibid., 293.

[6]Ibid., 295 and 297. In the original French edition, *L'histoire notable de la Floride* (Paris, 1586), fol. 13v, one of these pillars is described as "une borne taillee en façon de colomne, en laquelle les armoiries du Roy de France estoient gravees."

[7]Quinn, *New American World*, 2:309.

fleurs-de-lis, surmounted by a crown, with the date 1561.[8] The pillar was formally flung to the ground and then removed to the boats.

Music, in the form of trumpet calls, was associated with the act of conquest from an early date. There were musicians of one sort or another on all the French expeditions cited above, and it is likely that they participated in the ritual, even though the sources give no details.[9]

An early English act of possession took place during Cabot's 1497 voyage to Newfoundland, when, according to John Day's brief report, royal banners were formally raised on land.[10] It was not until 1577, however, during Frobisher's second voyage in search of a northwest passage, that the first significant English ritual was enacted in the New World. Surviving accounts make it clear that trumpeters played an important part. In 1576 Frobisher had returned from Baffin Island with specimens of rocks that were believed to contain gold. His 1577 voyage, promoted by Michael Lok's newly formed Cathay Company, which could boast Queen Elizabeth herself as one of its subscribers, had the dual objectives of mining ore and continuing the search for the northern route to Cathay. Frobisher's acts of possession were thus motivated by the need to validate the company's claim on the gold rather than by any serious intention to establish a permanent settlement. On 18 July 1577, Frobisher landed on Hall's Island with "his best companie of Gentlemen and Souldiers, to the number of fortie persons" and climbed to the highest point. There, in a formal ceremony, he named the place Mount Warwick. Best, in his narrative, described the scene thus:

> We passed up in to the Countrey about two English miles, and recovered the toppe of a high hill, on the top whereof our men made a Columne or Crosse of stones heaped up of a good heigth togither in good sort, and solemnely sounded a Trumpet, and saide certaine

[8]Ibid., 316.

[9]The name of one of the trumpeters on Cartier's 1535 expedition—"Pierres Marquier, trompecte"—is known from a document in Saint-Malo. See H. P. Biggar, *A Collection of Documents Relating to Jacques Cartier and the Sieur de Roberval* (Publications of the Public Archives of Canada, No. 14; Ottawa, 1930), 55. That there were other trumpeters and musicians with Cartier is evident from his meeting with the Iroquois: "our Captaine commanded Trumpets and other musicall instruments to be sounded, which when they heard, they were very merie." See Hakluyt, 8:236.

[10]D. B. Quinn, *New American World*, vol. 1: *America from Concept to Discovery. Early Exploration of North America* (London, 1979), 98.

> prayers kneeling about the Ensigne, and honoured the place by the name of Mount Warwicke, in remembrance of the Right Honourable the Lord Ambrose Dudley Earle of Warwicke.[11]

In Settle's account, *A true reporte of the laste voyage into the West and Northwest regions* (1577), the formal act of colonization takes place immediately after the landing, with Frobisher taking possession of the land in the name of his Queen. Only then, according to this version, did the party of Englishmen march through the country, heaping up stones on high hills "in token of possession." Two editions of Settle's account were published. Both are dated 1577. Significantly, the description of Frobisher's formal claim occurs in only one of them. This has given rise to the suggestion that details of the act of possession were hastily inserted into a new edition when the possible consequences of their omission from the first version were appreciated. The inclusion of the extra material may well have been suggested by members of the company, who were about to promote a third voyage, in order to establish in print the validity of their claim to the area.[12]

In Best's narrative, reference is made to a further ceremony on the mainland:

> Tuesday the three and twentieth of July, our Generall with his best company of gentlemen, souldiers and saylors, to the number of seventie persons in all, marched with ensigne displayde upon the continent of the Southerland (the supposed continent of America) where, commanding a Trumpet to sound a call for every man to repaire to the ensigne, he declared to the whole company how much the cause imported for the service of her Majestie, our countrey, our credits, and the safetie of our owne lives.[13]

Frobisher's first act of possession, which ended with his men kneeling in prayer round the ensign, is reminiscent of the ceremony conducted by Cartier in 1534. Details of Spanish and French acts of conquest in the New World were known to English readers in published translations, and it is conceivable that Frobisher was influenced by these. An English translation of Cartier was not published until 1580, but the original French account, *Brief Récit de la*

[11]Hakluyt, 7:292.

[12]G. B. Parks, "The Two Versions of Settle's Frobisher Narrative," *HLQ*, 2 (1938–1939), 59–66.

[13]Hakluyt, 7:297.

navigation faict es isles de Canada (Paris, 1545), was perhaps one of the "French bookes ij smalle" provided for the 1576 voyage together with André Thevet's *The New Founde Worlde, or Antarctike* (London, 1568).[14]

The next English claim to territory in the New World was enacted by Sir Humphrey Gilbert in 1583 from a tent pitched on a hillside above the harbor of St John's, Newfoundland. Gilbert's patent entitled him "to discover, finde, search out, and view such remote, heathen and barbarous lands, countreys and territories not actually possessed of any Christian prince or people."[15] To mark the occasion, a significant one in the history of North America, Gilbert received "a rod and a turffe of the same soile" and he caused a monument to be erected—"the Armes of England ingraven in lead, and infixed upon a pillar of wood."[16] The trumpeters and the band of "Cornets and Haughtboyes" doubtless took part in this ceremony.

The fullest description of the musical elements in an English act of possession comes in an account of Robert Dudley's voyage to the West Indies in 1594. Dudley, apparently on his own initiative, decided to claim the Island of Trinidad for Elizabeth, which he did by engraving the Royal Arms on a piece of lead with an appropriately bombastic inscription, and hanging the plaque ceremoniously on a convenient tree near the top of a mountain:

> And soe marchinge forth in good order, wee came unto the place wheare this our service was to be accomplished, the which wee finished after this sorte: firste wee caused the trumpetts to sownde solmlie three severall times, our companie troopinge rownde; in the midst marched Wyatt, bearinge the Queenes armes wrapped in a white silke scarfe edged with a deepe silver lace, accompanied with Mr. Wright and Mr. Vincent, each of us with our armes, haveinge the Generalls collers displaid, both with the trumpetts and the drome before us, after the cheifest of the troopes, then the whole troope, thus marchinge up unto the top of the mounte unto a tree the which grew from all the rest, wheare wee made a stande. And after a generall

[14]D. B. Quinn, *New American World* vol. 4: *Newfoundland from Fishery to Colony. Northwest Passage Searches* (London, 1979), 197. Extracts from the accounts of the Frobisher voyages in the London Public Record Office (E 164/35).

[15]D. B. Quinn, *New American World*, vol. 3: *English Plans for North America. The Roanoke Voyages. New England Ventures* (London, 1979), 186.

[16]D. B. Quinn, *The Voyages and Colonising Enterprises of Sir Humphrey Gilbert*, vol. 2 (*HS*, 2nd series, vol. 84; London, 1940).

> silence Wyatt red it unto the troop, first as it was written in Lattin, then in English; after kissinge it [he] fixed it on the tree appointed to bear it and, having a carpender placed alofte with hammer and nailes readie to make it fast, fastned it unto the tree. After wee pronounced thease wordes that "the Honourable Robert Duddeley, sonn and heyre unto the Right Honourable Robert, Earle of Leicester, Leiftenante of all Her Majesties fortes and forces beyonde the seas, Lord High Stewarde of her Majesties Howseholde, Knight of the most honourable order of the Garter, hath sent us heather and in his name to accomplish this honorable acte dedicated unto the service of his most gratious soveraigne and benifitt of his countrey, and this with his sworde, God favoringe his intent, doth hee sweare to make good against anie knight in the whole worlde." This beinge ended, the trumpetts and drome sownded, the whole troope cryed "God save our Queene Elizabeth"; and havinge thus, as solmlie as wee coulde, accomplishte this committed unto our chardge, wee marched downe the mounte, and havinge equallie ladende our men with that ore with the which the place did abownde, wee sett forwarde towards our shippinge. And by foure of the clock wee had recovered the same, and beinge sett aborde wee gave an accounte unto our honorable Generall what wee had done.[17]

The Englishmen's ritual conquest was not the first such act on Trinidad. In 1592 Domingo de Vera had claimed the Island for Spain in similar fashion. Having raised a forty-foot wooden cross, the Spanish commander ceremonially swept his sword round, cutting down plants, and then declared the island the property of the King of Spain, vowing to defend it against any challenger, armed or unarmed, to all of which his soldiers responded with shouts of "Biba el ray."[18] It seems unlikely that Dudley knew about the earlier Spanish ritual; even if he had, it would merely have reinforced his determination to make a rival claim. The resemblance between the two declarations of intent, both made with drawn sword in hand, is certainly striking, but the unsheathing of a weapon on such occasions was a well-established practice that can be traced back as far as Balboa.

The music performed during Spanish acts of conquest at this period was more elaborate than that of the English ceremonies

[17]G. F. Warner, *The Voyage of Robert Dudley to the West Indies 1594–1595* (*HS*, 2nd series, vol. 3; London, 1899), 27–28.

[18]G. Carmichael, *The History of the West Indian Islands of Trinidad and Tobago 1498–1900* (London, 1961), 22–23.

described above, with the celebration of mass forming an integral part of the ritual. Accounts of the act of possession staged by Pedro Fernandez de Quiros in the New Hebrides in 1606 and the subsequent celebration of the Feast of Corpus Christi give us a vivid picture of the musical elements, military and religious, that were part of a Spanish territorial claim.[19]

Quiros, a Portuguese navigator in the employ of Spain, ranks as one of the most enigmatic figures of his age, an extraordinary amalgam of skilled pilot, religious mystic and utopian idealist. Having sailed with Mendaña to the South Seas in 1595, he came under the influence of the myth of "Terra Australis," the vast southern continent that was supposed by some to link Tierra del Fuego with New Guinea. His vision was of a land where Spaniard and native could live together in fraternal harmony. Having reached the largest island of the New Hebrides, which he named La Austrialia del Espíritu Santo in the belief that it was the southern continent, he performed a ritual on a scale commensurate with his great dream. On the eve of the Feast of Pentecost, the day upon which possession of the new continent was to be taken, Quiros announced to the assembled company the creation of a new order, the Knights of the Holy Ghost, the insignia of which was to be a blue cross. During the night, the Spanish ships celebrated with a display of rockets, firewheels, and gunfire. There was much music on board: "We sounded drums, rang the bells, had music and dancing, and had other forms of rejoicing, in which the men showed great pleasure" ("sonaron cajas, repicáronse campanas, hubo músicos y bailes porfiados, y se hicieron otras fiestas en que se mostró bien grande alegría").[20] Early next morning, an altar was set up on shore under a canopy. The royal ensign was taken on shore, and then a cross was delivered to the Father Commissary, who received it with great devotion, singing the hymn "Vexilla Regis." The cross was raised and taken to the "church" in a solemn procession, during which the "Lignum" was sung. The

[19]Five volumes of the Hakluyt Society are concerned with Quiros: C. Markham, *The voyages of Pedro Fernandez de Quiros, 1595–1606* (*HS*, 2nd series, vols. 14 and 15; London, 1904); H. N. Stevens, *New Light on the discovery of Australia, as revealed by the journal of Captain Don Diego de Prado y Tovar* (*HS*, 2nd series, vol. 64; London, 1930); C. Kelly, *La Austrialia del Espíritu Santo* (*HS*, 2nd series, vols. 126 and 127; London, 1966).

[20]D. J. Zaragoza, *Historia del descubrimiento de las regiones Austriales* (Madrid, 1876), 1:311.

cross was planted and a formal document read out. This was followed by the proclamation of six documents in which Quiros took possession of the land in the names of the Holy Trinity, the Catholic Church, St. Francis and his Order, John of God and his Order, the Order of the Holy Ghost, and finally Phillip III. Three masses were then said and a fourth sung, after which the colours were dipped and consecrated. At a prearranged signal, guns were fired and rockets let off.

Ten days later, the Feast of Corpus Christi was celebrated with equal splendor to confirm the Spanish claim. The path to the church was strewn with flowers. Three triumphal arches had been put up, made from palms, green shoots and flowers. The day was clear and serene with birdsong. Three masses were said and then the procession began. A soldier went first carrying the heavy wooden cross and next a lay brother with a gilt cross accompanied by acolytes with candlesticks and red cassocks. Three companies of soldiers followed, each with their banner and a drum ("caja") sounding a march.[21] There followed eleven boys, dressed in red and green silk with bells ("cascabales") on their feet, who danced with much grace and dexterity "to the sound of a guitar" ("al son de una vihuela"), played by an old and respected sailor. They were followed by eight more boys, dressed in brown, blue and grey silk, with garlands on their heads and white palms in their hands. Bands of bells were tied round their ankles and they danced, singing their "motetes" to the sound of a "tamborin" and a "flauta." Then came the royal standard and the sacrament accompanied by priests singing the "Pange Lingua." At the entrance to the church, bells were rung, the banners were lowered three times, "the drummers beat the drums for battle" ("los atambores tocaban apriesa las cajas á son de batalla") and guns were fired.[22] During the siesta that followed the ceremony, there were "dances, music, and pleasant conversations" ("músicas y bailes y buenas conversaciones").[23]

The basic ingredients of the sixteenth-century act of possession—Spanish, French, or English—remained the same: a procession, an oration, the erection of a monument, religious consecration. However, the different military and religious traditions upon which these rituals were based, the particular circumstances of each claim

[21]Ibid., 328.

[22]Ibid., 329.

[23]Ibid., 330.

to territory, and the flamboyant personalities of the men in command, often combined to give such occasions a distinctively national character. The English privateers under Dudley raised their standard on Trinidad at the height of the Anglo-Spanish conflict. The trumpets, drums, and jingoistic (not to say ludicrous) military ritual expressed their purpose accurately enough. The exalted religious idealism of Quiros, on the other hand, resulted in ceremonies that were deeply imbued with the traditional pageantry of Hispanic Catholicism, adapted to the purposes of his own bizarre vision.[24]

In a curious way, these very different ceremonies both marked an end rather than a beginning. Although the West Indian waters were, as one writer has put it, "literally infested with English corsairs" during the 1590s,[25] the failure of the last great voyage of Drake and Hawkins in 1595 marked something of a lull in large-scale English interest in the Caribbean at this period. As for Quiros, the realization that his great continent was but a dot in the vast southern reaches of the Pacific was not long delayed. In reality, the act of possession was not a particularly difficult piece of theatre to stage; the marching, the rhetorical speeches, the music and the ceremonial firing of salutes gave to the participants a sense of occasion. But the sequel was often an inglorious departure, as the problems of establishing permanent settlements became apparent. Even Sir Humphrey Gilbert, whose claim, unlike those of Dudley or Quiros, was one of considerable historical significance, remained for only a few weeks on American soil before setting sail.

[24]On the history of music for Corpus Christi processions, see E. A. Bowles, "Musical Instruments in the Medieval Corpus Christi Procession," *JAMS*, vol. 17 (1964), 251.

[25]B. Penrose, *Travel and Discovery in the Renaissance 1420–1620* (Cambridge, Mass., 73 1952), 191.

CHAPTER 9

Military Occupation

The involvement of musicians in the protracted struggle to establish permanent settlements in North America marks their first contribution to the real occupation of the continent as opposed to its symbolic conquest. The military requirements for exploring and settling the vast territories of the New World were quite different from those needed to establish and maintain coastal bases. The Spanish gained early experience of the rigors and rewards of interior exploration in Central America, and this was put to good use when the North American land mass was first explored. Setting out into an unknown region was an extremely hazardous undertaking, no matter how well prepared the expedition, and any musicians accompanying the commander would have needed both physical fitness and resourcefulness. It is evident from reports of Cortez's march across the Yucatan peninsula to the Honduras in 1523 that some were certainly not equal to the task. Gruesome details of the fate of the shawm and sackbut players are given by Stevenson.[1] According to Bernal Diaz, the five "chirimías y çacabuches y dulçaynas" were unable to endure the hardships of the march. Eventually four of them died from starvation, and the music of the remaining man was cursed by the soldiers as no better than the sound of foxes or the howling of jackals. Stevenson further records the admission of the surviving musician, a shawm player from Toledo cathedral, that he had eaten the brains and intestines of his fellow musicians in order to survive. This, no doubt, is an extreme case, but death through hunger or disease must

[1]R. Stevenson, *Music in Aztec and Inca Territory* (University of California Press, 1976), 222–23.

have been commonplace among musicians taking part in such explorations.

What soon became apparent during long interior marches of this kind was the absolutely crucial signalling function of trumpeters and drummers. During long marches such as that of Hernando de Soto in the region north of the Gulf of Mexico or Francisco Vásquez de Coronado in the Grand Canyon area, parties sent to forage or spy out the way ahead must frequently have got lost.[2] The very lives of those separated depended on their finding the main party again. In these circumstances, trumpet signals could convey a much more definite message than the sound of distant gunfire. In his account of Coronado's expedition, Castañeda described how every night the soldiers played "trombetas" and "atambores" to help guide hunting parties back to camp.[3] The effect of a distant trumpet call on a group of men separated from their fellows and facing possible death is strikingly described in the account of a later English voyage—that of Gosnold to New England in 1602. After three days without contact, the demoralized men were struck with "dumpish terrour," but then: "we heard at last, our Captaine to lewre unto us, which made such musicke as sweeter never came unto poore men."[4]

In the vast interior lands of North America there was little chance of Spanish armies encountering rival European forces, but in the coastal regions there were inevitable conflicts with the English and the French. The part played by naval trumpeters during skirmishes between Spanish and English forces is well documented. Accounts of two related engagements that took place on the Spanish Main during the early years of Elizabeth's reign are well known: the attack on Hawkins in the harbour of San Juan de Ulúa; and Drake's revenge raid on Nombre de Dios. The story begins in 1568 when Hawkins, having loaded his cargo of slaves on the west coast of Africa, crossed the Atlantic and began to trade. His ships by now in

[2]For references to trumpeters and drummers see: Fernández de Oviedo, *Historia general y natural de las Indias*, Book 17, Chapters 6 and 7; and D. B. Quinn, *New American World: A Documentary History of North America to 1612*; vol. 2: *Major Spanish Searches in Eastern North America. Franco-Spanish Clash in Florida. The Beginnings of Spanish Florida* (London, 1979), 174 and 179.

[3]G. P. Winship, "The Coronado Expedition, 1540–1542," *Fourteenth Annual Report of the Bureau of Ethnology* (1892–1893), 443. Quinn, *New American World*, 1:387.

[4]D. B. and A. M Quinn, *The English New England Voyages 1602–1608* (*HS*, 2nd series, vol. 161; London, 1983), 137.

very poor repair, he put in at the port of San Juan de Ulúa, where he was surprised by a Spanish fleet carrying the new Viceroy of Mexico. This man was determined to launch an attack but decided that surprise was a better tactic than frontal assault. He accordingly negotiated an agreement with Hawkins which allowed him to repair his ships and restock them with food and water. Ten hostages were exchanged, the agreement was signed and sealed, and "forthwith a trumpet blowne with commandement that none of either part should be meane to inviolate the peace upon paine of death." In a deposition concerning the incident, Jean Turren, Hawkins's French trumpeter,[5] stated that it was he who had sounded to announce the agreement.[6]

Meanwhile, planning a surprise, the Viceroy concealed a force of soldiers in a Spanish vessel. His plan of attack was as follows: the soldiers, hidden in an apparently empty cargo boat, were to approach the English fleet at a prearranged hour, and when they were close enough to board, a white flag was to be waved to the Spanish flagship, where a trumpeter was to sound a signal to alert the other forces.[7] The English had their suspicions of the cargo ship, and Hawkins sent Robert Barrett, master of the *Jesus*, to protest to the Viceroy. According to English accounts of what followed, Barrett's arrival convinced the Spaniard that his plan was about to be discovered: "which seeing the vice Roy that the treason must be discovered, forthwith stayd our master, blewe the trumpet, and of all sides set upon us."[8] Miles Phillips confirms that this was the sequence of events as seen by the Englishmen: "The Viceroy then perceiving that their treason was thoroughly espied, stayed our Master, and sounded the trumpet, and gave order that his people should upon all sides charge upon our men."[9]

But a very different story emerges from the deposition of the Viceroy, which states that his plan went very wrong. The soldiers concealed in the ship were accompanied by a man whose responsi-

[5]J. A. Williamson, *Sir John Hawkins, The Time and the Man* (Oxford, 1927), 194.

[6]C. R. Beazley, *Voyages and Travels mainly during the 16th and 17th centuries*, vol. 1 (London, 1903), 114.

[7]I. A. Wright, *Spanish Documents Concerning English Voyages to the Caribbean, 1527–1568* (*HS*, 2nd series, vol. 62; London, 1929), 131–34.

[8]Hakluyt (1589), 555.

[9]Ibid., 565.

bility it was to give the signal at the prearranged time. Contrary to orders, however, the signal was given early, while his ship was still some distance from the English vessels. This error apparently enabled Hawkins to make his escape. Even if on this occasion the plan was only partly successful, the potential for a single naval trumpeter to coordinate a devastating attack is evident. This accounts for the fear that an unexpected blast on a trumpet could cause and why, except in special circumstances, trumpet calls were so strictly forbidden at night.

Both Hawkins and Drake escaped from San Juan de Ulúa. News of the attack spread quickly in England and inflamed public opinion. In 1572 Drake, bent on revenge, set sail for Nombre de Dios in Panama. The part played by trumpeters during his night attack on the town suggests that he had learned much from his experiences in 1568 about the value of trumpet calls in surprise warfare. There are two versions of the Nombre de Dios attack in Hakluyt, both derived from a document supposedly written by Lopez Vaz, a Portuguese pilot captured by the Earl of Cumberland in 1586.[10] The status of these accounts is uncertain, since Vaz was probably not himself an eyewitness to the raid. The account *Sir Francis Drake Revived* (1628) tells the story in colorful but not necessarily inaccurate terms.[11] The Spanish depositions published by Wright contain less detail than the English narratives but provide crucial contemporary corroboration of the affair.[12]

On the night of 28 July, Drake and his men approached the town of Nombre de Dios in four pinnaces. The company included "two Drums and two Trumpets." Drake's first action upon landing was to take the fort on the shore and disable the guns. Next, leaving men to protect the pinnaces, he advanced on the town. Panic seized the inhabitants, which was evident "not only by the noyse and cries of the people, but by the Bell ringing out, and Drums running up and downe the Towne." Drake then divided his force into two, one section entering the market place at the far end, the other passing up the main street "with sound of Drum and Trumpet." The firepikes were divided between the two companies and "served no lesse for

[10]Hakluyt, 10:76; also Hakluyt, 11: 227–28.

[11]I. A. Wright, *Documents Concerning English Voyages to the Spanish Main 1569–1580* (*HS*, 2nd series, vol. 71; London, 1932), 245–326.

[12]Ibid., docs. 17–28, 30 and 31.

fright to the enemy than light of our men, who by this means might discerne everie place verie well, as if it were neere day, whereas the inhabitants stood amazed at so strange a sight, marvelling what the matter might be and imagining, by reason of our Drums and Trumpets sounding in so sundry places, that we had beene a farre greater number then we were." One of the Spanish witnesses confirms that the Englishmen sounded trumpets in the streets as they entered the town. This was a classic military tactic, familiar to any military commander who knew his Bible.[13] A small force, suddenly appearing in the night with firepikes and the noise of guns, trumpets and drums, terrified the inhabitants into believing that their town was under attack from a large army. A number of Spaniards, however, organized themselves to resist, and during an exchange of gunfire in the market-place, the English trumpeter was killed. All reports agree that this was the only English fatality, although several others, including Drake himself, were wounded. The trumpeter's body, "his trumpet in his hand," was left in the market-place.

Up to this point, all the narratives are in substantial agreement. Lopez Vaz, however, goes on to relate how the death of the trumpeter led directly to the English withdrawal from Nombre de Dios. Drake had apparently left one of his trumpeters in the fort close to the place where the pinnaces were moored, before marching upon the town. The other narratives make no mention of this, but it was normal practice for a trumpeter to stay with the men guarding the boats, so that signals could be sent to the force inland (Plate 12). After the death of the English trumpeter, his colleague in the fort sounded his instrument, but received no reply, whereupon the men in the fort, assuming from the silence and the general noise of gunfire that the English attackers had been routed, fled to the pinnaces. When Drake's party arrived back at the fort, they found it deserted and likewise fled ingloriously to the boats.

[13]Judges, Chapter 7, verses 16 and 20–21: "And he divided the three hundred men into three companies, and he put a trumpet in every man's hand, with empty pitchers, and lamps within the pitchers. And the three companies blew the trumpets, and brake the pitchers, and held the lamps in their left hands, and the trumpets in their right hands to blow withal: and they cried, The sword of the Lord, and of Gideon. And they stood every man in his place round about the camp: and all the host ran, and cried, and fled."

Plate 12. The circumnavigation of Joris van Spilbergen in 1614: a young trumpeter and a young sailor remain on guard with the boats for a landing party. *Oost ende West-Indische Spieghel* (Leyden, 1619) plate 15. By permission of the British Library.

The vital importance of the military musicians attached to the first fortified settlements is even clearer in accounts of the tragic demise of the Huguenot colony at Fort Caroline in the 1560s.[14] The trumpeter who accompanied the French leader, René de Laudonnière, played an important part in the events surrounding the loss of the fort. He is first mentioned in the description of the religious ceremony enacted by Laudonnière[15] before he began work on the construction of the fort:

> On the morrow about the breake of day, I commaunded a trumpet to be sounded, that being assembled we might give God thankes for our favourable and happie arrivall. There wee sang a Psalme of thankesgiving unto God, beseeching him that it would please him of his grace to continue his accustomed goodnesse toward us his poore servants, and ayde us in all our enterprises, that all might turne to his glory and the advancement of our King. The prayer ended, every man began to take courage.[16]

The summer months of 1565 saw the arrival of two further bands of musicians, accompanying Jean Ribault's reinforcements, and the Spanish army sent to destroy the French settlement. Shortly after the

[14] T. E. Warner, "European musical activities in North America before 1620," *MQ*, 70 (1984), 77–95.

[15] R. de Laudonnière, *L'Histoire Notable de la Floride* (Paris, 1586), 45 .

[16] The English translation, *A notable history containing foure voyages made by certeine French captaines unto Florida* (London, 1587), is in Quinn, *New American World*, 2:325.

arrival of the Spanish ships off the coast of Florida, there was a brief skirmish with Ribault's fleet, which began in the usual way, with the trumpeters of the rival ships hailing each other.[17] Having established his base at San Agostín, the Spanish commander, Pedro Menéndez de Avilés, prepared to attack Fort Caroline. On the eve of his departure, "trompetas, pifanos y tambores" were sounded in a display of bravado.[18] In planning his assault, Menéndez hoped to achieve surprise, but if his men were discovered, he intended to mislead the French defenders about his strength and then send them a trumpeter to offer terms for surrender. Laudonnière described how the Spaniards were first spotted:

> In the meane while one which had something to doe without the fort, and my trumpet which went up into the rampart perceived a troupe of Spanyards which came downe from a little knappe. Where incontinently they beganne to cry alarme, and the Trumpetter also.[19]

Caught off their guard, the French offered little resistance. The occupants of the fort, according to a Spanish account, were terrified by two trumpeters "sounding victory" ("tocando vitoria") on the ramparts.[20] A few Frenchmen escaped from the fort and fled to their ships. Menéndez immediately sent a trumpeter to order them to surrender. Under a white flag of truce, this man "sounded a parley" ("tocar con señal de paz"), but to no avail.[21]

In his account of the capture of the fort, Laudonnière wrote scathingly of the quality of the men at his disposal, doubtless in an attempt to divert attention from his own failings:

> Among those that were without the fort, and which were of the foresaid company of Captaine Ribault, there was a Carpenter of threescore yeeres olde, one Beere-brewer, one olde Crosse-bow maker, two Shoomakers, and foure or five men that had their wives, a player on the Virginals ["un joueur d'espinette"], two servants of Monsieur de Luys, one of Monsieur de Beauhaire, one of Monsieur de Grange. . . ."[22]

[17]E. Ruidíaz y Caravia, *La Florida* (Madrid, 1893), 76: "y entonces hizo tocar las trompetas, salvando los enemigos, y los enemigos le respondieron salvándole con las Suyas . . .".

[18]Ibid. 88.

[19]Quinn, *New American World*, 2:358.

[20]Ruidíaz y Caravia (1893), 97.

[21]Ibid., 98. See also N. le Challeux, *Discours de l'Histoire de la Floride* (Dieppe, 1566), 33.

[22]Laudonnière (1586), 108v.

According to the deposition of a young Frenchman who escaped execution, the only French captives to be spared with him were three "taborins," one from Dieppe and two from Normandy, and four "trompetes," three from Normandy and one, named Jacques Dulac, from Bordeaux. Another survivor, the artist Jacques Le Moyne also reported the reprieve granted the musicians; he named two men, a drummer from Dieppe called Dronet, and a fife and fiddle player called Masselin, who was spared to play for dancing.[23] His first objective achieved, Menéndez returned to San Agostín, leaving a garrison in Fort Caroline. Upon his return, he was met by a procession singing the "Te Deum."[24]

In the meantime, groups of Frenchmen who had escaped from Fort Caroline were making their way to the sea. Nicholas Le Challeux, a carpenter, recounts how he came upon a party of stragglers which included Laudonnière himself and his trumpeter.[25] A French ship was sighted and hailed, and Laudonnière decided that the only sensible course of action was to return to Europe.

Further south, near San Agostín, a further disaster had already struck the French with the loss of Ribault's fleet in a storm. Several hundred Frenchmen were left defenseless. Their brutal execution and the reprieve granted to the musicians are recorded in both French and Spanish sources. Le Challeux, who by that time had left Florida and was thus not an eyewitness, reported that the Spaniards had massacred their captives to the sound of "phiffres," "tabourins," and "trompes."[26] Gonzalo Solís de Méras, an eyewitness and author of the most detailed account, described how Menéndez came upon the demoralized Frenchmen by a river. When they first caught sight of the Spaniards, they arrayed themselves in military formation, "playing their fifes, and beating their drums in very good order" ("tocando pifanos e atambores con muy buena orden").[27] The martial music of the Frenchmen, however, was deliberately ignored by the Spanish commander.[28] The French drummers and fifers soon ceased playing and a "clarín" was sounded under a white flag.[29] Menéndez

[23]P. Hulton, *The Work of Jacques le Moyne de Morgues* (London, 1977), 137.

[24]Ruidíaz y Caravia (1893), 109.

[25]Le Challeux (1566), 40.

[26]Ibid., 50.

[27]Ruidíaz y Caravia (1893), 119.

[28]Ibid., 2:102.

[29]Ibid., 1:120.

called upon his own "clarín" (described in one source as "muy bueno"—a very good one) and waved a flag in return. After negotiations, the French gave themselves up and were ferried across the river. Menéndez ordered the hands of his captives to be bound, and questioned them about their religion. Ribault, probably realizing what was about to happen, admitted that his men were Protestants. He began to sing—"Domine, memento mei."[30] The French captives were marched along the shore and at a prearranged place the Spaniards butchered them with knives. According to Solís de Méras, sixteen men were spared, four Catholics and twelve musicians ("atambores y trompetas"), but in his letter to Philip II, Menéndez claimed that he had found no Catholics and that he had spared only five, two young gentlemen, a "pífano," a "tronpeta" and an "atanbor."[31]

Some days later, reports reached Menéndez of another band of Frenchmen further south in Cape Cañaveral, who were building a fort to protect themselves. The Spanish commander set out with a large force, but discovered that the Frenchmen had already abandoned their position and taken refuge in dense woods. Menéndez now made good use of Ribault's trumpeter, whom he sent into the woods with the message that if the fugitives surrendered, their lives would be spared.[32] On this occasion, the promise was honored.

Having thus rounded up the last remnants of the French forces, Menéndez was now in a position to consolidate the Spanish presence in Florida. The problem of establishing good relations with the Indians of the area was one that now occupied much of his attention. On one visit to an Indian leader, he was accompanied by "two fifes and drums, three trumpets and one harp, one bowed vihuela and one psaltery" ("dos piphanos y atanbores, tres tronpetas y Una harpa, Una bigüela de arco y Un salterio"). The Spanish musicians performed for the Indians and then "five or six gentlemen who had very good voices sang" ("despues cantaron cinco o seys gentiles hombres que tenian muy buenas boces"). According to Solís de Méras, author of this report, Menéndez was a "lover of music" ("amigo de musica") and always traveled with the best musicians that were available.[33]

[30]Ibid., 126.

[31]Ibid., 126 and 2:103.

[32]Ibid., 1:131.

[33]Ibid., 158 and 163.

The final act in the tragedy of Fort Caroline was the arrival in 1568 of Dominique de Gourgues, a Catholic, whose sole purpose in Florida was to avenge the atrocities perpetrated by Menéndez. He was accompanied by the trumpeter who had escaped with Laudonnière:

> Afterwards perceiving the shore to bee covered with Savages with their bowes and arrowes, (besides the Signe of peace and amitie which he made them from his ships) he sent his Trumpetter, to assure them, that they were come thither for none other ende but to renew the amitie and ancient league of the French with them. The Trumpetter did his message so well (by reason he had bene there before under Laudonniere) that he brought backe from King Satourioua, the greatest of all the other kings, a kidde and other meat to refresh us, besides the offer of his friendship and amitie.[34]

The trumpeters and drummers accompanying De Gourgues are mentioned twice in Spanish reports of the raid.

The part played by military musicians during the years of the French colony in Florida reinforces a high estimate of their military value as signallers and messengers. Although accounts vary widely as to the numbers involved, there is complete agreement that, apart from a few young Catholics, musicians were the only men to be spared. Which of several possible considerations led to their survival is hard to say. There was certainly a tradition of regarding musicians as non-combatants, and Menéndez himself is known to have enjoyed music, but their practical value was probably uppermost in the Spaniard's mind when he granted them a reprieve. An experienced trumpeter had skills that were not lightly to be thrown away, as shown by the use of Ribault's trumpeter by Menéndez at Cape Cañaveral and De Gourgues's employment of Laudonnière's trumpeter.

[34]Laudonnière (1586), 115.

CHAPTER 10

Early Settlements

An examination of the part played by musicians in the first English-speaking settlements of North America should begin with the colony established at Jamestown in Virginia in 1607. Evidence concerning some aspects of the musical life of this, the first successful English colonial venture in North America, is admittedly meagre, but a more rounded picture may be obtained by taking into account the Virginia Company's sister colony on Bermuda and the small English outpost established on Newfoundland in 1610.

The function of drummers in the life of the early Jamestown colony is described fully in William Strachey's *For the Colony in Virginea Britannia. Lawes Divine, Morall and Martiall* (London, 1612). Strachey's pamphlet gives details of the disciplinary codes of conduct that were enforced in Jamestown in 1610. In the words of Quinn, "it was calculated to make any person who read it wary of setting foot in Virginia as a soldier or settler, unless he was determined to behave himself with the utmost probity and obedience (or else hope that such severe laws would not be enforced)."[1] No other work of the period gives so clear a view of the duties of the drummer in an overseas settlement, and for this reason we shall look at its evidence in some detail.

Strachey begins with a series of general instructions. Item 6 reads: "Everie man and woman duly twice a day upon the first towling of the Bell shall upon the working daies repaire unto the Church, to heare divine Service upon pain of losing his or her dayes

[1]V. Yellin, "Musical Activity in Virginia Before 1620," *JAMS* , vol. 22 (1969), 284–89, and Warner (1984), 77–95.

allowance for the first omission." A second offence would lead to a whipping and a third to the gallies. Concerning the working day, it was ordained in Item 28 that: "No souldier or tradesman, but shall be readie, both in the morning, and in the afternoone, upon the beating of the Drum, to goe out unto his worke, nor shall hee returne home, or from his worke, before the Drum beate againe . . . " The general martial laws included the following instructions to soldiers: Item 5: "That Souldier that shall march upon any service, shall keepe his Ranke, and marching, the Drum beating, and the Ensigne displayed, shall not dare absent himselfe, or stray and straggle from his ranke, without leave granted from the cheefe officer, upon pain of death." Item 33: "He that shall not appeare upon the guard, or not repaire unto his colours, when the Drum upon any occasion shall beate either upon an Alarum, or to attend the buisinesse which shall be then commaunded, shall for his first offence lie in Irons upon the court of guard all one night, and for his second be whipt, and for the third be condemned to the Gallies for one yeare." Item 49: "Whosoever shal not retreat when the drum or trumpet soundeth the same, whether it be uppon any sallies, made out of any town or fortres, or in skirmish, or in any incounter, shall be punished with death." In battle, ill-disciplined heroics, such as the failure to respond to a signal to retreat, could be every bit as dangerous as desertion.

Strachey next gives instructions for various ranks from captains down to rank-and-file soldiers. These show the extent to which the daily routine of the whole colony was regulated by the sound of the drum. The instructions for the captain of the watch included the following orders:

> It shall bee his duty the time beeing come, when the general morning worke is to be left off, to cause the Drum to beate, and with his Guard of Rounders to assist the Captaines or Capt. to bring the laborers in to the Church to heare divine service. . . .
>
> At the time or houres appoynted for the afternoone worke of the Colony, every labourer to his worke, and every crafts man to his occupation, Smiths, Ioyners, Carpenters, Brick makers etc. He shall cause the drumme to beate again, to draw and call forth the people unto their labour, when againe, the worke on all hands towards night being to bee left off, he is to cause the drumme likewise then to beate, and as before assist the Capt: with the whole company to bring them to evening prayer.

> It shall be his duty halfe an houre before the divine Service, morning and evening, to shut the Ports and place centinels, and the Bell having tolled the last time, he shal search all the houses of the towne, to command every one, of what quality soever (the sick and hurt excepted), to repaire to Church, after which he shall accompany all the guards with their armes, (himselfe being last) into the Church, and lay the keyes before the Governor.[2]

Having set forth the duties of captains, Strachey works his way down the ranks. Ensigns, "at the beating of the Drum," were responsible for conducting their squadrons to the captain; sergeants, "when the Drum shall call them forth to worke," were to check for absentees; corporals, "when the Drum beateth," were to ensure a general state of readiness. Finally, the ordinary soldier "must learne the severall sounds of the Drumme . . . for the Drum often-times is the voice of the Commander."

For soldiers and workers alike, there seem to have been four main divisions to the day which were marked by five regular rounds by the drummers:

Table 4

DRUM (daybreak)	morning work / guard duties
DRUM (9. 00 a.m.—10. 00 a.m.)	church service / guard duties lunch and recreation
DRUM (2. 00 p.m.–3. 00 p.m.)	afternoon work / guard duties
DRUM (5. 00 p.m.–6. 00 p.m.)	church service / guard duties evening meal
DRUM (night)	setting the watch

The pattern established at Jamestown was soon copied on Bermuda. The author of "The Historye of the Bermudaes or Summer Islands" mentioned that the Governor set his course "after the Virginian rule," in particular "imitatinge divers orders digested by Sir Thomas Dale, while he was marshall ther, a copy whereof he had brought with him"—a palpable allusion to Strachey's pamphlet.[3] The

[2]D. B. Quinn, *New American World;* vol.5: *The Extension of Settlement in Florida, Virginia, and the Spanish Southwest* (London, 1979), 221.

[3]J. H. Lefroy, *The Historye of the Bermudaes or Summer Islands* (*HS*, vol.65; London, 1882), 76–77.

duties of drummers on Bermuda included sounding the signal for laborers to assemble at the town wharf. Another passage refers to the use of drums to place the colony in a state of alarm—again, one of the duties prescribed by Strachey. One evening as the watch was about to be set, a fleet of ships was observed out at sea. Nathaniel Butler, the Governor, mobilized his forces thus: "Secretly callinge for the drumme of his owne Company, he commanded him, in stead of his wonted settinge of the watch, to beate an alarme, the which being well and speedely answered by the garrison at the towne, and all of them quickly brought together and in armes upon the warfe. . . ."[4] As it turned out, the ships belonged to Englishmen who were night-fishing for sharks.

Given the significance of their role in the daily routine of the first English colonies, it is hardly surprising that drummers appear in lists of settlers and drums in inventories of their possessions. A list of the planters in Virginia who remained after Newport's departure in 1607 includes one "Nicholas Skot, Drum."[5] A later document detailing payments made in Bristol in 1609 while one of the Virginia Company's ships was being equipped, includes a payment of 35 shillings "ffor a drum" and half a crown "to one Hale a drummer by m^r^ Thorpes appoyntm^t^."[6] Even in the fledgling colony sponsored by the Newfoundland Company at Cupid's Cove, "one drume" is recorded among the meagre possessions of the settlers in August 1611.[7] No matter how small the settlement or how remote its location, the drum was an ever-present symbol of order and authority.

The trumpeters mentioned in some early reports of the Jamestown settlement were not long-term residents of the colony. They were employed on the Virginia Company's ships during the transatlantic crossing and would then disembark for a period of service on shore, remaining on American soil only until their captain returned to England. At his first arrival in 1607, Newport's "noise" of trumpets marked the occasion with an appropriate fanfare.[8] The

[4]Ibid., 236.

[5]P. L. Barbour, *The Jamestown Voyages under the First Charter*, vol. 2 (*HS*, 2nd series, vol. 137; Cambridge, 1969), 383.

[6]S. M. Kingsbury, *The Records of the Virginia Company of London*, vol. 3 (Washington, 1933), 187.

[7]G. T. Cell: *Newfoundland Discovered: English Attempts at Colonization, 1610–1630* (*HS*, 2nd series, vol. 160; London, 1982), 66.

[8]Purchas, 19:55.

adverse effect of trumpet calls on the Indians was soon noted by residents of the new colony. During a period of imprisonment at the hands of Powhatan, John Smith, perhaps with self-preservation in mind, described to the Indian chief the frightening effects of the English military instruments: "I gave him to understand the noyse of Trumpets, and terrible manner of fighting [that] were under Captain *Newport*. . . ."[9] In his *Historie of Travell into Virginia Britania*, Strachey wrote: "the noyse of our drumms of our shrill Trumpetts and great Ordinance terrefyes them so as they startle at the Report of them, how far soever from the reach of danger. . . ."[10]

In view of such reactions, the silencing of the trumpets and drums could be made a fairly effective guarantee of a truce. After the infamous kidnapping of Pocahontas during a trading expedition up the Potomac in 1612, Captain Argall agreed during the negotiations that followed that "if they would fight with us, they should know when we would begin by our Drums and Trumpets,"[11] a concession that may have been viewed as much as a threat as a promise. Argall's trumpeters were later encountered by a French priest, Father Biard, during the attack on the French colony at Port Royal in 1613. The English flagship, he wrote, approached with "three trumpeters and two drummers playing with all their might" ("trois trompettes et deux tambours faisants rage de sonner").[12]

Daily life in the Jamestown Colony centered around the morning and afternoon services to which the residents were summoned by the tolling of a bell. The Jamestown Church apparently had two bells: "It is in length threescore foote, in breadth twenty foure, and shall have a Chancell in it of Cedar, and a Communion Table of the Blake Walnut, and all the Pewes of Cedar, with faire broad windowes, to shut and open, as the weather shall occasion, of the same wood, a Pulpet of the same, with a Font hewen hollow, like a Canoa, with two Bels at the West end. . . ."[13] The tolling of the bell, a sign for

[9]P. L. Barbour, *The Jamestown Voyages under the First Charter*, vol.1 (*HS*, 2nd series, vol. 136; Cambridge, 1969), 187.

[10]L. B. Wright and V. Freund: *The Historie of Travell into Virginia Britania (1612) By William Strachey, gent.* (*HS*, 2nd series, vol. 103; London, 1953), 105.

[11]J. Smith, *The Generall Historie of Virginia, New England and The Summer Isles*, vol. 1 (Glasgow, 1907), 220.

[12]R. G. Thwaites, *The Jesuit Relations and Allied Documents* (Cleveland, 1896), 3:278.

[13]Purchas, 19:56.

the drummers to escort all except the sick and those engaged in guard duties to church, was part of the daily routine, but it could also be used as an emergency signal to congregate at other times. When Sir Thomas Gates and Sir George Somers arrived at the stricken colony in 1610, they "caused the Bell to be rung" as a sign for the surviving settlers to assemble.[14] The Bermuda Church also had at least one bell. During their enforced stay on the island after the wreck of 1609, Gates and Somers recalled that "at the ringing of a Bell, wee repayred all to publique Prayer. . . ."[15]

It is certain that psalm singing was an integral part of public worship in the early seventeenth-century Jamestown Church, but there is a regrettable lack of evidence. Only once does John Smith mention psalms. During his travels amongst the Indians in 1608, he reported: "Our order was, dayly, to have prayer, with a psalm: at which solemnity the poore Salvages much wondered."[16]

Useful information about the early Bermuda Church, however, survives in the works of a Welsh preacher, Lewis Hughes. In a document entitled "The Maner of the Publicke Worship and Service of God in the Summer Ilands" (written in March 1618), Hughes gave details of the liturgy that he had personally devised for his congregation.[17] His suggested order of worship allowed for four psalms to be sung: (i) before the minister's call to worship; (ii) after the Old Testament reading; (iii) before the sermon; (iv) after the celebration of Holy Communion. The Governor of Bermuda, with whom Hughes had quarrelled, complained to a bishop in England of the preacher's "irregularities in not conformeinge himselfe in the Sommer Ilands to the booke of Common Prayer."[18] This unnamed ecclesiastic—evidently a judicious man—refused to take action "in respect the place was so farre remote of his diocesse." Later, during the governorship of Nathaniel Butler, Hughes's liturgy was still a cause of dissension. By now, there were two rival preachers, neither of whom subscribed to the Book of Common Prayer. Their differences made both the subject of ridicule. It was put to them that the liturgy

[14]Ibid., 44.

[15]Ibid., 37.

[16]P. L. Barbour, *The Jamestown Voyages under the First Charter*, vol. 2 (*HS*, 2nd series, vol. 137; Cambridge, 1969), 408.

[17]V. A. Ives, *The Rich Papers: Letters from Bermuda 1615–1646* (London, 1984), 336–46.

[18]Lefroy (1882), 112.

in use on Guernsey and Jersey should be adopted, and this proved an acceptable compromise.[19]

After his return to England in 1621, Hughes published *A Plaine and True Relation of the Goodnes of God towards the Sommer Ilands* which includes a catechism. This gives a moderately informative, if idealistic picture of the role that Hughes envisaged for psalm singing on Bermuda. Concerning the observance of the Sabbath, he wrote: "if the Minister and people be praying or singing of Psalmes, we ought presently without any delay to ioyne with them. . . ." In answer to the question, "Is merry talking and iesting and singing of merry Songs a breach of the Sabaoth?," we read: "Yes, and that not onely in him that useth it, but also in others, in that it causeth them to withdraw their mindes from holy meditations to hearken thereunto." Concerning the choice of psalms on the Sabbath, Hughes wrote: "They [the Jews] had singing of Psalmes; the 92. Psalme [It is a good thing to give thanks unto the Lord] was made of purpose to be sung on the Sabaoth day, to stirre up the people to acknowledge God, and to praise him in his workes, and therefore in the title of it, it is called a Psalme for the Sabaoth." Finally, Hughes recommended that psalms be sung "in a knowne tonge, with our spirits and understanding, and with grace in our hearts to the Lord. . . ."

The importance of psalm-singing in the early years of the Bermuda colony is also evident in the journal of Richard Norwood, a surveyor by profession, who was employed to map out the islands and divide them into "tribes." In 1616 he underwent a conversion after which he was assiduous in his devotions. He wrote: "That night after supper we sang a psalm, and from thenceforth, both there (being in Smith's Tribe) and in all the other Tribes as I came to lay out the shares, all the people that were near, which was then almost all in the Tribe, met after supper at the Overseer's house where I was, and we read a chapter, sang a psalm, and went to prayer together."[20] This presents an attractive picture of psalm-singing as the accepted musical expression of faith among the isolated groups of English settlers.

Life for the first English colonists was arduous, but there were periods of relaxation, notably during the middle of the day and in the

[19]Ibid., 171.

[20]W. F. Craven and W. B. Hayward, *The Journal of Richard Norwood, Surveyor of Bermuda* (New York, 1945), 83.

evenings, when laborers and off-duty soldiers could engage in hobbies such as music. There may even have been some professional musicians among the early settlers. A list of "Walloons and French" who applied for permission to emigrate to Virginia in August 1621 includes two men, George Wautre and Martin Framerie, who are both described as musicians.[21] The Virginia Company had no objection to their request, provided that they agreed to take the oath of allegiance to the King, but no assistance with their passage was offered. At this stage, the fledgling colonies were far too small to be able to support resident musicians. Any instrumentalists who emigrated would certainly have been employed in other trades, perhaps on the understanding that they would be released from their duties if their musical skills were required.

Ballad-singing and dance music seem to have been the most popular forms of musical entertainment in the Jamestown and Bermuda settlements. One ballad singer resident in Bermuda is known by name. The author of "The Historye of the Bermudaes" referred to the man in 1618: "this Grove was a fellowe sent out of England by Sr. Edwin Sands, and it is sayd he was a ballade-maker and streete-singer of them ther, but now, by the wise choyce of the Governour, made the Provost Marshall, though at that present, by reason of some sawecynesse, in some deiection."[22] Grove, again described as a "ballad-singer," was later reported to have been dismissed for his "insufficiencye and knaverie."[23]

In a letter from Virginia dated 31 March 1623, William Capps made an obscure allusion to two popular tunes, probably ballads, that may have been known in the Colony. Referring to the provision of slaves to work on a fort, he remarked cryptically: "but before I deliver them up I will make them sing new Toes, old Toes, no Toes at all, because they shall not outrun me, for I am sure they have made us sing a song this twelve moneth to the tune of O man where is thy hart. . . ."[24] Ballads, either unaccompanied or else sung to a popular instrument such as the fiddle, may also have been used for dancing.

[21]W. N. Sainsbury: *CSP, Colonial Series, 1574–1660*, vol. 1 (London, 1860), 498–99.

[22]Lefroy (1882), 137. A Francis Grove (active between 1623 and 1661) published a number of ballads in England. See C. M. Simpson: *The British Broadside Ballad and its Music* (Rutgers University Press, 1966), 99.

[23]Lefroy (1882), 249.

[24]Kingsbury (1935), 4:77.

In 1621 Guy Fawkes Day was celebrated on Bermuda with great solemnity. In the morning, the Governor went to church with "an extraordinary garde of halberds and musketts," while the afternoon was given over to a period of recreation, with "musick and dancinge."[25]

[25]Lefroy (1882), 274.

CHAPTER 11

The Growth of Colonies

The final stage in the long process of colonisation saw the gradual evolution of the first small-scale settlements into large more-or-less unified colonial territories. The cultural, linguistic and religious character of each colony was that of the mother country in Europe, or, in the case of dissenting settlements, that of the minority population from which the immigrants were drawn. It was perhaps only during this period of consolidation that the distinct musical identities of the colonies began to emerge. It is not my intention to examine in detail the history of music in the Spanish and Portuguese colonies in Central and South America[1], but in order to put developments in the English-speaking colonies in a fair perspective, it will be helpful to look firstly at New France, the jewel in the crown of England's most vigorous colonial competitor in North America.

For an account of music in the short-lived French colony at Port Royal we are indebted to Marc Lescarbot's *Histoire de la Nouvelle France* (Paris, 1609). Trumpeters are first mentioned when, shortly after the arrival of the French ships in 1604, a priest went missing: "Finally, they sounded a Trumpet thorow the Forrest, they shot off the Canon divers times, but in vaine: for the roaring of the Sea, stronger then all that, did expell backe the sound of the said Canons and Trumpets."[2] The arrival of supply ships was invariably marked with gunfire and trumpet calls. François du Pontgravé was saluted

[1]For bibliographies of Latin American music see G. Chase, *A Guide to the Music of Latin America*, 2nd ed. (Washington, 1962). See also G. Béhague, *Music in Latin America* (Prentice-Hall, 1979).

[2]Purchas, 18:230.

in this way[3], and in 1606 the Frenchmen left behind to occupy the fort were hailed by the returning colonists "with three Canon Shots, and many Musket Shots ... at which time our Trumpeter was not slacke of his dutie."[4]

During the summer of 1606, Sieur de Poutrincourt embarked upon an exploration of the region around Fundy Bay, leaving Lescarbot in charge at Port Royal. Poutrincourt was careful to preempt possible attacks from Indians by setting the watch to the sound of the trumpet "at every houres end, as Captaine James Quartier did."[5] The consequences of failing to maintain an adequate watch were soon to become apparent. A small group of Frenchmen were attacked. Poutrincourt, his trumpeter and several other men rushed to assist them, but not before two men had been killed. As the dead were being buried, the Frenchmen chanted funeral prayers and hymns, while the Indians, exaltant at their success, "danced and howled in the distance." To mark Poutrincourt's return to Port Royal, Lescarbot arranged an entertainment which was entitled "Le Theatre de Neptune en la Nouvelle-France." It was enacted on deck.[6] A trumpet call announced the opening speech of the First Triton, and at one point the followers of Neptune were required to sing a chanson in four parts ("a quatre parties").

The winter of 1606 was a mild one, and Lescarbot paints an idyllic picture of life in Port Royal: "On a Sunday, the fourteenth day of the moneth, in the afternoone, wee sported our selves singing in Musicke ["chantans Musique"] upon the River l'Esquelle ..."[7] The arrival of a ship with news of the revocation of the monopoly enjoyed by Sieur de Monts brought to an end the first phase of the Port Royal Colony. Before their departure, the French colonists celebrated the birthday of the Duke of Orleans with gunfire and sang the Te Deum.

In 1610 Poutrincourt returned to Port Royal, and the following year he was joined by two Jesuit priests, Father Pierre Biard and

[3]Ibid., 245.

[4]Ibid., 257.

[5]Ibid., 271.

[6]M. Lescarbot, *Les Muses de la Nouvelle France* (Paris, 1609). See E. B. Holman, *Neptune's Theatre: The First Existing Play Written and Produced in North America, by Marc Lescarbot, 1606* (New York, 1927).

[7]Purchas, 18:275.

Father Enemond Massé. It was their practice "to sing solemnly" on Sundays and feast days to attract the Indians.[8] Hymns were particularly popular.[9] Lescarbot, whose *Relation Derniere* (Paris, 1612) recounts events in the Colony during the years 1610 and 1611, reported that the Te Deum was sung before the baptism of Indians.[10] More interestingly, he also stated that services at this period were "usually sung to music composed by Poutrincourt" ("ordinairement chanté en Musique de la composition dudit Sieur").[11]

In most respects the place of music in the short-lived colony at Port Royal–it was destroyed by Captain Argall on behalf of the English Virginia Company in 1613–resembles that of earlier settlements, but even at this stage there are some signs, notably in the fervent use of music to evangelise the Indians, of the distinctive way in which music in French America was to develop.

The best source for the study of music in Quebec, the first successful French colony in North America, is *The Jesuit Relations and Allied Documents*, a monumental work which includes the reports published every year in France to inform the public of the progress of the mission, and the "Journal des Jesuites," an internal record of life in the church between 1645 and 1668. There are many references to music and musicians, and it is perhaps the single most informative source about European music in America at this period.[12]

The arrival of Father Paul Le Jeune in 1632 marked the beginning of an intensive drive by the Jesuits to convert Indians. Le Jeune immediately opened a school, and in 1635 a house was built to accomodate the growing number of pupils. In 1639 the Ursulines took over the instruction of girls. A fire destroyed the church and school house in 1640, but both were rebuilt on a larger scale. In the *Relation* for 1633, Le Jeune wrote of the successful use of music to teach the Indian children, who were summoned to catechism by the sound of a small bell ("une petite clochette").[13] Having taught the

[8]R. G. Thwaites, *The Jesuit Relations and Allied Documents* (Cleveland, 1896), 2:6.

[9]Ibid., 36.

[10]Ibid., 136.

[11]Ibid., 147.

[12]On the early history of Canadian music, see H. Kellman, *A History of Music in Canada 1534–1914* (Toronto, 1960).

[13]Thwaites, 5:186.

children to pray in Latin, the Jesuits later heard them "humming the Pater noster."[14] Le Jeune described the scene in his schoolroom:

> When everyone is seated, I repeat slowly the Pater or the Credo which I have arranged in verse so that it can be sung; they follow me word for word, learning it very nicely by heart, and having learnt several couplets or strophes, we sing it, in which they take much pleasure; the older ones even sing with them.[15]

The sights and sounds of Indian children singing the hymns and prayers of the Christian Church with such devotion were reported, in these early optimistic days of mission, with great enthusiasm. In 1640, for example, Father Berthelemy Vimont described the singing of the children thus:

> They sing the *Ave Maris Stella* and the *Gloria Patri*, bowing as they see us do, and if they do not know a hymn by heart, they sing it twenty or thirty times without stopping, thinking that they are praying in a way pleasing to God; such innocence is truly charming.[16]

Instruments were also taught to Indian children. One of the Ursulines instructed her pupils "to sing and play on a viol the notes of the chants" ("à chanter et à toucher sur la viole, la note des cantiques spirituels").[17] The children often sang at services, their music giving great pleasure to those who heard it.

The official Jesuit reports which recount with such pride the achievements of Indian children, rarely give details of the music in the Quebec church. The compilers of the Journal, however, were clearly interested in the subject. A few weeks after the Journal begins in 1645, there was a wedding service at which two violins ("deux violons") are reported to have been played.[18] At Midnight Mass that year, a small ensemble provided music: "Then we began to sing two airs, *Venez mon Dieu* and *Chantons noe;* Monsieur de la Ferté provided the bass ("faisoit la basse"), St. Martin played a violin ("Ioüoit du violon") and there was also a German flute ("une fluste d'alemagne") that was found to be out of tune."[19] On Christmas Day the psalms

[14]Ibid., 138.

[15]Ibid., 11:222.

[16]Ibid., 19:40.

[17]*Les Ursulines de Quebec* (Quebec, 1863), 41.

[18]Thwaites, 27:100.

[19]Ibid., 112.

were sung "en faux-bourdon" (i.e. in simple, parallel note-against-note harmonisations).[20] In 1646 the three regular musicians were joined by a soldier: "As this soldier was musical and knew how to sing a treble part ("chanter un dessus") we began on St. Thomas's Day to sing in four parts ("a quatre parties").[21] The singers were usually provided with a meal after they had sung, probably as part or all of their payment.[22] The Christmas music of 1648 again included instruments: the three psalms were sung "en faux-bourdon," the responds "en musique," and at the Elevation and during Communion, there was music with viols ("musique avec violes").[23]

In the second half of the 17th century, the organisers of music in the Quebec church had access to a growing number of performers, both vocal and instrumental. In 1652 Father Paul Raguena reported that the new church had eight choirboys and singers,[24] and by 1661 an organ had been installed.[25] In March 1663 a service was sung with instruments[26], and at the Feast of St. Matthias in 1664, the sermon was followed by organ music.[27] About this period, the suggestion was made that the musicians should be given a meal before the service, to enable them to sing better! It seems that they were having to struggle to make themselves heard. On one occasion, the compiler of the Journal noted that the Benediction had been given at the screen near the organ; it went well, he reported, except that the voices and instruments were considered too "weak" for a building of that size.[28]

Limited though its chronological coverage is, the Journal illustrates the central role of the Catholic Church in the development of musical culture in New France. Qualitative judgements are difficult, but the musical life of Quebec seems curiously unsophisticated, even amateurish, when compared with the more vigorous approach adopted in Portuguese India or Spanish America. This may be a

[20]Ibid., 116.

[21]Ibid., 28:248.

[22]Ibid., 30:188.

[23]Ibid., 31:108.

[24]Ibid., 36:174.

[25]Ibid., 46:162.

[26]Ibid., 298.

[27]Ibid., 48:228.

[28]Ibid., 230.

consequence of the fact that the Journal was a private document in which Jesuits felt able to record candid assessments of reality rather than the usual propaganda for consumption back at home, but it may also reflect the fact that French missionaries working in North America did not feel the same need to compete with a sophisticated indigenous culture as their colleagues in the East.

Notwithstanding the lengthy list of settlements founded before 1620—San Agostín; Fort Caroline; Roanoke; Jamestown; Bermuda; Cupid's Cove; Port Royal; Quebec; and others, notably in the Spanish south—historians of American music have traditionally regarded, and to some extent still do regard, the arrival of the *Mayflower* as the most significant point of departure.[29] The founding of the Plymouth Colony certainly marked the beginning of large-scale English immigration into North America, and settlements quickly grew up in Massachusetts Bay, Rhode Island, Connecticut, New Haven, New Hampshire and Maine. In addition to the New England and Virginia Colonies, there were also English-speaking settlements in the Caribbean.

A celebrated passage in Winslow's *Brief Narration* (1646) describes the psalms sung by the congregation at Leyden before the departure of the "Pilgrims":

> And when the ship was ready to carry us away, the bretheren that stayed having again solemnly sought the Lord with us and for us, and we further engaging ourselves mutually as before, they, I say, that stayed at Leyden feasted us that were to go, at our pastor's house, being large; where we refreshed ourselves, after tears, with singing of psalms, making joyful melody in our hearts, as well as with the voice, there being many of our congregation very expert in music; and indeed it was the sweetest melody that ever mine ears heard.[30]

Like the earlier colonists in Virginia, the New England settlers carefully nurtured the practice of psalm singing in the New World. The growth of an indigenous American tradition of psalmody has been well documented, and there is no need to do more here than to repeat

[29]In *The New Grove* (London, 1980), Gilbert Chase wrote: "Although the ill-fated settlement at Jamestown in Virginia dates from 1607, it is with the Plymouth Colony that the history of American music properly begins." Others, however, give greater emphasis to earlier developments, see R. Stevenson, *Protestant Church Music in America* (New York, 1966). See also Yellin (1969), and Warner (1984).

[30]P. A. Scholes, *The Puritans and Music in England and New England* (London, 1934), 3.

the point that there was a gradual decline in the use of psalters imported from Europe in favour of those published in the colonies. The psalters used by the first settlers, Henry Ainsworth's *Book of Psalmes* (Amsterdam, 1612), Thomas Ravenscroft's *Whole Booke of Psalmes* (London, 1621) and Sternhold and Hopkins, were joined in 1640 by the *Whole Booke of Psalmes* (widely known as the *Bay Psalm Book*) which was published in Cambridge, Massachusetts and went into many editions.

Psalm singing, as characteristic a feature of life in the English settlements in the New World as it was in the Eastern factories, was normally unaccompanied at this period. Not until the early 18th century are there reports of organs in church. On 29 May 1711 Joseph Green wrote in his diary: "I was at Mr. Thomas Brattle's: heard ye organs and saw strange things in a microscope.[31] Brattle bequeathed the instrument to the King's Chapel in Boston. Whether this instrument can sustain a claim to be the first organ in use in an English-speaking church in the New World is uncertain, as organs were beginning to appear in the Caribbean settlements about this time. John Atkins, who visited Bridgetown, Barbados in 1721 wrote: "There is only one large Church, with an Organ, and about twenty Chappels at different parts of the island, all Episcopal ..."[32]

The drum was as vital an instrument of time-keeping and discipline as it had been in the Jamestown colony. In 1627 Isaac de Rasières, secretary to the Dutch colony at Manhattan, reported during a visit to the Plymouth settlement: "They assemble by beat of drum, each with his firelock or musket, in front of the Captain's door."[33] Scholes cited an ordinance, promulgated in the Plymouth colony in 1658 that points to the widespread use of the instrument: "Enacted that every towne that shalbee defective in the want of a drum att any time for the space of two moneths shall forfeit the sum of forty shillings to the collonies use."[34] On some plantations it may have been the policy to equip a band to undertake the duties of waits. In 1633 at Newitchwanick in New Hampshire an inventory records "15 recorders and hoeboys," and at Pascattaquack "hoeboys and recorders 26" and "1 drume."[35]

[31]Ibid., 250.

[32]J. Atkins, *A Voyage to Guinea, Brasil, and the West-Indies; in His Majesty's Ships the Swallow and Weymouth* (London, 1735), 206.

[33]Scholes (1934), 22.

[34]Ibid., 23.

[35]L. Pichieri, *Music in New Hampshire 1623–1800* (New York, 1960), 13.

Military duties apart, the main function of the trumpeters and drummers was the traditional one of providing ceremonial salutes. The arrival at Port Royal, Jamaica, of the Duke of Albermarle in 1687 was marked by fanfares. According to John Taylor, he was greeted with gunfire while "the drums and trumpets joyfully sounded their marshall blasts."[36] After lunch, "the drums beating several points of turn," several regiments of infantry paraded before him. The day ended thus: "All the night the drums continued beating and the trumpetts joyfully sounding on shore, with other musick, with boon fires, and all other possible signals of joy ..." The trumpeters traditional perk, playing in the New Year for a gratuity, is recorded in New England by Judge Sewell. In 1696: "One with a Trumpet sounds a Levet at our window just about break of day, bids me good morrow and wishes health and hapiness to attend me."[37] In 1701: "Just about Break-a-day Jacob Amsden and 3 other Trumpeters gave a Blast with the Trumpets on the common near Mr. Alford's. Then went to the Green Chamber, and sounded there till about sunrise."

Evidence of non-military professional musicians in the English-speaking colonies is exceedingly scanty. This is hardly surprising since there were few opportunities to work in the service of the church, the main source of employment for such men in the French and Spanish colonies. In the late 1640s Richard Ligon and a few of his musical friends among the planters on Barbados discussed the possibility of bringing over the band of musicians who had played at Blackfriars Theatre in London until its closure in 1642:

> As for Musick, and such sounds as please the ear, they wish some supplies may come from *England*, both for Instruments and voyces, to delight that sense, that sometimes when they are tir'd out with their labour, they may have some refreshment by their ears; and to that end, they had a purpose to send for the Musick, that were wont to play at the *Black Fryars*, and to allow them a competent salary, to make them live as happily there, as they had done in *England*: And had not extream weaknesse, by a miserable long sicknesse, made me uncapable of any undertaking, they had employed me in the businesse, as the likeliest to prevail with those men, whose persons and qualities were well known to me in *England*.[38]

[36]M. Pawson and D. Buisseret, *Port Royal, Jamaica* (Oxford, 1975), 111–13.

[37]Scholes (1934), 42.

[38]R. Ligon, *A True and Exact History of the Island of Barbados* (London, 1657). Cited by C. D. S. Field, "Musical Observations from Barbados, 1647–50," *MT* (1974), 565–67.

The plan, however, remained unfulfilled, and Ligon went on to imply that though there were a few kindred spirits on the island, the majority of the planters were so engrossed by the land and its profits that they had been known to remark that "three whip Sawes, going all at once in a Frame or Pit, is the best and sweetest Musick that can enter their ears."

The prospect of a consort of professional musicians from London earning a "competent salary" on Barbados was never a very realistic one in the 1640s, but there were no doubt opportunities for individual fiddlers to make a living by playing at dances and providing music at the tables of the gentry. Later, towards the end of the century, small bands of professional musicians became more readily available. Francis Hanson summarised the style of living on Jamaica in 1683 as follows: "The manner of living there for gallantry, good Housekeeping and Recreations (as Horse-Races, Bowls, Dancing, Musick, Plays at a publick Theatre etc) sufficiently demonstrate the flourishing condition of the Island.'[39] In New England, Judge Sewell records several occasions on which he"had musick," or, as the case might be, "had no musick" at dinner, which suggests that by then there was a class of musicians who earned at least part of their living from such engagements.[40]

The slow growth in the ownership of musical instruments for amateur recreation can be traced in all the English-speaking colonies in the New World. The idea that music was absent from the Puritan homes of 17th-century New England was effectively rebutted by Scholes, and more recent research by Lambert has demonstrated that in the second half of the century instrument ownership was far more widespread than has hitherto been believed.[41] During the first hundred years of the settlement in Suffolk County (which includes Boston) she has found references in inventories to some 70 instruments, including 13 citterns, four guitars, seven viols, nine violins and 13 pairs of virginals. A wide range of mainly middle-class occupations—doctors, farmers, merchants, clergymen—are represented among the owners. Similar bequests have been noted in the Virginian records.[42]

[39]F. Hanson, *The Laws of Jamaica* (London, 1683), fol. d5.

[40]Scholes (1934), 42.

[41]B. Lambert, "The Musical Puritans," *Bulletin of the Society for the Preservation of New England Antiquities*, vol. 62 (1972), 66–75. See also S. E. Morison, *Harvard College in the Seventeenth Century*, vol. 1 (Cambridge, Mass., 1936), 115. Pichieri (1960), 16–17.

[42]P. A. Bruce, *Economic History of Virginia in the Seventeenth Century*, vol. 2 (New York, 1896), 175.

Despite this evidence of instrument ownership, the impression still remains that expatriate musical culture in the English-speaking New World grew in a slow, almost desultory fashion for much of the 17th century. Not until the 18th century is it possible to speak of a fully-developed musical society in the American settlements. This pattern of slow growth from small beginnings contrasts markedly with the process of impoverishment that has been observed in Hispanic colonial cultures. As Seeger has pointed out, the vigorous implantation of the choirschools and fine instruments of Spanish catholicism, proved, after an often successful early phase, unsustainable.[43] Eventually, "the social conditions for the cultivation of fine and popular idioms as practised in the mother countries existed to an almost negligible extent." A revival did not occur until the emergence of a prosperous class of colonial administrators in the 18th century, who had the time, resources and inclination to offer patronage to professional musicians. One factor contributing to the slow growth of a distinctive musical culture in English-speaking America was the process of dispersal itself. Comparison with the eastern settlements is instructive. Typically, an English trading station in India concentrated its resources (including musical ones) into a small area, and, with rival factories often located nearby, the potential for the development of closely-knit networks of amateurs, resulting eventually in an audience for the professional musician, was there at an early stage. In North America, by contrast, with the boundaries of settlements receding ever further into the interior, potential musical resources were ever more widely scattered, stunting to some small degree growth in the major centres such as Boston. The range of musical activity in the East was undoubtedly enhanced further by the fact that from the beginning the trading companies employed many men with middle-class skills, such as merchants, writers, linguists and accountants. By contrast, the initial need in the the New World was for farmers, artisans and soldiers. Finally, the North American settlements were not able to avail themselves of the services of visiting ships' musicians, since, after the initial Elizabethan voyages, professional consorts were deemed wholly unnecessary on the routine transatlantic routes, whereas, at least until the mid 17th century, the musical life of the eastern trading stations was invigorated by a constant supply of visiting consorts on the ships of the trading companies. The legacy of these circumstances can be seen even at the end of the 18th century when, arguably, Calcutta could still be said to rival Boston as the most vital centre of English culture outside Europe.

[43]C. Seeger, *Studies in Musicology 1935–1975* (University of California Press, 1977), 188.

TRADE IN THE EAST

The long quest for eastern trade, which had so dominated the thinking of Elizabethan colonial advocates, eventually bore fruit in 1600 with the formation of the East India Company. For advice on how to conduct their affairs in the East, the Council of the newly-formed company turned to Hakluyt, the acknowledged authority in the field of overseas exploration. In a memorandum entitled "Certain notes gathered of such as have had much familiaritie with the Portugales that trade in the East Indies," he commented that "certain musisians" were very necessary for the planned voyage.[1] The East India Company accepted this advice and began to make use of musicians as an integral part of its trading strategy.

[1]E. G. R. Taylor, *The Original Writings and Correspondence of the two Richard Hakluyts*, vol. 2 (*HS*, 2nd series, vol. 77; London, 1935), 482.

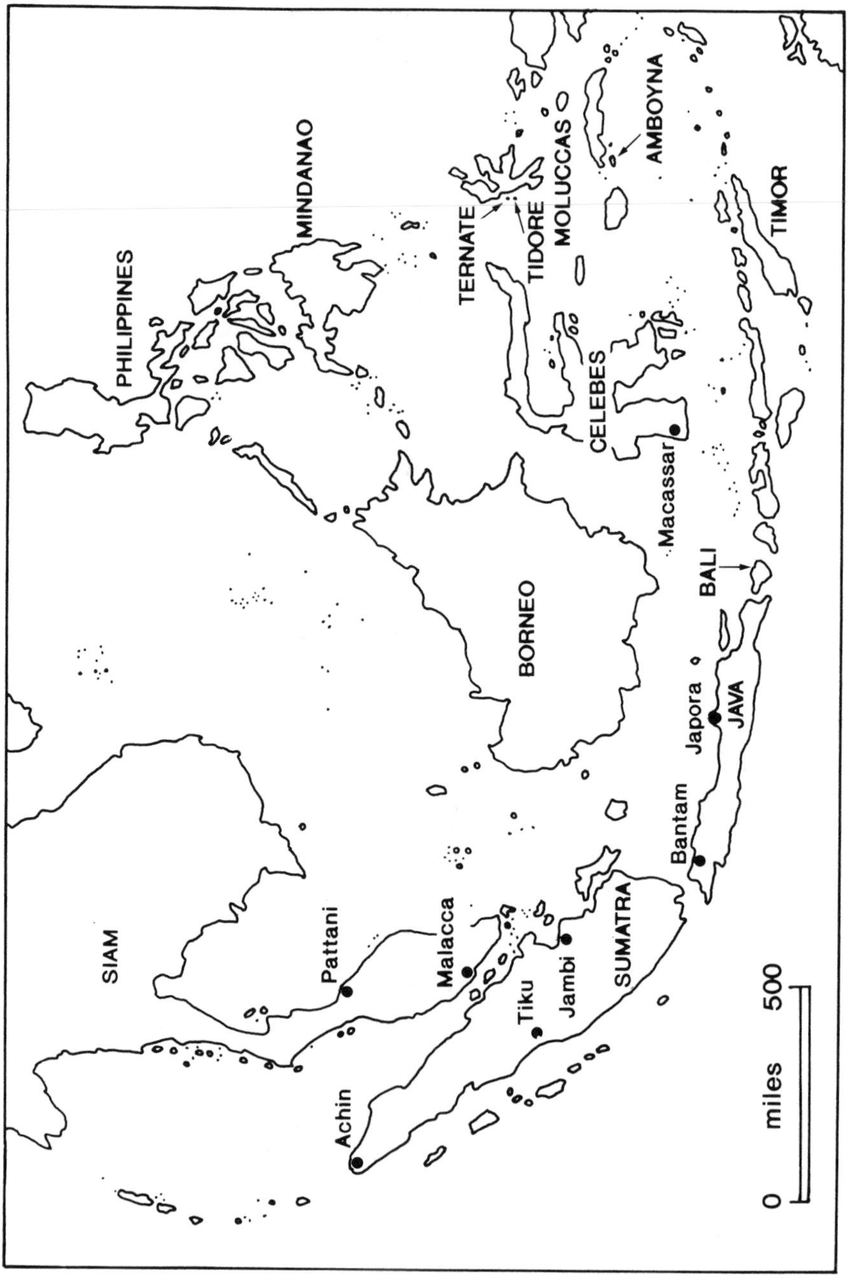

Plate 13. The East Indies.

CHAPTER 12

Establishing the Routes

The experience of the Portuguese had shown it was neither possible nor desirable to sail directly to India. Several stops at strategic points on the southern and eastern coasts of Africa were necessary. With even further to sail, English ships had a correspondingly greater need for such bases. The potential benefits of strategically-placed ports and islands along the trade route around Africa were considerable: ships could be restocked with water, fresh fruit, poultry, and cattle; the injured and infirm could disembark to recover their strength; and any damage sustained during storms could be made good. Sometimes, it was even possible to leave letters for later ships with valuable advice and intelligence. For these reasons, company policy was to promote good relations wherever possible. When their ships arrived in the East, the need for this kind of diplomacy, far from diminishing, increased still further, as the Company, faced with competition from other well-established European interests, endeavored to gain trading concessions.

The key element in this diplomatic campaign was the musical banquet. The lavish ship-board feast with incidental music was not a new idea as it was a form of hospitality extended as a matter of course to important visitors to Elizabethan ships. Following a pattern established by Drake and Cavendish, guests were escorted on board with trumpet fanfares and volleys of shot, and would then be treated to a banquet in the captain's cabin during which the musicians would perform. When leaving, they would be presented with gifts and escorted back to land with equal ceremony. For those unwilling to risk coming on board, the entertainment, with no less pomp, could be provided on their own boats, or, as was often the practice, in tents pitched on the shore. The provision of a banquet was not simply a matter of introducing guests to the everyday food of the English. Great care was taken to provide delicacies suited to the most refined of tastes. A document drawn up in 1580 for the Russia Company made suggestions for the entertainment of "persons of credit": sweet perfumes were to be set under the hatches before the arrival of visitors; delicacies to be served included marmalade, figs, prunes, walnuts, dried pears, almonds, olives, and "the apple John that dureth two yeeres to make shew of our fruits."[1] It was normal practice for some of these foods to be packaged as gifts for guests to take with them when they left—a necessary precaution during Ramadan when followers of Islam could be expected to refuse food served during the day.

The captain of the First Voyage of the East India Company, James Lancaster, knew from personal experience what could happen when the confidence of an African ruler was not won. As a member of George Raymond's expedition of 1591, he witnessed the massacre of thirty Englishmen at the Comoro Islands to the north of Madagascar.[2] The local chief had been entertained on board, but the English, through inexperience, were imprudent enough to send their only boat on shore with an inadequate guard. Lancaster would also have been informed by John Davis, his pilot, of the loss of thirteen Dutchmen in similar circumstances during the voyage of Houtman in 1598.[3] When his ships called at Saldanha Bay to restock, the English captain, therefore, ordered the most stringent of precautions to be observed by his men as they engaged in barter with the local populace. The evil reputation of Saldanha Bay (subsequently a regular staging post) is manifest in the commission given to Middleton for the Second Voyage of the Company in 1604: "we requier you to shun this place, as our expresse order and will herein."[4] When he sighted the Cape,

[1]E. G. R. Taylor, *The Original Writings and Correspondence of the two Richard Hakluyts*, vol. 1 (*HS*, 2nd series, vol. 76; London, 1935), 154–55.

[2]W. Foster, *The Voyages of Sir James Lancaster to Brazil and the East Indies 1591–1603* (*HS*, 2nd series, vol. 85; London, 1940), 6.

[3]Ibid., 80.

[4]W. Foster, *The Voyage of Sir Henry Middleton to the Moluccas 1604–1606* (*HS*, 2nd series, vol. 88; London, 1943), 9. The English no doubt acquired their distrust of the Cape Hottentots from the Portuguese. Ever since the killing of Almeida in 1509, the Portuguese had avoided the region "as they would shun the plague." See B. Penrose, *Travel and Discovery in the Renaissance 1420–1620* (Cambridge, Mass., 1967), 133.

Middleton's intention was to obey the instructions, but dysentery and scurvy were rampant on board the *Dragon*. Seeing the "swarme of lame and weake, diseased criples" outside his cabin door, he relented and weighed anchor. The Africans were reluctant to approach a large force and so Middleton sent four men to them with a bottle of wine and food, with a "taber and a pipe."[5] Reassured by this, they drank the wine and danced to the sound of the music. But the lack of discipline shown by some English sailors hampered Middleton's attempts at bartering. One incident ended with a large company of soldiers scattering in pursuit of fleeing natives in complete defiance of a retreat signalled by Middleton's trumpeter.[6]

Accounts of the Third Voyage illustrate with particular clarity the lengths to which the Company's representatives were prepared to go to maintain at least a measure of good faith. When the *Hector* and the *Dragon* called at Sierra Leone, the local chief was entertained in the usual fashion, and the English began to barter for supplies. On 29 August, Anthony Marlowe recorded in his journal that "this day Walther Stere on[e] of our Trumpeters, beinge sent in the long Boate to wood [to gather wood], did straggle from his fellowes, and was surprised by the negros, and was carryed prysoner 6 myles into the Countrye to one of there houses all night."[7] The following day, Captain Keeling went ashore to investigate the reasons for this hostile act. Having discovered that the trumpeter was being held prisoner nearby, he dispatched a strong force to retrieve him. As there was evidently some cause for complaint, Keeling took the trumpeter back on board, leaving two hostages on land so "they should see that yf any offence were found donne by our men Justice should be exsecuted." Several men were examined, and one confessed that goods had been stolen. These were returned and punishment meted out to the culprits to the evident approval of the Africans. The trumpeter, Walter Stere, "being cleard of the Robberye was for his stragling sett in the Bilboas."

The most interesting account of the part played by musicians in entertaining guests during an early voyage of the East India Company is that of the historic voyage of John Saris to Japan. Two versions of his journal are extant: a manuscript in his own hand in the India Office

[5]Foster (1943), 10.

[6]Ibid., 14.

[7]The journal of Anthony Marlowe is in the British Library, ms. Cotton Titus B VIII.

Library,[8] and the account printed by Purchas.[9] Saris, if not actually a musician himself, was, at any rate, well informed on the subject. He records the presence of his musicians at banquets more frequently than any of his contemporaries. The objectives of his voyage were summarized in a commission dated 4 April 1611.[10] Three ships, the *Clove*, the *Hector*, and the *Thomas*, were to sail for Surat in India. If this could not be done by the required date, Saris was then to trade at Mocha, near the entrance to the Red Sea. The fleet was next to sail for Bantam in Java, whence the *Clove*, alone, was to proceed to Japan. The three ships set out on 18 April 1611, and rounded the Cape of Good Hope during August. On 26 October, they reached the Island of Mohilla in the Comoros, where Saris stopped to replenish his supplies. Having done so, he "invited the king of Moyella [Mohilla] beeing a Mahometan aboord the Clove, and intertained him with a noyse of Trumpets, and a consort of Musique, with a Banket, which he refused to eate of, because it was then his Lent [Ramadan], but hee tooke away with him the best of the Banket to carrie to the Queene his Mother, saying, thay would eate it when the Sunne was downe."[11]

Saris continued northwards along the coast of Africa, arriving at the Island of Socotra on 17 February 1612. He disembarked and was feasted and entertained by Amr-bin-Said. He heard news of Sir Henry Middleton's escape from Mocha and decided to begin trading in the Red Sea. This course of action was soon frustrated, however, by the reappearance of Middleton, bent on vengeance. After a heated disagreement, Saris set sail for Bantam. Following the Company's instructions, the *Clove* was then prepared for her forthcoming voyage to Japan. The route led Saris through the Moluccas. At Ternate, he received word the ruler's son was coming to visit him. The usual entertainment was prepared: "At coming he Rowed 3 tymes Round about the shipp, having divers other Great Corra Corras [boats] with him, and at enterance I ordered 5 peeces ordenance, bringing him to my cabbyn, wheare was provided a suffityent bankett to have been sett to his Father, with musicke and all necessarye, which much contented him."[12] The day after this reception, Saris described in his journal the reaction of the Dutch who were intent

[8]E. M. Satour, *The Voyage of Captain John Saris to Japan, 1613* (*HS*, 2nd series, vol. 5; London, 1900).

[9]Purchas, 3:357–514.

[10]Satour (1900), x–xv.

[11]Purchas, 3:363.

[12]Satour (1900), 40.

on hindering him at every opportunity: "a Curra Curra of the Flemmings came rowing by the ship using a song of scoffing and mocking our people, as they had done manye times before." When they returned "singing and scoffing according to there custome," Saris attempted to ram their boat. He was eventually compelled to leave because the Moluccans were unwilling to risk the wrath of the Dutch by trading with him.[13]

The *Clove* finally arrived at the port of Firando in June 1612. Her musicians now embarked on an intensive period of entertaining, while Saris, on behalf of the Company, sought permission to open the first English trading factory on Japanese soil. The *Clove* anchored on 11 June, and Saris immediately welcomed aboard the "king," Matsura Ho-in, whom he entertained with "a banquet of severall sorts Conserves furnished all in a Glasse, which gave him great Content" and also "a consort of good musick, where in he tooke great pleasure."[14] A large crowd of Japanese later boarded the *Clove* to examine the ship and her contents. The following day Saris again permitted a number of Japanese into his cabin and was amused to see them fall down and worship a picture of Venus "verye lasiviously sett out," as though she were the Madonna.[15] Matsura Ho-in returned later with four of his own women who performed music for Saris. A four-string lute played by one of them caught his attention:[16]

> The Kings women seemed to be somewhat bashfull, but he willed them to bee frollicke. They sung divers songs and played upon certain Instruments (whereof one did much resemble our Lute) being bellyed like it, but longer in the neck, and fretted like ours, but had only foure

[13]The singing of anti-English songs seems to have been a propaganda tactic favored by the Dutch. Cocks wrote in his diary on 16 April 1618, "There were rymes cast abrode and song up and downe towne [Firando] against Matinga and other English mens women. Wherupon matters being brong in question to put them all away, noe proofes could be fownd against them, but a mater donne of spyte by their evell willers, all the neighbours coming to speake in their behalves, affermyng all was lies and that they would take such order that handes should be laid upon such as were heard to sing it hereafter and punishment inflicted upon the offenders. I imagen they were set on by the Hollanders, songs haveing byn made against them to lyke effect before, but not against us." See E. M. Thompson, *The Diary of Richard Cocks*, vol. 2 (*HS*, 2nd series, vol. 67; London, 1883), 31.

[14]Satour (1900), 80.

[15]Ibid., 83.

[16]Ibid., 84.

> gut-strings. Their fingring with the left hand like ours, very nimbly: but the right hand striketh with an Ivory bone, as we use to play upon a Citterne with a quill. They delighted themselves much with their musicke, keeping time with their hands, and playing and singing by booke, prickt on line and space, resembling much ours heere.

After this meeting, Matsura Ho-in agreed to allow Saris to rent a house on shore. During the next few days the English were very active. There were frequent receptions, and the customary presents were exchanged. On 21 June, Matsura Ho-in returned with his women to the *Clove,* and on this occasion Saris's musicians were present: "I intreated them kindly with musicke and a bankett of Conserves of divers sorts, which the King tooke verye well."[17] On 28 July, the musicians again played for a reception: "The young King and the cheife of the nobillyty came with a great trane to vizit me. I intertaned them fitting there worth with a rich bankett and musick, which they tooke great pleasure in."[18]

On 7 August, Saris left Firando to visit the interior of Japan. The English house was left in the charge of Richard Cocks, while most of the crew remained on board the *Clove.* In his journal, Cocks hinted that, after the departure of Saris, the novelty of the English presence was beginning to pall. He continued to entertain, but his efforts now sometimes went unnoticed. On 19 August, anticipating a visit, he made ready a banquet, but no one turned up. On 24 August, Cocks was informed that Matsura Ho-in's grandson and Nobusone, his younger brother, would visit the English house upon their return from the festivities that night. Cocks watched the party set out in style: "the yong king and his brother were mounted on horse-back, and had Canopies caried over them; the rest went on foote, and the musicke was Drummes and Kettles, as aforesaid; and Nabesone winded a Phife."[19] Cocks "sate up untill after midnight," having a banquet in readiness, but the Japanese revellers drifted back "confusedly, and out of order," none entering the English house. The only mention of music at the English house during Saris's absence is on 10 October when Cocks was visited by two Japanese: "I entertayned them in the best sort I could, and shewed them our commodities, and after made them collation and gave them Musicke, Master Hounsell

[17]Ibid., 91.

[18]Ibid., 108.

[19]Ibid., 145.

and the Carpenter by chance being heere."[20] This last remark, however, suggests an *ad hoc* performance, put on by any musicians, including amateurs, who happened to be available.

The journal of a single voyage may give a good impression of the immediate impact of the musical entertainments arranged by the East India Company, but its value in assessing their effect in the longer term is minimal. It will, therefore, be useful to look at a series of reports of visits made by ships of the Company to a single location—the Island of Socotra. Situated off the Horn of Africa, within easy sailing distance of the Red Sea, the Gulf of Persia, and the coast of India, Socotra was ideally placed for the purposes of the Company. The island had been occupied by Tristão da Cunha in 1507, but by the beginning of the seventeenth century was under the control of Sultan Amr-bin-Said, the "king" so often mentioned in English reports. Musicians played a notable part in fostering Amr-bin-Said's goodwill.

At their first meeting in 1608, Amr-bin-Said and William Keeling were both accompanied by their musicians. Anthony Marlowe wrote in his journal: "Our Generalls trumpettes and the kinges drumes and one trumpet for joye sounded at theyr meetinge." Two days later when Keeling and his merchants again disembarked, the English trumpeters were presented with banners by the Sultan. On the morning of 17 May, "the Generall went ashore in good manner w[i]th his noyse of trumpettes drume and fiffe," and later Amr-bin-Said escorted him to his residence, "the Kinges drumes, pipes and voyses, and the Generalls Trumpettes drum and fiffe soundinge and playing all the waye before them." Keeling left a letter for future English visitors stating that he had been supplied with water and fresh provisions, but advising caution in any dealings with the people, "they beeinge Mores and full of deceipt."[21]

The next English ship to call at Socotra was the flagship of the Fourth Voyage of the Company, the *Ascension*, commanded by Alexander Sharpeigh. On 13 August 1609, John Jourdain, one of the factors on board, was sent on land with a present for Amr-bin-Said, "a vest of cloth, a peece and a sword blade."[22] He was entertained by

[20]Ibid., 159.

[21]C. R. Markham, *The Voyages of Sir James Lancaster, Kt., to the East Indies* (*HS*, vol. 56; London, 1877), 118.

[22]W. Foster, *The Journal of John Jourdain 1608–1617* (*HS*, 2nd series, vol. 16; Cambridge, 1905), 109.

the Sultan who communicated to him news of the doings of Keeling and Hawkins at Surat. The following day, Jourdain returned to bargain for cattle, which he purchased at the rate of one sword blade for four goats, three sword blades for a cow.[23] Having restocked with water, and leaving a letter for the next English ships, the *Ascension* set sail, only to be recalled by a signal from the shore. A boat was sent back which returned with the letter left the previous year by Keeling with its belated warning that the moors were a "treacherous people."[24] This letter was returned for the benefit of future arrivals. At this stage, the Sultan, despite his willingness to trade, remained cautious in all his dealings with the English, a sentiment fully reciprocated by the visitors.

When Sir Henry Middleton arrived in October 1610, he sent his chief merchant ashore "handsomely attendid," with a present consisting of "a faire gilt Cup of ten ounces, a Sword-blade, and three yards of Stammell broadcloth."[25] The chief merchant was received by Amr-bin-Said in an orange-tawny colored tent pitched close to the waterside. The next day, Middleton himself disembarked, "well attended on, and with a guard." The Sultan informed him of the wreck of the *Ascension*, but was unable to produce the letter left by Sharpeigh: "the Sulltaun of Sacatoria sayd that the letter was loste: that it was guiven to one of his servantes and hee loste it."[26] When Middleton returned to Socotra in August 1611, after his escape from captivity at Mocha, he left letters for the next ship in the usual way, this time with a more urgent and personal message concerning the dangers of trading in the Red Sea.

Captain Saris arrived at Socotra in February 1612. His chief merchant, Richard Cocks, was sent ashore in a skiff "well appointed" and was entertained by Amr-bin-Said.[27] He returned with the letter left by Middleton the previous September. Saris kept the original and returned a copy for the benefit of future ships. The following day Saris himself disembarked "in solemnest manner" and was feasted with many "complements and curtesies." Notwithstanding the warning left by Middleton, he decided to follow the Company's

[23]Ibid., 110.
[24]Ibid., 112.
[25]Purchas, 3:206.
[26]Foster (1905), 112.
[27]Purchas, 3:370.

instructions and sail to the Red Sea. The well-established practice of leaving letters in Amr-bin-Said's keeping was now beginning to pay dividends. Two months after Saris had left, Middleton was once again in the area, and one of his men was shown the letter containing news of his voyage to the Red Sea.[28] Middleton was then able to alter his plans accordingly.

None of these accounts mentions musicians, but it is certain that when Middleton, Saris and others are reported as having disembarked "handsomely attended," "well attended on," "in a skiffe well appointed," or "in solemnest manner," they did so with their musicians, probably the wind band with trumpeters sounding fanfares.

When Downton arrived at Socotra in September 1614, he ordered all his ships to salute Amr-bin-Said in recognition of his friendship. A present was selected for the Sultan "which neither exeeded what formerlie other of our comaunders had geven him (for makeing a bad president) nor lessned, leaste we geve him cause of dislike."[29] The gift consisted of: "Tow damasked fouleinge peces; tow veste of broade clothe; tow Turkie sworde blaides; eighte knives, in one cace; one lookinge glass; with divers instreuments and 40 li corne poother [granulated gunpowder]." Amr-bin-Said received the English delegation in his tent at the waterside. Music was provided by four of his attendants, "two men playinge upon kettell drumes and two men upon winde instrumentes, not muche unlicke in sownde to baggepipes."[30] As usual, Downton was shown the letters left by previous English captains, the most recent having been written by Saris upon his return from the Red Sea in September 1612. While the aloes purchased by Downton were being packed, Amr-bin-Said took the chance to improve his knowledge of the English nation. He was greatly pleased by the performances of Downton's musicians: "the Kinge earnestlie intreted to heare some of our musicke; which he semed mutch to delighte in, requestinge dailie our companye duringe our staie thire."[31] He debated the Christian religion with his visitors, acknowledging Jesus to have been a great prophet but, in accordance with the tenets of Islam, denying his position as Savior.

[28]Ibid., 280.

[29]W. Foster, *The Voyage of Nicholas Downton to the East Indies, 1614–15* (*HS*, 2nd series, vol. 82; London, 1939), 75.

[30]Ibid., 60.

[31]Ibid., 77.

When he asked about England, Downton sent for "Speedes Cronicle [John Speed: *Theatre of the Empire of Great Britaine*, 1611]" and pointed out to him "all the cheeffe citties, townes, sheres and counties within our Kinges domynions, allsoe the fortes and castells upon the sea coastes."[32] The Englishmen admired the Sultan's knowledge of navigation and astronomy, and his collection of geographical instruments, "celestiall and terrestriall globes, instruments and astralabe," which, he told them, was increased every year by gifts and purchases from the English, Dutch, Portuguese, and Spanish ships which called at his Island.[33] On the day of his departure, Downton again saluted the Sultan with the noise of "sea-musicke (great gunnes and trumpets)."[34]

In 1615, Sir Thomas Roe called at Socotra on his way to the Court of the Great Mughal. As was by now customary, the English party was received in a tent pitched at the waterside. The Sultan was attended by his bodyguards and "a few Kettle Drummes and one Trumpet."[35] Keeling (whom the Sultan had already met) was rowed ashore in a boat with his wind band. Roe noted Amr-bin-Said's comments on the English music: "hearing our hoy-boyes in the Generals boat, hee asked if they were the Psalmes of David? and being answered yes: hee replyed, it was the invention of the Devill, who did invent it: for King David, who before praysed God with his lips and heart in devotion, but after it was left to senceless Instruments."[36] Keeling's reply to this observation is not recorded, but Edward Terry, Roe's chaplain, whose ship was prevented by adverse winds from calling at Socotra in 1616, was told of the Sultan's views and added his own riposte:

> The immediate yeere before our English fleet touching at this Iland, learned this Apothegme from the petie King thereof, who comming to the water side, and hearing some of our winde Instruments, asked if they played Davids Psalmes (of which, being a Mahometan, he had heard.) Hee was answered by one that stood by, they did; He replyed thus, That it was an ill invention of him that first mingled Musicke with Religion; for before (said he) God was worshipped in heart, but

[32]Ibid., 78.

[33]Ibid., 132.

[34]Ibid., 133.

[35]Purchas, 4:320.

[36]Ibid., 322.

> by this in sound. I insert not this relation to condemne musick in Churches, Let him that bids us prayse the Lord with stringed Instruments and Organs, plead the Cause."[37]

By the time Roe called at the Island, the Company's relationship with the ruler of Socotra had developed to the point that little further progress could be made without establishing a permanent base. Keeling, Hawkins, and others clearly valued Socotra, but Roe, an altogether more cynical observer, recommended that outward-bound fleets should avoid the place. He was damning in his comments on the quality and price of the supplies on offer: "the victualls is both carrion, and deare as in England, goodnesse considered."[38] He also pointed out the dangers of restocking with water on such rocky terrain. Notwithstanding Roe's observations, letters of friendship were later exchanged between James I and Amr-bin-Said.

The East India Company's captains made frequent use of small musical trinkets. Interestingly, the "instrument" most frequently coveted was not the small bell or jews harp, but the silver whistle, the badge of authority of the boatswain. Sometimes the whistle itself was the attraction, but more often than not its silver chain was the object of desire.[39] Requests for silver whistle chains were especially prone to occur at ports visited regularly by European ships. When Downton's fleet called at St. Augustine's Bay in Madagascar in 1614, it was quickly realized that, as John Monden put it in his journal, "English money and little silver chaines such as botsuns doe hang their whissels in ar best to buy vittailes heere."[40] Since the purser was not provided with a stock, two or three chains were supplied by boatswains. Thomas Elkington, one of the chief factors on the voyage, later wrote to the East India Company, advising that Downton had been obliged to use all the "white whistle chaynes in the fleete," and recommending that future ships should carry a supply.[41]

[37]Purchas, 9:6.

[38]Purchas, 4:323.

[39]On the history of the naval whistle, see J. S. Corbett, "The Lord Admiral's Whistle," *MM*, vol. 3 (1913), 353–358. G. E. Manwaring, "The Whistle as a Naval Instrument," *MM*, vol. 5 (1919), 72–76. G. E. Manwaring, "The Lord Admiral's 'Whistle of Honour'," *MM*, vol. 9 (1923), 75–77.

[40]India Office Library, East India Company, Marine Records, vol. 20, 6 August 1614

[41]Foster (1939), 195.

A French captain, Augustin de Beaulieu, calling at Madagascar in 1620, tried to pass off fake chains, but without success.[42] He ordered those of his men who possessed "siflets d'argent" to hide them, but several attempts to purchase cattle with chains made from cheaper metals, including a pewter chain manufactured by a goldsmith on board, failed. The local chief was impressed by the French "trompettes" and their "tambours" and offered an ox for one of either, but this suggestion was unacceptable for obvious reasons. Beaulieu was therefore obliged to bargain with sections of the silver chains worn by his men.

The attitude of the Company towards minor figures like the rulers of Socotra or Madagascar was determined by one consideration only: the need to achieve its purposes with a minimum of expenditure. Costly gifts were essential, as we shall see, for men upon whose word depended permission to engage in substantial trade. But for the innumerable subordinates and petty officials with whom the Company also had to deal, relatively inexpensive gifts would often suffice, provided that their manner of presentation was glamorous, with trumpets sounding, drums beating, guns firing salutes, musicians playing, colorful uniforms, banners, streamers, and pendants. Their value in helping to conserve as much as possible the merchandise of their ship is surely the reason why musicians were so evidently considered cost-effective by the East India Company at this period. Once trade routes had been secured, however, the employment of five or six professional musicians on every flagship could no longer be justified. With the arrival and departure of ships becoming an ever more routine occurrence, a professional consort seemed more and more an unnecessary luxury, except for embassies of unusual importance. It was also increasingly realized that the target audience was interested not in the music itself, but in the manner of its performance. Trumpeters and well-dressed amateur musicians from the crew would usually suffice for this purpose.

A different perspective on the entertainments given by musicians serving on ships bound for the East Indies may be found in a series of early seventeenth-century Dutch publications, many of which include copious illustrations. Pictures of trumpeters, drummers and other musicians were included in accounts of six Dutch

[42]M. Thévenot, *Relations de divers voyages curieux (1663–1672)*, part 2, *Memoires du Voyage aux Indes Orientales du General Beaulieux*, entry for 22 May 1620.

voyages—those of Mahu (1598), Van Neck (1598), Spilbergen (1601 and 1614), Le Maire (1615), and Bontekoe (1618)—and also in one report of an English voyage, the Fourth Voyage of the East India Company (1609).

Interpreting this type of pictorial evidence is no easy matter. Early seventeenth-century book illustrations were certainly not intended as photographic records, that is, as detailed, accurate, and complete representations of each event as it actually occurred. On the other hand, neither are they necessarily to be viewed merely as imaginative reconstructions of written descriptions. Published illustrations of voyages were often based on drawings supplied by an artist employed specifically to record the flora, fauna, and ethnography of the places visited by his ship. The illustrator would naturally incorporate any official sketches made available to him and he might also have access to drawings made by other crew members or even published pictures. He could, in addition, make his own interpretations of the written and oral descriptions to which he had access. Some of the more elaborate illustrations are obviously conflations of several smaller drawings. A series of successive occurrences which took place during a brief stop at an island may be combined in one illustration. Discrepancies of scale—the prerogative of the illustrator who seeks to enlarge and therefore clarify matters of particular interest to his readers—are everywhere apparent. These plates, therefore, were imaginative constructions in the sense that their design, balance, and content were determined by their function as text illustrations. However, the possibility that their source materials may have been authoritative drawings made by an experienced, on-the-spot artist suggests they should not be dismissed as mere flights of fancy.

An illustration of musicians serving on an early seventeenth-century East India Company ship was published by De Bry (Plate 14). It depicts the disembarkation of Captain Robert Coverte on one of the Comoro Islands in 1609. In his own account, Coverte described the scene thus:

> The 29. day I went ashore againe, with our Master, master Tindall, master Iordan, and our whole noise of Trumpeters, and at the shore side were very kindly entertained by the Interpreter, who brought us to the King, being then by his Pallace side . . . .[43]

[43]B. Penrose, *The Travels of Captain Robert Coverte* (Philadelphia, 1931), 23.

Plate 14. The Fourth Voyage of the East India Company in 160[illegible] Captain Robert Coverte disembarks with his "noise" of trumpets on the Comoro Islands. De Bry: *India Orientalis*, vol. 11 (Oppenheim, 1618) plate 2. By Permission of the British Library.

In the background, the illustration shows a ceremonial landing from an English ship. Coverte is followed by his "noise" of trumpets. Two trumpeters are depicted sounding their instruments, a third with his trumpet slung behind his back. The "interpreter" advances to meet the Englishmen and behind him is the native leader with his men. Other incidents are pictured in the middle- and foreground, culminating in the violent encounter which first attracts the eye.

Three pictures of trumpeters who sailed with Jacob Mahu in 1598 were published by De Bry. The first of these (Plate 15) shows his fleet at anchor. The obvious disparity between the size of the ships and the size of the men enables the reader to see clearly what the trumpeters are doing. There are two points to note. First, the illustrator has depicted two trumpeters on each of the larger ships, but a

Plate 15. The voyage of Jacob Mahu in 1598: trumpeters sound. De Bry: *America*, part 9, appendix (Frankfurt, 1602) plate 17. By Permission of the British Library.

single trumpeter only on the smaller vessels, thus symbolising the normal deployment of trumpeters—a full "noise" of anything up to four or five men on an admiral or on a vice-admiral, a smaller number, often only one, on lesser ships. Secondly, the position of the trumpeters is unusual. Their regular station was on the poop deck above or next to the captain's cabin, but in this picture (with one exception) they appear on the forecastle because of the proximity of land. This kind of detail is rarely if ever mentioned in written accounts. Two pictures take as their subject a "noise" of five trumpets with their captain during meetings with an African chief. (Mahu's fleet called at Guinea before crossing the Atlantic to the Straits of Magellan.) The scenes illustrated here—the "noise" sounds in honor of the chief, and the "noise" attends the captain—(Frontispiece and Plate 16) are unusually detailed. Worth noting is the characteristic position of the trumpet (slung behind the back) when not in use.

Plate 16. The voyage of Jacob Mahu in 1598: the "noise" of five trumpeters sound during their captain's meeting with an African chief. De Bry: *America*, part 9, appendix (Frankfurt, 1602) plate 19. By Permission of the British Library.

Two plates depicting the work of trumpeters employed on the voyage of Jacob van Neck were published in *Journael oft Dagh-Register* (Amsterdam, 1601). This fleet of eight ships sailed to Bantam and then to various destinations. Four ships called at Java; the Dutch trumpeters are shown saluting the "king" on his elephant (Plate 17). Two ships called Ternate; the Dutch trumpeters, their duties temporarily over, are here depicted on a log outside the circle where the meeting is taking place (Plate 18).

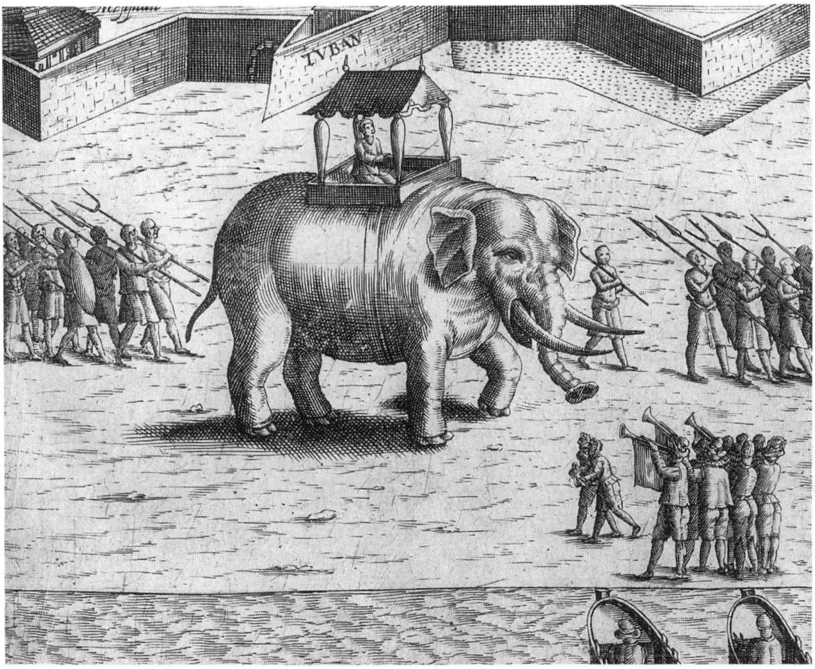

Plate 17: The voyage of Jacob van Neck in 1598: trumpeters salute the King of Tuban in Java. *Het tweede Boek, Journael oft Dagh-register* (Amsterdam, 1601) 51. By permission of the British Library.

Plate 18: The voyage of Jacob van Neck in 1598: trumpeters wait while their captain meets the King of Ternate in the Moluccas. *Het tweede Boek, Journael oft Dagh-register* (Amsterdam, 1601) 22. By permission of the British Library.

The musicians and trumpeters who accompanied Spilbergen to Ceylon in 1601 (whose performances at sea were noted by Pyrard de Laval[44] from his ship, the *Corbin*) are depicted in *Het Journael van Joris van Speilberghen* (1605). During the Dutch fleet's stop at the Comoro Islands, two musicians, Hans Rempel, a trumpeter, and Erasmus Martsberger, performed on "diversche instrumenten," giving much pleasure to a local official who had some knowledge of musical instruments and asked about a dulcimer ("een Hackebert") and harpsichord ("claversingels").[45] When the Dutch arrived in Ceylon in June 1602, Spilbergen disembarked with his musicians and, again, his journal records a performance upon "diversche instrumenten."[46] A depiction of Spilbergen's formal meeting with the Ceylonese on 5 June illustrates a column of Dutch soldiers approaching with musicians—five trumpeters on one side, players of the lute, fiddle and shawm with singers on the other, forming a guard of honor (Plate 19). When Spilbergen set off into the interior, he was accompanied by the musicians, and, on entering Kandy, was preceded by three trumpeters displaying the colors of the Prince of Orange.[47] The performances of the Dutch musicians so delighted the Ceylonese ruler that Spilbergen presented him with the two musicians, Rempel and Martsberger, "who could play very well on all instruments" ("die seer wel op alle Instrumenten costen spelen"). As a mark of favor, Martsberger was made "secretary" to the ruling family.[48]

The musicians who accompanied Spilbergen on his circumnavigation in 1614 are not known by name. They make their first appearance in the published account, *Oost ende West-Indische Spiegel* (1619), when, having made a successful rendezvous with the ships of his fleet in the Straits of Magellan, Spilbergen invited all the principal officers to dinner at which they enjoyed "a fine consort of various instruments" ("een schoon accort van veelderley instrumenten") playing "music of many parts" ("Musijcque van vele stemmen").[49] A month later, at an island off the coast of Chile, the Dutch

[44]A. Gray, *The Voyages of François Pyrard of Laval to the East Indies, the Maldives, the Moluccas and Brazil*, vol. 2, part 2 (*HS*, vol.80; London, 1890), 397–98.

[45]F. C. Weider, *De Reis van Spilbergen naar Ceylon, Atjeh en Bantam 1601–1604* (*LV*, vol. 38; The Hague, 1933), 29.

[46]Ibid., 39.

[47]Ibid., 43.

[48]Purchas, 5:209.

[49]J. A. J. de Villiers, *The East and West Indian Mirror* (*HS*, 2nd series, vol. 18; London, 1906), 45. *Oost ende West-Indische Spieghel* (Amsterdam, 1621), 38.

Plate 19: The voyage of Joris van Spilbergen in 1601: as Spilbergen approaches Baticaloa in Ceylon in 1602, his musicians (two singers and players of the fiddle, shawm and lute) and his "noise" of five trumpets line up to salute him. *Het Journael van Joris van Speilberghen* (Amsterdam, 1605) fol. 30. By permission of the British Library.

landed to barter, and the trumpeters and "other musicians" ("andere musijckanten") entertained the local populace with "a fine consort" ("een schoon accort"). The engraving (Plate 20) depicts three trumpeters and a fife player. In September 1616, as Spilbergen was passing through the East Indies, he encountered Captain William Keeling who described the meeting at which the Dutch musicians were present:

> We were doing businesse ashoare, and this day Gll [General] Spilberk] (who came w[i]th 5 shipps by the Streight of Magellan hether) came aboord me who I wellcomed w[i]th 7 pcs [pieces], and at p[er]ting 9: he came like a Gll [General] in a Japan boate finelye built, all her p[or]ts full of silke streamers displayed, rowed by 40 or 50 Japanezes all well clad and dulye armed: his noyse of trumpetts and other musique.[50]

An illustration of Dutch musicians playing on the shore of a Pacific island is to be found in the second part of the *Spieghel* which gives an account of Jacob Le Maire's 1615 voyage around Cape Horn

[50]M. Strachan and B. Penrose, *The East India Company Journals of Captain William Keeling and Master Thomas Bonner, 1615–1617* (Minneapolis, 1971), 148.

and across the South Pacific to the East Indies. At a small atoll named Cocos Island, the local chief was honored with drums ("Trommeln") and trumpets ("Trompetten"), the sounds of which caused great astonishment.[51] At Horn Island, which the Dutch ships reached some days later, the chief developed a great liking for the sound of the trumpets. On one occasion, the captain went on shore with his "Trompetters" because, as the author put it, the king "liked to hear them blow."[52] On another occasion, having been invited to a feast, the Dutch went on shore with "four trumpeters and a drummer" ("vier Trompetters mit een Trommelslager"), who played before two "kings" to their great delight.[53] The artist responsible for the plates in the *Spieghel* included a picture of this particular encounter (Plate 21); it makes an interesting case study of the way such illustrations were put together. In the background, the reader is given a general impression of the terrain of Horn Island and the Dutch ship at anchor at the mouth of a river. In the distance is the "royal" hut of the "king" (labelled "O"). On the right hand side of the picture, in the middle background, are the two "kings" (labelled "A") making obeisances to each other, while in the middle foreground is a close-up of the hut (labelled "O") with the two "kings" seated on mats as described in the text. In the foreground is a still closer view of the "king" (labelled "F") showing his crown of feathers and his long plait of hair. The accompanying notes explain further points of interest. Note "K," for instance, draws the reader's attention to the fact that the women of the Island wore their hair short. The four trumpeters and one drummer mentioned in the text are reduced, perhaps for the purposes of clarity, to two trumpeters and a drummer. A fifer, however, has been added. Vigor and panache, as shown in the drummer's demeanor, were doubtless the qualities most likely to succeed in such situations. This illustration, then, takes the meeting of the two "kings" and the performance of the Dutch musicians as its central focus, but at the same time shows the setting in which the encounter took place and presents the reader with close-ups of some of the participants.

[51]De Villiers (1906), 202, *Spieghel*, 170.

[52]De Villiers (1906), 208, *Spieghel*, 175.

[53]De Villiers (1906), 211, *Spieghel*, 178.

Plate 20. The voyage of Jacob le Maire in 1615: the "noise" of trumpets on an island off the coast of Chile. *Oost ende West-Indische Spieghel* (Leyden, 1619) plate 4. By permission of the British Library.

Plate 21. The voyage of Jacob le Maire in 1615: two Dutch trumpeters, a drummer and a fifer play on Horn Island. *Oost Ende West-Indische Spieghel* (Leyden, 1619) plate 25. By permission of the British Library.

Plate 22. The circumnavigation of Joris van Spilbergen in 1614: Dutch musicians perform on Horn Island. De Bry: *America*, part 11 (Oppenheim, 1620) plate 6. By permission of the British Library.

A second illustration of the same scene was published by De Bry (Plate 22). Very different in style and composition, it is nonetheless related to the *Spieghel* illustration in some of its detail; compare, for example, the representation of the two "kings" greeting each other, the two "kings" seated in the open hut, and the small group of figures around the dish. Whether these details were taken directly from one illustration into the other, or whether the designers of both pictures had access to the same source materials, is, in a sense, unimportant. What these different interpretations do show is how pre-existing details could be incorporated into an overall design. It is clear that however much they may have taken from their sources, the illustrators always retained final control over the composition. The Dutch musicians, as depicted in De Bry, are not, it is interesting to note, directly related to those in the *Spieghel* except in their general position and demeanor.

[54]*Iournael ofte Gedenckwaerdige beschrijvinghe vande Oost-Indische Reyse van Willem Ysbrantsz Bontekoe van Hoorn* (Amsterdam, 1646), 10.

Plate 23. The voyage of Willem Ysbrantsz Bontekoe in 1618: a Dutch fiddler plays for dancing on Madagascar. *Journael ofte Gedenckwaerdige* (Amsterdam, 1646) plate 1. By permission of the British Library.

The final example comes from a popular account of a journey to the East Indies made in 1618.[54] The author, Willem Ysbrantsz Bontekoe, describes how the Dutch disembarked at Madagascar with a musician who accompanied the dancing of the local inhabitants with his "fiddle" ("fioel"). This kind of scene is frequently described but rarely illustrated (Plate 23).

The evidence of these illustrations, and the accompanying written accounts, suggest that the duties of the trumpeters, drummers, and other musicians on the Dutch East-Indian fleets (some of whom were, of course, Englishmen) were essentially those of their counterparts employed by the English East India Company. Despite the large imaginative element in their construction, they do give us, as they must have given the reading public of their day, a fair impression of the manner in which European musicians performed their diplomatic entertainments in conditions far removed from those experienced by men who stayed at home.

[54] *Iournael ofte Gedenckwaerdige beschrijvinghe vande Oost-Indische Reyse van Willem Ysbrantsz Bontekoe van Hoorn* (Amsterdam, 1646), 10.

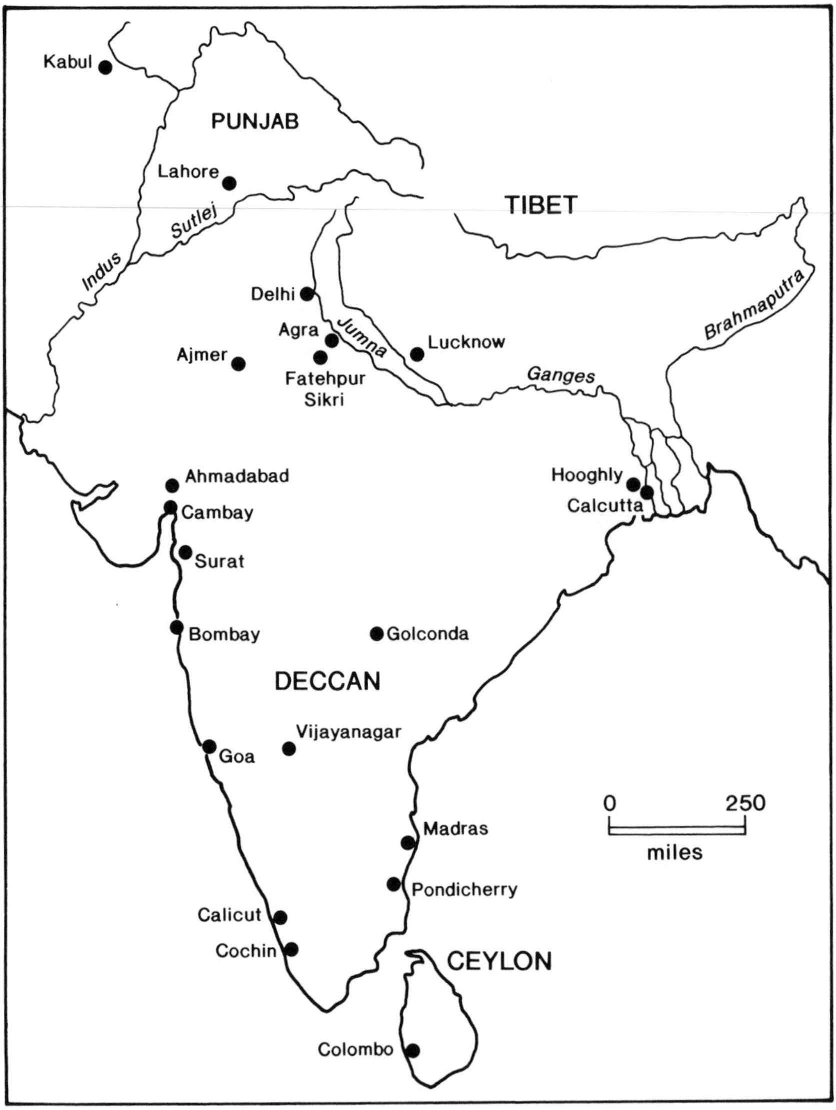

Plate 24. India.

CHAPTER 13

Permission to Trade

The giving of gifts, or "bribes," in return for permission to trade was an immutable fact of life in oriental society which Europeans travelling to the East in the service of commercial interests had no choice but to accept. Permission to open a factory would rarely be granted without a present of some substance. The initial gift, moreover, would inevitably inspire demands by subordinate officials in whose hands lay considerable power to disrupt the ordered patterns of daily life. The choice of suitable objects for presentation was thus an abiding concern of every European organization with interests in the East. There was general agreement that cheap trinkets of the kind which might be used to "buy off" an African chief along the trade route would be regarded as an insult in any of the great oriental courts. To appear before the Sultan or the Great Mughal with a feeble or even mildly inadequate offering was to put at risk the very interests in which gifts were given. Failure to please could be doubly damaging if a rival European organization were able to make good the disappointment. So a balance had to be struck between the need for goods displaying the best aspects of European artistry, craftsmanship, and mechanical ingenuity, and the need to keep costs to a reasonable level. The musical gift most closely matching these requirements was a keyboard instrument: a harpsichord, for instance, could be painted attractively and displayed as an *objet d'art;* with its method of sound reproduction, it could also be presented as a mechanical device; it was certain to be regarded as a novelty; and, most important of all, the costs of its manufacture and transportation, and the wages of the single musician hired to accompany it, would not be prohibitive.

The practice of presenting organs, musical clocks, and other automata as diplomatic gifts can be traced back to the eighth-century Byzantine Empire. Many chroniclers record the "organum" given to Pepin, King of the Franks, in 757.[1] There is no evidence, however, that Western keyboard instruments were sent out to the Far East until the thirteenth century. At this period, the Mongol Empire was receptive to European travellers, and at least one creator of automata, a Parisian by the name of William Bouchier, is known to have resided there. In 1254, William de Rubruquis examined one of Bouchier's creations—a silver tree which functioned as a drinks-dispensing machine. At the sound of a trumpet, it could provide milk or a choice of four other beverages, some alcoholic. By the time Rubruquis saw this curiosity, its bellows had failed, and air pressure for the trumpet was being provided by a man concealed inside.[2] It is probable that some keyboard instruments found their way into the Far East at this period. There are, for example, reports of an organ of ninety pipes having been sent from an Arab court to China some time during the thirteenth century.[3]

Whether the Portuguese knew anything of the previous history of such presentations when, in the fifteenth century, they began to make use of musical gifts in their newly acquired overseas empire is doubtful. It is perhaps more likely they rediscovered the attraction of the keyboard instrument in the East through the experiences of their own missionaries who took many portable organs and small harpsichords for use in mission schools. An early reference to a missionary organ, taken to Africa by Portuguese Franciscans, comes in Ruy de Pina's *Chronica d'El Rei Dom João II*. According to this account, the missionaries, accompanying De Sousa's expedition to the Congo in 1490, took with them vestments, crosses, books, and "orgãos."[4] The first portable organ to be landed on Indian soil was probably an instrument taken by the Franciscans who accompanied Cabral in 1500. (It is not known whether Vasco da Gama had any keyboard instruments with him in 1497.) His party of missionaries included an

[1]P. Williams, "Organ," The New Grove Dictionary of Music and Musicians (London, 1980), XIII, 727.

[2]W. W. Rockhill, *The Journey of William of Rubruck to the Eastern Parts of the World* (*HS*, 2nd series, vol. 4; London, 1900).

[3]Williams (1980), 727.

[4]R. Stevenson, "The Afro-American Musical Legacy to 1800," *MQ*, vol. 54 (1968), 478.

organist, Frei Maffeu, and a singer, Frei Neto.[5] The success of these purely functional instruments may well have opened the way for more ornate presentation keyboards.

The first recorded instances of the use of organs and harpsichords in an overtly diplomatic role in the Portuguese Empire come in accounts of two embassies which were sent out from Goa in 1520—one to Vijayanagar, the other to Ethiopia. Until her capture by the Mughals in the mid-sixteenth century, Vijayanagar, the great capital of the Deccan, was a dominant power in the area. During their early years in India, the Portuguese made few contacts with their inland neighbors, but, in 1520, it was decided to send a mission on the relatively short journey from Goa to Vijayanagar. According to the narrative of Domingo de Paes, the Portuguese ambassador, Christovão de Figueiredo took with him a selection of gifts which included an organ ("horgãos").[6] The King is reported as having been especially delighted with the musical part of the present.

A report by Francisco Alvares of the expedition to Ethiopia gives details of the keyboard instruments taken and the uses to which they were put. Although there are some discrepancies between the original Portuguese account, *Ho Preste Joam das Indias* (Lisbon, 1540), and the version in the first volume of Ramusio's *Delle navigazioni e viaggi* (Venice, 1550), the basic facts are not in doubt.[7] Accompanying Alvares was Manoel de Mares, "tangedor dorgãos," and the gifts destined for the Court of Prester John included "orgãos"[8]—"un organo" according to Ramusio.[9] When the Portuguese arrived at their destination, they appeared before the King. A request was made "that they should sing to a clavichord" ("que cantassem a hum manicordio") and dance.[10] Ramusio refers to the instrument as "un organo"[11]—a discrepancy which might be explained as a simple error.

[5]W. B. Greenlee, *The Voyage of Pedro Alvares Cabral to Brazil and India* (*HS*, 2nd series, vol. 81; London, 1938), 201.

[6]D. Lopes, *Chronica dos Reis de Bisnaga* (Lisbon, 1897), 92. For an English translation of the narrative of Paes, see R. Sewell, *A Forgotten Empire (Vijayanagar)* (London, 1900).

[7]The account in Ramusio is based partly on F. Alvares *Ho Preste Joam* (1540) and partly on a lost source. See the introduction to C. F. Beckingham and G. W. B. Huntingford, *The Prester John of the Indies* (*HS*, 2nd series, vols. 114 and 115; Cambridge, 1961).

[8]Alvares (1540), fol. 3.

[9]Ramusio (1550), fol. 206.

[10]Alvares (1540), fol. 60v.

[11]Ramusio (1550), fol. 241v.

On another occasion, however, the King again sent for the Portuguese: "Then our people began to sing songs to a harpsichord which we had here" ("Eloguo começaram hos nossos de cantar cantiguas em hum cravo que hi tinhamos").[12] Ramusio this time confirms the instrument: "Subito li nostri cominciarono à cantar canzoni in un clavocimbalo, che havevamo portato noi."[13] The Portuguese evidently took two instruments—an organ and a string keyboard of some type. The precise identification of the latter is difficult, since confusion between the terms for the harpsichord ("cravo") and the clavichord ("manicordio") is commonplace in journals written by non-musicians. What seems likely is that the harpsichord or clavichord was played during the entertainments, and that the organ was reserved for the celebration of Mass.

By the mid-sixteenth century, keyboard instruments had spread throughout the Portuguese Empire. Fine organs and harpsichords were as popular as ever as diplomatic gifts. The first such presentation in Japan, the jewel in the crown of the Portuguese East, was made by Francis Xavier himself in 1551. Cosme de Torres referred to the instrument as a "monacordio," while a later historian, Antonio de San Roman, reported (with what authority is not known) that the musical part of the present consisted of "algunas vihuelas de arco y clavicordio."[14] In the years after Xavier's gift, there was an extraordinary influx of small keyboard instruments into Japan, where the desire for Western music grew to an intensity not matched elsewhere. Organs, harpsichords, and clavichords are mentioned scores of times in the letters of Jesuit missionaries working in Japan during the 1560s and the 1570s, and keyboard playing soon became an integral part of the syllabus of Jesuit seminaries. In 1580, Alessandro Valignano wrote in his "Regimento pera os semynarios de Japan" that students were taught "to sing and play harpsichord, viols and other instruments" ("de cantar e tanger cravo e violas e outros semelhantes instrumentos").[15]

The most significant diplomatic harpsichord recital to be staged in Japan took place at the zenith of this fashion for Western culture.

[12]Alvares (1540), fol. 89v.

[13]Ramusio (1550), fol. 253.

[14]*Cartas* (Alcala, 1575), fol. 48v. A. de San Roman, *Historia General de la Yndia Oriental* (Valladolid, 1603), 664.

[15]J. F. Schütte, *Valignanos Missiongrundsätze für Japan* (Rome, 1958) II:479.

The occasion, as was often the case with such presentations, was the accession of a new ruler. The death, in 1582, of Oda Nobunaga, who had favored the Portuguese and was said to have been delighted by the sound of a "clavio,"[16] obliged the Jesuits to win over a new dictator, Toyotomi Hideyoshi. Shortly before Nobunaga's death, Valignano had left Japan with an embassy to the Pope which included four young Japanese noblemen. Harich-Schneider has described the musical experiences of the Japanese legates in Europe and their prowess on the "clavicembalo."[17] Towards the end of their stay in 1586, Ascanio Colonna presented them with a valuable instrument. Described as "a rich harpsichord decorated with mother-of-pearl" ("un ricco clavicembalo ornato di madre perle"), it was reported to have been made in Rome "at great cost."[18] During their long absence, Hideyoshi's attitude towards the Jesuits became unpredictable and, without warning, he issued an edict against Christianity. Although this was not fully enforced, the warning signs were clear, and Valignano, returning from Rome, recognized the need to present Hideyoshi with the best gifts that could be procured. At this critical moment, he placed his trust in the four Japanese and their musical instruments, the most obviously eye-catching of which was Colonna's harpsichord. When the legation came before Hideyoshi, the Japanese performed upon the "gravecimbalo," the "harpe," the "leuto," and the "ribeca" with such grace that the dictator's attention was immediately attracted. He asked for the music to be repeated three times and then took the instruments into his own hands, asking questions about each one in turn.[19] The musicians' success was such that they were feted as celebrities, but the advantages won by the embassy were short-lived as political realities reasserted themselves. Persecution and the horrors of mass martyrdom were soon to become the lot of the Jesuits in Japan.

The part played by keyboard recitals in Portuguese Eastern diplomacy did not pass unnoticed in other European nations with commercial ambitions in Asia. English merchants were quick to

[16]E. Harich-Schneider, *A History of Japanese Music* (London, 1973), 463.

[17]E. Harich Schneider, "Renaissance Europe through Japanese eyes," *EM*, vol. 1 (1973), 19–25.

[18]G. Galtieri, *Relationi della Venuta degli Ambasciatori Giaponesi* (Rome, 1586), 153 and 159.

[19]*Lettera del Giapone degli anni 1591 et 1592* (Rome, 1595), 40.

realize such presentations could form a valuable and relatively inexpensive weapon in their diplomatic armory. Musical gifts were sent out, first by the Barbary Company, the Russia Company, and the Levant Company, and then, on two occasions, by the East India Company.

The first musical instrument known to have been presented by English merchants in return for trading concessions was not in fact a keyboard instrument but a bass lute. The circumstances of the gift are recorded in Edmund Hogan's account of his embassy to Morocco.[20] Having arrived on the North African coast in May 1577, Hogan disembarked with ten men of whom three were trumpeters. On being presented to the "Emperor," he delivered the Queen's letters and explained her requests. Later the same night, he had a longer meeting at which there was a favorable reaction to Elizabeth's demands. This was clearly the moment for the presentation. Hogan described the scene thus:

> After the end of this speech I delivered Sir Thomas Greshams letters, when as he tooke me by the hand, and led me downe a long court to a palace where there ranne a faire fountaine of water, and there sitting himselfe in a chaire, he commaunded me to sit downe in another, and there called for such simple Musicians as he had.
>
> Then I presented him with a great base Lute, which he most thankfully accepted, and then he was desirous to heare of the Musicians, and I tolde him that there was great care had to provide them, and that I did not doubt but upon my returne they should come with the first ship. He is willing to give them good intertainment with provision of victuall, and to let them live according to their law and conscience wherein he urgeth none to the contrary.

It is curious that Hogan had not come prepared with a musician which, perhaps, suggests a certain inexperience with this type of presentation. On the other hand, he may have been expecting, not without reason, to find a competent lutenist in Morocco. Hogan, however, was quick to reassure the Emperor that musicians would travel out on the next ship. The conditions offered to any English musician willing to serve in Morocco seem to have been quite favorable. In some places, European musicians were required to undergo circumcision and renounce their Christian faith. In return

[20]Hakluyt, 6:285–93.

for the bass lute, the English Ambassador was given a rich dagger set with two hundred stones. A number of concessions were granted, including the promise of safe conduct for all English ships bound for the Levant.

It is uncertain whether the Barbary Company made any further gifts of musical instruments during the period of its charter. In 1588, Don Christoval embarked upon a trading mission for the Company, taking with him "diversos ynstrumentos de musica," but these may simply have been for the use of his own musicians. Three years after the expiry of the Company's charter, however, a group of merchants, hoping to recover some of their debts, did seek permission to export a musical gift to Morocco. The list of presents in the Privy Council Register (20 July 1600) included a "Wynde Instrument,"[21]—possibly an organ of some sort. Whether the shipment was actually made is not known.

The Russia Company was the first to include keyboard instruments among the gifts it sent abroad. During the early years of Elizabeth's reign, the Company sent several embassies to Tsar Ivan IV. In 1569, Thomas Randolph delivered to Ivan "a notable great cuppe of silver curiously wrought with verses graven in it," a common enough gift by the standards of the age.[22] Like other trading organizations, the Russia Company soon discovered that an initial series of presents was not enough; if they wished to protect their privileges from competition, a constant supply was necessary. Companies were at particular risk in times of political uncertainty following the demise of a ruler. After the death of Ivan IV in 1584, the accession of Fyodor, and the effective assumption of power by Boris Godunov, the Russia Company found itself in the position of having to renegotiate the terms of its trade, and at first the terms on offer were less good than those agreed by Ivan. It was in these circumstances that Sir Jerome Horsey was sent as an ambassador in 1586. The quality and range of presents, assembled with the help of Sir Francis Walsingham and the Lord Mayor of London, is a good pointer to the gravity with which the Company viewed the situation. These included: "my provicion of lyons, bulls, doggs, guilt halberds, pistolls, peces, armor, wynes, store of druges of all sorts, organes,

[21]T. S. Willan, *Studies in Elizabethan Trade* (Manchester, 1959), 307.

[22]T. S. Willan, *The Early History of the Russia Company 1553–1603* (Manchester, 1956), 105.

virgenalls, musicions, scarletts, perrell chaines, plate of curious makinge and of other costly things of great value, according to my commissions."[23] Horsey was presented to the Tsar to whom he delivered the letters from Elizabeth. When asked for the presents, he replied that "they wear such in nature as did requier som longer tyme for transportacion." The curiosity of the Tsar was aroused and he ordered fifty huntsmen to travel down river to speed up the delivery of his gifts.

The convoy arrived and on the appointed day Horsey, with twenty liveried attendants, rode to the Tsar bearing the gifts. An impressive display was staged outside the palace windows:

> A goodly fare white bull, all spotted over with black naturall dappell, his crop or gorg hanging down to his knees before him, guilt fals horns, coller of green vellett studded and redd roep; made kneell down before the Emperowr and Emporis, standes uppe and loeks gasinge and feersly one everie side, appearing to the people to be some other strainge beast called *bueval;* twelve goodly large mastive dogs lead with twelve men, daect with rozes, collers, etc, in like fashion; two lyons brought forthe of their cages (drawen upon sleades) by a littell Tartar boye with a wand in his hand, standinge in awe of noe other. These wear left before the Pallace to the lokers on.[24]

Horsey was then invited into the Tsar's presence. Boris Godunov spent a whole day examining the "jewels, chaynes, perrell, plate, gilt armour, halberds, pistolls and peces, white and reedd, scarlett velletts," and was well pleased. The musical instruments were outstandingly successful, being admired especially by the Tsarina:

> And the Emporis his sister, invited to behold the same, admired especially at the organes and vergenalls, all gilt and enambled, never seinge nor heeringe the like before, woundered and delighted at the lowd and musicall sound thereof. Thousands of people resorted and steyed aboutt the pallace to hear the same. My men that plaied upon them much made of and admitted into such presence often wher myself could not com.[25]

[23]E. A. Bond, *Russia at the Close of the Sixteenth Century* (*HS*, vol. 20; London, 1856), 217.

[24]Bond (1856), 220.

[25]Ibid., 222.

In 1599, Dallam, as a musician, was to experience a similar freedom of access to restricted areas in the Sultan's seraglio, though it nearly cost him his life. From the description of the loud sound made by at least one of Horsey's instruments, it seems likely that a pair of regals had been included. Horsey himself began to reap some reward for his success: "The sighte of these rarieties, bull-doggs, lyons, orgaines, mussicke and other delights, made me continewally to be thought upon, with gold wraught handkerchers, towells, shirts, cannapies, carpetts, dietts and such daintes as the lord protectors and his frendes good will and favour did afford." Even allowing for the exaggerations in his own account, Horsey's mission was, for the moment, undoubtedly a success, and the privileges granted to the Russia Company were more favorable than those offered before. As was so often the case, however, generous concessions granted during the excitement of an unusually lavish mission were not long observed in full. After Horsey's departure, commercial realism reasserted itself. By the time Giles Fletcher, the Company's next ambassador, arrived in Russia in 1588, he had to report he "founde noe priviledge."[26]

The Levant Company's first charter was granted by Elizabeth in 1581.[27] During the following year, the Company petitioned the Queen for financial assistance with the proposed embassy to the Sultan. Some of the documents from this correspondence which survive provide us with valuable evidence of contemporary attitudes to the giving of presents.[28] In an undated document (*c*1582) William Harborne petitioned the Queen for the dispatch of an ambassador on behalf of the Company. Specific pleas for help were submitted, among which was the following:

> For soe mutch of necessetye a present muste be firste geven to the gran Sig*nio*r from her Mag*es*tie (accordinge to usuale Costomes of all other pryncesthe ire Imbassators or Agents at theire firste Comynge in token of theire M*aste*r his good will and friendshipp) that it would please her Mag*es*tie to doe the lyke, for that the same muste be presented as a gifte sent him from her Mag*es*tie w*hi*ch in valure maie amounte to one thowsand pound starlinge.

[26]Willan (1956), 172.

[27]On the general history of the Levant Company, see A. C. Wood, *A History of the Levant Company* (Oxford, 1935).

[28]The transcriptions quoted here are from A. Skilliter, *William Harborne and the Trade with Turkey 1578–1582* (Oxford, 1977), 184 and 191.

Also, "at the Change of everie Gran Sig*nio*r a preasent, as aforesaid." The Company, then, regarded a gift to the value of £1000, renewable for every Sultan, as the basis for the establishment of trading rights.

A quite different view is argued in an undated memorandum from the same period which raises a series of questions about the proposed embassy to the Sultan:

> Whether it be requysitte, to gyve any present to the Grand-Signor, yn the name of her Ma*jes*tie. Sythe he taketh all presentes of the Chrystian prynces, to be as Tributes: And for suche are they regystred in his Recordes. Whiche beynge ones begonne, he lookethe for the contynuance thereof, as of dutye. And the greater value that the presente ys made, the greater dutye and subiection he takethe hold of therbye.

The author of this document was right to point out that the Sultan would require an "ongoing" series of presents. All the English trading companies had to cope with this phenomenon. But his second point—that the magnificence of the present would have been in some way regarded as an indication of weakness—is implausible. In practice, rival trading organizations attempted to outdo each other in the munificence, real or apparent—preferably apparent—of their gifts. Subsequent embassies sent by the Levant Company did indeed take valuable presents, culminating in Dallam's magnificent mechanical organ. The real issue behind these documents, however, was Elizabeth's reluctance to finance any ambassador sent on behalf of a trading company. Although, as a matter of courtesy, the presents would come "from the Queen," the costs were usually borne by the company.

An account of the Levant Company's first official embassy, undertaken by Harborne in 1583, was published by Hakluyt.[29] After his arrival in Constantinople on 26 March, Harborne quickly showed himself skilled in the art of diplomacy by presenting subordinate officials with presents suited to their rank: to the Great Bassa "sixe clothes, foure cannes of silver double gilt, and on piece of fine holland"; to the Second, Third and Fourth Bassas "foure clothes." When he was presented to Sultan Murad III, Harborne summoned his assistants with the Company's gifts:

> Twelve fine broad cloths, two pieces of fine holland, tenne pieces of plate double gilt, one case of candlesticks, the case whereof was very large, and three foot high and more, two very great cannes or pots,

[29]Hakluyt, 5:243–58.

> and one lesser, one basin and ewer, two poppinjayes of silver, the one with two heads: they were to drinke in: two bottles with chaines, three faire mastifs in coats of redde cloth, three spaniels, two bloodhounds, one common hunting hound, two greyhounds, two little dogges in coats of silke: one clocke valued at five hundred pounds sterlinge: over it was a forrest with trees of silver, among the which were deere chased with dogs, and men on horsebacke following, men drawing of water, others carrying mine oare on barrowes: on toppe of the clocke stood a castle, and on the castle a mill. All these were of silver. And the clocke was round beset with jewels.

This was the gift that the Company later tried to surpass with Dallam's organ. The expenditure represented by these items amounted to slightly over £1000, the sum originally suggested by the Company. A document in the possession of John Sanderson valued the present thus: the clock at £304. 8s. 6d; the cloth at £443. 11s. 10d; the plate at £298. 2s. 7d; the dogs at £36. 3s. 8d; the total value being £1082. 6s. 7d.[30] Concessions were granted to the English and a trading factory was opened at Constantinople.

A second gift to Murad was sent in 1593 with Edward Barton who replaced Harborne as the Company's agent at Constantinople.[31] The Venetian ambassador reported that the Englishmen had arrived "to the accompaniment of the sounds of trumpets" ("accompagnate da suoni de trombe").[32] His gift, according to the description in Hakluyt, consisted of "12 goodly pieces of gilt plate, 36 garments of fine English cloth of al colors, 20 garments of cloth of gold, 10 garments of sattin, 6 pieces of fine Holland, and certaine other things of good value." Other gifts were presented to the Sultana and leading officials.

The death of Murad III in 1595 obliged the Levant Company (exactly as they had predicted) to seek a renewal of all their agreements with the new Sultan. On this occasion, the Company commissioned from the organ maker, Thomas Dallam, the most magnificent musical gift sent by any English company—the celebrated mechanical organ.[33] The choice of an elaborate musical automaton may have

[30]W. Foster, *The Travels of John Sanderson in the Levant 1584–1602* (*HS*, 2nd series, vol. 67; London, 1931), 277.

[31]Hakluyt, 6:94–113.

[32]H. F. Brown, *CSP, Venice 1592–1603* (London, 1897), 107.

[33]Dallam's diary was published by J. T. Bent, *Early Voyages and Travels in the Levant* (*HS*, vol. 87; London, 1893). S. Mayes, *An Organ for the Sultan* (London, 1956) is based

been influenced by the Company's earlier success with their clock, possibly also by recent reports from the Russia Company of the good reception given to Horsey's keyboard instruments. There can be little doubt, however, that the principal objective was to outshine their competitors. A comment made shortly before Dallam's departure was unequivocal on the point: "Here is a great and curious present going to the great Turk which no doubt wilbe much talked of and be very scandalous among other nations specially the Germanes."[34] Even before the organ was presented, it was the subject of much speculation. The Venetian ambassador to Constantinople, Girolamo Capello, reported the gift thus: "the present, then, will be a most cunningly wrought organ ("un artificiosissimo organo") that acts as a clock and that plays several pieces ("diversi moteti") by itself."[35]

The long delay in sending the present caused the Company's agents some alarm. On 29 September 1597, Barton wrote to Sanderson at Aleppo (where the Company maintained a consul): "We heare

---

on this account and also incorporates material from the Public Record Office. Praetorius, in *Syntagma Musicum*, vol. 2, *De Organographia* (Wolfenbüttel, 1618), tells the story of an earlier presentation organ sent by Francis I to Suleiman some time after *c*1525 during the period of the Franko-Turkish alliance. According to this seemingly fanciful account, the Sultan at first approved of his gift, but later ordered the instrument to be smashed and burned and the French musicians sent home, because he feared that his people would become effeminate through listening to it.

[34]Public Record Office, S. P. 31 January 1599. In the late sixteenth century, German craftsmen were renowned for their mechanical instruments and musical clocks—hence the allusion. Their instruments were highly prized throughout Europe. In *A true relation of all the remarkable places and passages observed in the travels of the right honourable Thomas Lord Howard* (London, 1637), William Crowne described a collection of musical clocks kept in the treasure room of the Emperor of Bohemia at Prague: "Then in the middle of the roome are rare clocks of all kinds; the first was like a globe with musicke; the second was set round about the middle with little pillars, and a bullet running round in a cresse out and in, and over it hung two litle cords, which being puld, wee heard sweet musike, but could not discerne from whence it was; the third had a faire lively face and hand looking out, and musike with voyces singing, not to be discovered; the fourth a close clock, and by it a faire table of Mozaique worke; the fifth, with four ascents set severally with pillars, and a bullet running round in a cresse up to the top, playing with musike; the sixth, like the top of a globe, the gold coloured like a green field, and a Bucke running round in and out, and hounds after making a noyse, and beneath musike and Anticks, dancing in a round within it. . . ."

[35]Brown (1897), 375.

so smalle comfort of the present. And I marvaille our frinds in Aleppo doe not more dilligently sollicitt the same, for there owne benefitt and surtie of there trade, knowing that our privileges be not yet confirmed. I cannot wright to the Company more than I have therup-pon, and therfore will expect ther resolutione." Then, on 2 March 1598, Henry Lello, the Ambassador, wrote to Sanderson: "I praye you be earnest with the Company for sendinge the present; for that importuneth much their wellfaier in these parts." The French were claiming there would be no present from England. Again, on 18 March, Lello told Sanderson "I have written to the Company at large howe necessary itt is the present be hastened," because the Turks "doe daly demaunde the same."[36]

Dallam eventually set sail from Gravesend on 18 February 1599. His list of personal expenses included "a pare of virginals" priced at £1. 15s. 0d. In his own words, "I wente aborde our shipp, Called the Heckter, and thare placed my chiste, my bedinge, and a pare of virginals, which the martchantes did alow me to carrie, for my exersize by the waye." Since the organ was packed up in chests in the hold, the provision of a pair of virginals upon which Dallam could practice was deemed a reasonable expense. Off the Kent coast, the wind dropped and some of the men disembarked "to make our selves merrie." The ship's band of five trumpeters was soon reduced to four in a manner familiar to brass players down the years:

> When the wynde came fayer, it was in the nyghte, and diverse of us that weare passingers, and also som saylers, weare in the towne of Deale, wheare som of our company had dranke verrie moche, espetialy one of our five Trumpeters, who, beinge in Drinke, had Lockid his Chamber dore; and when he that came from the ship to call us went under his chamber wyndoe and caled him, he Came to the wyndoe and insulted him; whear upon we wente all a waye a borde our shipp, and lefte that Dronkerde be hinde.[37]

On 28 June, the *Hector* called at Rhodes to replenish the stock of fresh water. The Governor of the town came aboard and was entertained in the gunroom: "Our gonroume was one of the fayerest Roumes in the ship, and pleasant to com into. In the gonroume I had a pare of virginals, the which our Mr. goner, to make the better

[36]Foster (1931), 173–75.

[37]Bent (1893), 2–5.

showe, desired me to sett them open." Various Turks and Jews entered to view the instrument and wondered what it was. When Dallam played for them, "they wondered more." Dallam continued: "Diveres of them would take me in there armes and kis me, and wyshe that I would dwell with them." One of the Turks who heard (and kissed) Dallam, later came to his assistance when a small group of Englishmen, somewhat rashly sight-seeing in the town, were confronted by hostile Turks.[38]

The *Hector* arrived at Constantinople on 15 August. The present was taken to the Ambassador's house, but because there was no room high enough for it, a special room was hastily erected in the courtyard so that "it myghte there be made perfitt before it should be carried to the surralia." When Dallam began to unpack the organ from the chests, he was horrified by its condition:

> We begane to louke into our worke; but when wee opened our chistes we founde that all glewinge worke was clene Decayed, by reason that it hade layne above sixe monthes in the hould of our ship, whiche was but newly bulte, so that the extremetie of the heate in the hould of the shipe, with the workinge of the sea and the hootnes of the cuntrie, was the cause of that all glewinge fayled; lyke wyse divers of my mettle pipes weare brused and broken.
>
> When our Imbassader [Lello], Mr. Wyllyam Aldridge, and other jentlmen, se in what case it was in, theye weare all amayzed, and sayde that it was not worthe ii *d.* My answeare unto our Imbassador and to Mr. Alderidge, at this time I will omitt; but when Mr. Alderidge harde what I sayede, he tould me that yf I did make it perfitt he wold give me, of his owne purss, 15 *li.*, so aboute my worke I wente.[39]

Lello, writing to Sir Robert Cecil, commented that the organ "in the voyedge have been evell handled and I doubte will be hardly brought to that perfection and rarenes, as the reporte have gone of itt, yett hath itt raysed sufficient matter for all Constantinople to talke of the same."[40] News of the instrument was spreading fast and important visitors arrived to view the present. Lello now wrote that the instrument "although at first here thought to be of small esteeme, yett now beinge sett up in my howse by the oppinion of such as have seene itt is thought 105 [the Sultan] will highly esteeme the same, if any of his

[38]Ibid., 35–37.

[39]Ibid., 58.

[40]Mayes (1956), 165.

people can mantayne the use thereof."[41] This last comment shows the Levant Company had not engaged Dallam to enter a period of service with the Sultan. (The East India Company on two later occasions employed a keyboard player on the understanding that he might be required to enter the service of the Great Mughal.)

The repaired organ was taken down again and transported to the Seraglio where Dallam spent several days erecting it. Then, on 24 September, the English Ambassador summoned Dallam and charged him to go to the Seraglio "and make the instrumente as perfitt as possibly I could, for that daye, before noune, the Grand Signor would se it." He warned Dallam not to expect a reward from the Sultan, nor, indeed, to be admitted to his presence, and once again he emphasized the crucial importance of the organ functioning correctly at its first appearance: "I car not yf it be non after the nexte, if it doo not please him at the firste sighte, and performe not those thinges which it is Toulde him that it can Dow, he will cause it to be puled downe that he may trample it under his feete. And than shall we have no sute grantede, but all our charge will be loste."[42] Dallam replied that the organ was now in an even better condition than when Elizabeth had viewed it in Whitehall.

On 25 September, the Sultan finally arrived to inspect the organ. Dallam's detailed description of the presentation is worth quoting in full. It is the only report we have of such an event, as seen through the eyes of the musician concerned:

> The Grand Sinyor, beinge seated in his Chaire of estate, commanded silence. All being quiett, and no noyes at all, the presente began to salute the Grand Sinyor; for when I lefte it I did alow a quarter of an houre for his cominge thether. Firste the clocke strouk 22; than The chime of 16 bels went of, and played a songe of 4 partes. That beinge done, tow personagis which stood upon to corners of the seconde storie, houldinge tow silver trumpetes in there handes, did lifte them to theire heades, and sounded a tantarra. Than the muzicke went of, and the orgon played a song of 5 partes twyse over. In the tope of the orgon, being 16 foute hie, did stande a holly bushe full of blacke birds and thrushis, which at the end of the musick did singe and shake theire wynges. Divers other motions thare was which the Grand Sinyor wondered at. Than the Grand Sinyor asked the Coppagawe yf

[41] Ibid., 170.

[42] Bent (1893), 64–65.

it would ever doo the lyke againe. He answered that it would doo the lyke againe at the next houre. Cothe he: I will se that. In the meane time, the Coppagaw, being a wyse man, and doubted whether I hade so appoynted it or no, for he knew that it would goo of it selfe but 4 times in 24 houres, so he cam unto me, for I did stand under the house sid, wheare I myghte heare the orgon goo, and asked me yf it would goo againe at the end of the nexte houre; but I tould him that it would not, for I did thinke the Grand Sinyor would not have stayed so longe by it; but yf it would please him, that when the clocke had strouk he would tuche a litle pin with his finger, which before I had shewed him, it would goo at any time. Than he sayde that he would be as good as his worde to the Grand Sinyor.

When the clocke began to strick againe, the Coppagaw went and stood by it; and when the clocke had strouke 23, he tuched that pinn, and it did the lyke as it did before. Than the Grand Sinyor sayed it was good. He satt verrie neare unto it, ryghte before the Keaes, wheare a man should playe on it by hande. He asked whye those keaes did move when the orgon wente and nothinge did tuche them. He Tould him that by those thinges it myghte be played on at any time. Than the Grand Sinyor asked him yf he did know any man that could playe on it. He sayd no, but he that came with it coulde, and he is heare without the dore. Fetche him hether, cothe the Grand Sinyor, and lett me se how he dothe it. Than the Coppagaw opened that Dore which I wente out at, for I stoode neare unto it. He came and touke me by the hande, smylinge upon me; but I bid my drugaman aske him what I should dow, or whither I shoulde goo. He answered that it was the Grand Sinyor's pleasur that I should lett him se me playe on the orgon. So I wente with him. When I came within the Dore, That which I did se was verrie wonderfull unto me. I cam in direcktly upon the Grand Sinyore's ryghte hande, som 16 of my passis from him, but he would not turne his head to louke upon me. He satt in great state, yeat the sighte of him was nothinge in Comparrison of the traine that stood behinde him, the sighte whearof did make me almoste to thinke that I was in another worlde. [Here Dallam describes the Sultan's attendants.]

When I had stode almost one quarter of an houre behouldinge this wonder full sighte, I harde the Grande Sinyore speake unto the Coppagaw, who stood near unto him. Than the Coppagaw cam unto me, and touke my cloake from aboute me, and laye it Doune upon the Carpites, and bid me go and playe on the organ; but I refused to do so, because the Grand Sinyor satt so neare the place wheare I should playe that I could not com at it, but I muste needes turne my backe Towardes him and touche his Kne with my britchis, which no man, in paine of deathe, myghte dow, savinge only the Coppagaw. So he smyled, and lett me stande a litle. Than the Grand Sinyor spoake againe, and the Coppagaw, with a merrie countenance, bid me go with a good curridge, and thruste me on. When I cam verrie neare the Grand Sinyor, I bowed my heade as low as my kne, not movinge my cape, and turned my backe righte towardes him, and touched his kne with my britchis.

He satt in a verrie ritche Chaire of estate, upon his thumbe a ringe with a diamon in it halfe an inche square, a faire simeterie by his side, a bow, and a quiver of Arros.

He satt so righte behinde me that he could not se what I did; tharfore he stood up, and his Coppagaw removed his Chaire to one side, wher he myghte se my handes; but, in risinge from his chaire, he gave me a thruste forwardes, which he could not otherwyse dow, he satt so neare me; but I thought he had bene drawinge his sorde to cut of my heade.

I stood thar playinge suche thinge as I coulde untill the cloke strouke, and than I boued my heade as low as I coulde, and wente from him with my backe towardes him. As I was taking of my cloake, the Coppagaw came unto me and bid me stand still and lett my cloake lye; when I had stood a litle whyle, the Coppagaw bid me goo and cover the Keaes of the organ; then I wente Close to the Grand Sinyor againe, and bowed myselfe, and then I wente backewardes to my Cloake. When the Company saw me do so theye semed to be glad, and laughed. Than I saw the Grand Sinyor put his hande behinde him full of goulde, which the Coppagaw Receved, and broughte unto me fortie and five peecis of gould called chickers, and than was I put out againe wheare I came in, beinge not a little joyfull of my good suckses.[43]

This description of the organ is very well known indeed. It is one of the most frequently cited passages in the whole diary. The *Illustrated London News* of 20 October 1860 published a drawing of an organ, with specifications (Plate 25), which is believed to have been Dallam's mechanical organ, but the original has not been traced.

[43]Ibid., 67–71.

Relics of the Past.

CURIOUS MUSICAL INSTRUMENT OF THE SIXTEENTH CENTURY.

Plate 25. Drawing of an organ believed to be the instrument built by Thomas Dallam and presented by the Levant Company to the Sultan in 1599. *Illustrated London News*, 20 October 1860. By permission of the British Library.

Several efforts were made to persuade Dallam to remain in the service of the Sultan, to which he replied (falsely) that he had a wife and child in England. Before he left, however, he dismantled the organ in order to explain how it was constructed. On one occasion, his work was interrupted by the unexpected arrival of the Sultan, and he was chased out of the Seraglio by four men brandishing scimitars. His mission successfully accomplished, Dallam returned home.

In view of the long history of oriental keyboard diplomacy and the recent success of the Levant Company's organ, the East India Company's decision to present two pairs of virginals to the Mughal Emperor is not in the least bit surprising.[44] The records of the Company in London enable us to reconstruct in some detail the part played by these musical missions in opening the subcontinent to English trade. The arrival of the East India Company placed the English in direct competition with the Portuguese, and a triangular relationship developed for a time between the two rival European interests and their Indian hosts. At the apex was the Mughal Court; at the two lower corners were the Portuguese Jesuits, the representatives of the old order, and the English factors, the newly arrived "interlopers." The Mughals' reaction to the English virginal recitals was thus influenced by the Portuguese, both indirectly, because their own musicians had already performed on keyboard instruments before the Emperor, and directly, because their opinion of the English performances was sought.[45]

The first formal contact between the Portuguese and a Mughal Emperor was made in 1579 when Akbar summoned a Portuguese mission to his court at Fatepuhr Sikri. Essentially a free-thinker in matters of belief, Akbar requested that Christian missionaries be sent to him.[46] Three Jesuits made the journey inland from Goa, carrying with them a copy of the Plantin polyglot Bible. Following the example of Xavier, they chose an organ as one of their gifts. The instrument was presented to Akbar and caused quite a stir. It is singled out for special comment by two Mughal historians whose descriptions pro-

[44]For a general history of the East India Company during its early years, see K. N. Chaudhuri, *The English East India Company* (London, 1965).

[45]On Portuguese music in the Mughal mission, see E. Maclagen, *The Jesuits and the Great Mogul* (London, 1932), 289–90. See also A. Camps, *Jerome Xavier S. J. and the Muslims of the Mogul Empire* (Freiburg, 1957), 228–35.

[46]The mission is described in C. H. Payne, *Akbár and the Jesuits* (London, 1926).

vide an insight into Indian reactions to the gift. The chronicler of Akbar's reign, Abul Fazl wrote:

> One of the occurrences was the arrival of Haji Habibullah. It has already been mentioned that he had been sent to the port of Goa with a large sum of money and skillful craftsmen in order that he might bring to this country the excellent arts and rarities of that place. On the 9th he came to do homage, attended by a large number of persons dressed up as Christians and playing European drums and clarions. He produced before H. M. the choice articles of that territory. Craftsmen who had gone to acquire skill displayed the arts which they had learnt and received praises in the critical place of testing. The musicians of that territory breathed fascination with the instruments of their country, especially the organ. Ear and eye were delighted, and so was the mind.[47]

Al-Badaoni attempted to describe the organ[48]:

> At this time an organ, which was one of the wonders of creation, and which Haji Habib-ullah had brought from Europe [i.e. Goa], was exhibited to mankind. It was like a great box the size of a man. A European sits inside it and plays the strings [i.e. keys] thereof, and two others outside keep putting their fingers on five peacock-wings [probably the bellows, shaped like peacock feathers], and all sorts of sounds came forth. And because the Emperor was so pleased, the Europeans kept coming at every moment in red and yellow colours, and went from one extravagance to another. The people at the meeting were astounded at this wonder, and indeed it is impossible to do justice to the description of it.[49]

The paintings presented by the Jesuits were also greatly admired and inspired a fashion among Mughal artists for copying and adapting European works. Organs, occasionally depicted in Mughal manuscript illuminations at this period (Plate 26), were thus probably copied from European originals.[50]

[47]H. Beveridge, *The Akbarnama of Abu-L-Fazl (ASB, Biblioteca Indica, new series, vol. 138, part 3; Calcutta, 1910–1939), 322–23.*

[48]W. H. Lowe, *Muntakhab-Ut-Tawáríkh by Abd-Ul-Qádir Bin Malúk Sháh known as Al Badáóní (ASB,* Biblioteca Indica, vol. 97, part 2; Calcutta, 1884–1898), 299.

[49]E. Rehatsek in *The Emperor Akbar's Repudiation of Esllám and Profession of his own Religion* (Bombay, 1866), 45, translates: "It looked like a large box as high as a man, and a European sitting within struck its chords, whilst two others were without, striking with their fingers five peacock-feathers and other things."

[50]Another organ illustrated by a Mughal artist is reproduced in E. Kühnel and H. Goetz, *Indian Book Painting* (London, 1926), plate 28.

Plate 26. Plato charming animals with the music of an organ. An adaptation of a European theme by a Mughal artist from the reign of Akbar, late 16th century. British Library, Or. 12208, fol. 298a. By permission of the British Library.

After the death of Akbar in 1605, Jahangir continued to show favor to the Jesuits. Like his father, he was undoubtedly familiar with the sound of Portuguese organs. On one occasion, he even hired an organ player. The story is told in Fernão Guerreiro's *Relaçam*. A captain of high rank at Agra had two black Christians in his service, for both of whom he had chosen a bride. The day before the marriages were due to take place, the pair escaped and asked for sanctuary with the Jesuits. From Agra they were sent to Lahore, where a native of Goa, thinking that he could gain favor with Jahangir, informed him of their whereabouts, adding that "one of them knew how to play the organ" ("que hum sabia tanger orgaons") and "sing Portuguese music" ("cantar musica Portugues"). Jahangir took the two men into his service and they were still at Lahore some time later.[51]

Reports from the Agra mission also imply that members of the Mughal Court sometimes attended Christian services at which organ music was performed. In 1610, Jahangir astonished the Jesuits by requesting the baptism of three of his nephews. The ceremony was performed on 5 September and was witnessed by William Hawkins, the East India Company's representative, who rode at the head of the procession under the flag of St. George. In the church there was organ music. One letter refers to "musica organa," another to "trumpets and organs playing together" ("tubis organisque concinientibus").[52] The Christmas services at Agra were the subject of much local interest. An organ, played perhaps by the black musician mentioned above, accompanied the Christmas services in 1610. Jerome Xavier gave details in a letter from Agra: "some songs suitable for the feast" ("alguãs cantigas aoproposito da festa") were sung "with the organs" ("com os Orgãos"); at midnight mass "chansonetas" were sung to the organ; "after these, a mass was begun which was sung throughout in four parts with the organ, with some very fine carols in the middle" ("essas acabadas se comecou a missa que se cantou toda a quatro vozes com os orgãos avendo no mejo de lla Cantigas do Natal muito boas").[53] At this period, the Mughal mission seemed to be flourishing, but in 1613, the three young converts apostatized, and relations

[51]F. Guerreiro, *Relaçam Annal das Cousas* (Lisbon, 1603–1611), V, 158v. For a translation of the parts of the *Relaçam* relating to the Mughal mission, see C. H. Payne, *Jahangir and the Jesuits* (London, 1930).

[52]Maclagan (1932), 289.

[53]British Library, Add. 9854, fol. 164v (an incomplete letter from Father Jerome Xavier at Agra, some time after 31 July 1611).

between the Mughals and the Portuguese declined to such an extent that the entrance to the Agra church was walled up. It was later reopened, but the optimistic hopes aroused by Jahangir in the early years of his reign were never fulfilled.

In 1612, the East India Company in London elected to present Jahangir with a pair of virginals. The proposed embassy was one of importance. Despite the efforts of William Hawkins, the Company had not yet been granted permission to establish a factory at Surat. Their choice of a musical instrument at this important juncture in their affairs was influenced by several considerations. They would undoubtedly have been aware of the success of Dallam's organ, and they may well have known of other such presentations. They also knew something of Jahangir's love of European novelties. A correspondent, writing from Surat on 30 August 1609, recommended as gifts, new drinking glasses, trenchers for sweetmeats, and large looking-glasses, with the comment that the Emperor affected not value but rarity "insomuch that some pretty new-fangled toys would give him high content, though their value were small, for he wants not worldly wealth or riches possessing an inestimable treasury." Jahangir's interest in music was also common knowledge. Even at this stage the Company was thus quite well informed about Jahangir's tastes, but what may not have been known was the extent to which his court had already become familiar with the sound of Portuguese organs. (Hawkins could certainly have told them, but he did not leave Agra until 1611 and died before reaching London.) With the information at its disposal, the Company's choice of a pair of virginals was thus a logical one. Their agents accordingly purchased an instrument and hired Lancelot Canning as a keyboard player.

When the English arrived at Surat, Captain Thomas Best disembarked in style. Having saluted the Indian reception party with gunfire, he landed with "100 Souldiers in armes, with our trumpetts and drumes, besides a dossen privatt attendants."[54] He opened negotiations and landed Jahangir's virginals so that the Governor of Ahmadabad could hear them, but refused to allow them to be sent to the Emperor himself until he had received confirmation of his acceptance of the Company's proposed articles of trade. Ralph Stand-

[54]W. Foster, *The Voyage of Thomas Best to the East Indies 1612–1614* (*HS*, 2nd series, vol. 75; London, 1934), 113.

ish, surgeon of the *Hosiander*, described in his journal the scene when on 21 October the virginals were first displayed:

> An Indian came and plaid upon a strang instrewmentt before our Generall. Afterwards our musittions plaid before the Governor off Amedevar and all the rest of the chieff; which muzick they did verie highlie comend. Our Generall caussed a paire of virginalls to be brought ashoare, and upon them one of our musitions plaid; which musick did please them the best of all. Our Generall left thes virginalls with the Governor of Amedevar, and tould him he would present them unto the Kinge, and he likewisse that plaid upon them; and in the meane tyme, so long as he staid ther, he should have both the man and the virginalls att his service.[55]

Best apparently thought better of this generous offer. After another public viewing, the present was taken on board again, pending the arrival of the Emperor's letter.

Best's own laconic journal records the discharge for service on shore of the virginalist Canning and a cornetto player, Robert Trully.[56] It is not clear whether Trully was ordered by the Company to go with Canning or whether, as musicians sometimes did, he decided to seek his fortune in a foreign land on the spur of the moment. Whatever his motives may have been, Trully's performances were to benefit the Company in the coming months. There was a delay, however, before the arrival of messengers from Jahangir. The long-awaited document, "covered with read silke and maid up in cloth," was finally delivered to Best on 11 January. He received it with appropriate ceremony, "our trumpetts afterwards soundinge, and a value [volley] or towe of shott."[57] Having shown the Indian delegation round the *Dragon*, Best accompanied them back as far as Swally: "so they in ther wagons, our Generall upon horsseback, repaired towards Swalley, and partted verie curtteouslie, [with] 2 valley of small shot [and] trumpetts soundinge."[58] Shortly after this, the virginals were dispatched to the Emperor. According to a letter sent to the East India Company by the three factors at Surat, Thomas Aldworth, William Biddulph, and Nicholas Withington, the Agra party with the present consisted of Mr. Paul Canning (the musician's cousin), two

[55] Ibid., 114.

[56] Ibid., 34.

[57] Foster (1934), 132.

[58] Ibid., 144–146.

of Best's men and "2 muzisions." In the same report, conscious perhaps of the good impression made by the virginals in Surat, they suggested to the Company that another instrument be sent with the next shipment, together with the usual knives, gloves, pictures, and dogs: "Wee thinke itt fittinge you sende for him a small pare of Orgaynes, havinge heere a skillful Muzition to play on them."[59]

The next report of the progress of the Agra delegation comes in the journal of Ralph Standish, who, with Captain Best, had completed the next stage of the voyage to Sumatra. On 26 May, a junk from Surat arrived with alarming news: "We understand that Mr. [Paul] Caneinge in his journey to Agra was assaulted by theves, and in resistaunce receved a shott in his bodie with an arowe and [was] dangerousslie wounded: and likewisse of Robert Trullie, one of his attendantts, was shott into the arme."[60] Even worse, after the robbers had been repulsed, the two non-musicians had deserted the party with the best horses and money. However, the depleted mission made its way to Agra. Nicholas Withington wrote in his journal: "soe Mr. Caninge proseeded on his journey, onlye attended with two musitians."[61] On 7 September 1613, Thomas Kerridge, one of the Company's factors, submitted a fascinating report to Thomas Aldworth and the Council at Surat describing in detail the delivery of their present and Jahangir's reaction to it:

> Lause [Lancelot] and his Virginalls presented hee playde on them butt nott esteemed, (a bagpipe had bene fytter for him) Rob: [Trully] thinkes Lause dyed wth Conceiptt, Roberts Cornett highely esteemed, the King putt ytt to his mouth keptt it from him Cawsed 6 others to be made, butt provd nott good, would have him serve him, he Refused itt offeringe to be att his Comand whyle hee stayed in the Countrye, the Kinge tooke displeasure there att, yett willed him to teach one of his Cheifest musycions, to whome hee sayd if thow canst learne this I will make thee a greate man, butt to Robertt promisd nothinge for learninge him the musycion in learninge tooke such paynes, y^{t} in 5 weekes hee playd before the Kinge who much delighted thereatt, butt before the seaventh weeke ended the skoller dyed of a fluxe wth over heatinge his bodye, in wch tyme the Kinge sentt often for Robertt, and

[59]Original Correspondence, vol. 1, no. 102.

[60]Foster (1934), 163.

[61]Nicholas Withington's journal has been lost. It was published in *A Journey over Land* (London, 1735), an edition of which is given in W. Foster, *Early Travels in India 1583–1619* (Oxford, 1921).

> especyally in thatt tyme when Pawle Can: had sentt him to seeke the boye mehomed, and returned in 4 dayes, the Kinge tooke itt ill yett still sentt for him, Robertt ill att ease sometyme returned wthout playinge, staying till mydnight and nott cald for, and as soone as hee was gone Called for, whereatt the Kinge was once exceedinge angrye yett never gave him any thinge only 50 Rupe: wch hee tooke so Indignantly y^{t} hee would skarcely play before him.[62]

The unpredictable reaction of rulers, like Jahangir, was a constant source of worry for the East India Company. "Noe man can tell what to advise for," wrote Sir Thomas Roe several years later in a candid assessment, "they change every yeare their fancy."[63] In this instance, the carefully chosen present was a complete flop, perhaps because keyboard instruments had lost their novelty value for Jahangir. The Great Mughal's reaction to Trully's cornetto playing, however, suggests that he had not heard the instrument before. Kerridge, incidentally, went on to blame the failure of Trully to receive proper recompense for his services on the malign influence of the Portuguese Jesuits who, for obvious reasons, would have been alarmed at the English musician's success. The Jesuits at Agra, he reported, asked Trully to teach the instrument to two of their servants, but he refused, even though they claimed that the request had come from Jahangir himself. Kerridge, noting that after this incident Trully had not been sent for again, linked the two events. Citing the example of a successful Neapolitan juggler, he observed bitterly that if his man had been presented by the Jesuits, he would by now have been a rich man, as Jahangir was "exceedingly delighted to heare his Cornett." But Trully was evidently a somewhat unpredictable character. Kerridge first reported that he was generally condemned by all the Christians in Agra for his drunkenness, whoring, and neglect of Mr Canning's interests, and then later, in the same letter, that he had "clean altered from his vein of drinking to a well governed man."

Thomas Aldworth, writing to the East India Company from Ahmadabad on 9 November, recorded the death (from natural causes) of Lancelot Canning, the unsuccessful player of the virginals.[64] Nicholas Withington wrote: "soone after his cominge to Agra, one of his musitians dyed (which was the chiefest present sent to the Kinge)."[65] The unfor-

[62]Original Correspondence, vol. 1, no. 110.

[63]W. Foster, *The Embassy of Sir Thomas Roe to India 1615–1619* (London, 1926), 449.

[64]Original Correspondence, vol. 1, no. 117.

[65]Foster (1921), 201.

tunate virginalist was buried, but a dispute arose between the English and the Portuguese over his grave. Withington wrote:

> Aboute the buriall of him Mr. [Paul] Caninge had much trouble with the Portungale Fathers, whoe would not suffer him to be buried in theire church-yarde (a place which the Kinge gave the Portungales for burriall of Chrystians); yet at laste Mr. Caninge buried him there. But the Portungales tooke him upp againe, and buried him in the heigh-way; which the Kinge hearing of, made them take him upp againe and bury him in the former place, threatninge them not onlye to turne them out of his kingdom, but allsoe theire dead bodies, theire countrimen, out of theire graves.[66]

Kerridge, however, gives a different version of events in which Paul Canning was not told of the disinterment of his cousin before his own death:

> They disinterred Launce Canning and buried him in another place, but his cousin never knew thereof so Robert [Trully] buried them both together in one side of these Jesuits' ground which they denied not, being a good distance from that place.[67]

Having settled the matter of his colleague's last resting place, Trully, by now the sole survivor of the original party, decided to seek his fortune further south. Withington takes up the story:

> Lykewise another of our companie, called Robert Trullye, which was an attendant to Mr. Caninge, whome hee lefte and wente to Decanne to the Kinge thereof, carryinge along with him a Germayne for his interpritor that understood the language; and cominge there, offred bothe to turne Moores, which was kyndlye accepted by the Kinge. So Trullye was circumsized, and had a newe name given him by the Kinge, with whom hee continued.[68]

The German, it was discovered, was already a "moor," and so he was refused employment, whereupon he returned to Agra and entered the service of a Frenchman, having turned Christian once again. Meanwhile, "hearinge reporte how Trullye was made of in Decanns courte," another Englishman, Robert Clarkson travelled there, but despite "havinge verye good allowance," returned to Surat. This is the last that is known of Trully.

[66]Ibid., 201.

[67]Original Correspondence, vol. 1, no. 110.

[68]Foster (1921), 204.

In London, the East India Company was already considering the advisability of purchasing another musical gift. On 14 October 1614, it was suggested that "a Plummer or twoe, a skillful person upon the harpe, and some virginalls" be sent to Surat, "for that yt is supposed the Emperor delighteth much in such kinde of musicke."[69] In December, however, the Company began to act on the Surat factors' earlier suggestion that a "small pare of orgaynes" would make a fitting present for him. The Court Minutes for 23 December, under the heading "orgaines," read as follows:

> Mr Middleton acquainted them that hee hath sene certaine Organs, one large that came out of a Church, annother of a middle sort pricd 28^{li}, and a third that is portrative of 25^{li} price, all very good ones, wch beinge painted and guilded will bee faire and very serviceable. Whereupon they ordered to have the partie whoe is enterteynd for an Organist to be sent unto to see them, and delyver his opinion of them, that yf it shall be thought convenyent both the lesser ones may be bought, beinge of such reasonable prices.[70]

On 4 January 1615, another suggestion was made that a "double virginall" be purchased:

> Mr Hanford acquainted them wth a virginall that may bee had of 14 or 15^{li} price for twoe to plaie upon at once, and by a pynne puld out one man will make both to goe, wch is a delightful sight for the Jacks to skipp up and downe, in such manner as they will, beside the musique, wch they thought fittinge to have bought, and ordered that the Organist should goe and see them, and mak reporte unto this Courte.[71]

The tone of Mr Handford's description of this double virginal shows the East India Company was well aware of the potential value of any European musical device exhibiting unusual mechanical ingenuity. Dallam's organ—admittedly a much more elaborate automaton—had been admired on similar grounds.

Meanwhile, in Ajmer, one of the Company's senior factors was renewing the suggestion that more musicians be sent out. Writing

[69]Court Book III, 247. The suggestion that the Company should hire a harpist is interesting. Had someone read António de Gouveia's *Relaçam em que se tratam as guerras e grandes victorias* (Lisbon, 1611), 209, in which the Shah is reported to have been greatly pleased by a performance upon the harp?

[70]Court Book III, 321.

[71]Ibid., 332.

on 26 February 1615, William Edwards recommended as presents, pictures, cross-bows, turkey-cocks, and hens; also "some extraordinary musition or two, one on the lute or other Instrumentes, the King would gladly entertayne for such tyme, as themselves should be willing to serve him, wth a sweete voyce or two, such thinges as those delights him much."[72] Unaware of this suggestion, the Company purchased a pair of virginals (presumably the instrument recommended by Mr. Handford) for the forthcoming embassy of Sir Thomas Roe.[73] The remainder of the present consisted of a coach (there is a clear parallel with Dallam's mission during which the Sultana was presented with a gilded carriage), a set of knives, and a richly embroidered scarf.

When Roe arrived at Surat, he had first to deal with the Governor, Zulfikar Khan, who demanded to see the coach and virginals. Roe replied it was not the custom to have the Emperor's presents viewed, but after some argument he relented. On 9 October, Roe showed the virginals "which he much misliked not."[74] Khan then asked for the coach. "When hee saw yt, he scornd yt and sayd it was little and poore." His attitude greatly angered Roe, who set down his complaints in "A Relation of such abuses as hath been done to the English merchants by Zulpherchacon and other subordinate officers under the great Mogull." Among these were "his ironical and mocking speeches of the Lord Ambassador's progression with the King's present, by saying he carried a cart and a pipe, in most contemptuous manner."[75]

In his correspondence to the Company in London, however, Roe himself was scathing about the quality of the presents sent:

> The presents yow have this yeare sent are extremely despised by those [who] have seen them; the lyning of the coach and cover of the virginalls scorned, being velvett of these parts and faded to a base tawny; the knives little and meane, soe that I am enforced to new

[72]Original Correspondence, vol. 2, no. 252.

[73]"The coppye of a generall letter and brief of the cargason sent to Mr William Edwardes" (Ahmadabad, 27 September 1615) values the "payre of virginalls with all necessaries" at £8. 5s. 2d., which suggests that the Company may have bought the instrument more cheaply. See British Library, Add. 9366, fol. 8.

[74]Foster (1926), 48.

[75]F. C. Danvers and W. Foster, *Letters Received by the East India Company from its Servants in the East* (London, 1896–1912) IV:78.

> furnish the case of my owne store; all those guilte glasses on paste, and the others in leather cases with handles, are soe mean, besides so ill packt, that noe man will except of them of guift, nor buy; they are rotten with mould on the outside and decayed within . . . the other things so decayed, as your guilded looking glasses, unglued, unfoyled, and fallen a peeices (and here no man taught to mend them) . . . your pictures not all woorth one penny . . . here are nothing esteemed but of the best sorts; good cloth and fine, and rich pictures, they comming out of Italy over land and from ormus; soe that they laugh at us for such as wee bring.[76]

As Dallam had found when unpacking his organ at Constantinople, six months in the hold of a ship can cause near irreparable damage to anything as sensitive as a musical instrument. Such gifts could not be expected to last long in extreme climates, but they did have to be in good condition for the presentation. The poor workmanship of goods was a perennial problem faced by the trading companies. Artifacts procured as gifts had to be of sufficient quality to attract the recipients, yet not so expensive as to diminish the profits of a voyage. The search for the ideal present, at once inexpensive and novel, was thus a constant one—the more so, since native craftsmen seem to have been adept at making facsimiles. The six cornetti copied for Jahangir from Trully's instrument may have been failures, but the very fact that copies were attempted at all bears out the truth of Roe's comment that local craftsmen "imitate every thing wee bring."[77]

Having heard the Governor's scornful comments on his gifts, Roe can hardly have been optimistic about their reception by Jahangir himself. The presentation, however, was a modest success as the Company's gifts had been augmented by one of Roe's personal possessions. In a letter from Ajmer dated 25 January 1616, Roe listed the objects given: "the virginalls, the knives, a scarfe all richly imbrodred, and a rich swoord of myne owne." He then commented on their reception: "He sitting in his state could not well descerne the coach, but sent many to see yt, and caused the musitian to play on the virginalls there, which gave him good content."[78] Later that night, the Emperor came down into a court and was driven about in the coach. Roe, somewhat to his surprise, had to admit that "he accepted your presents well." But then it came to his attention that Jahangir

[76]Foster (1926), 76.

[77]Ibid., 449.

[78]Ibid., 98.

had asked the Jesuits for an opinion of these gifts, "whether the King of England were a great kyng, that sent presents of so small valewe." Another sign of Jahangir's indifference to the Company's gifts was his early dismissal, without wages, of the musician, Thomas Armstrong. On the last day of 1616, William Biddulph informed the Company he had been obliged to pay Armstrong's wages from 4 August. The Emperor had given the musician a small gift of rupees which the Company, if it was deemed fit, could deduct from his wages when he returned home.[79] When Armstrong arrived back at Surat, he petitioned the Council for permission to travel home on one of the Company's ships, "for want of other employment," which request, being reasonable, was granted.[80] During the journey back to England on board the *Charles*, Armstrong made his will, which is dated 24 May 1618.[81] The goods acquired by the virginal player during his year in India included the following: "one pintadoe quilte"; "china dishes"; "one box of Amadavar [Ahmadabad] with a bracelett of beads"; "a remnant of Bengala stuffe"; "one half hundred weight of pepper"; "one shash and girdle wth a Japan box"; "one magull [mughal] scarfe"; "two paradise birdes"; "seaven hundred and a half of pepper of Tecoo"; "one peece of Bengala stuffe". This gives us an insight into the rewards of service in the East. Armstrong's effects hardly amounted to a fortune, but his estate was a more varied one than most common sailors were able to bequeath.

The apparent failure of Armstrong to impress the Mughal Emperor with his virginal playing was doubtless taken by the East India Company as an indication that the musical part of the gift had made little impression. Jahangir, however, may have been more attracted to the sound of the virginals than he was willing to admit to the English ambassador. A letter written by Father Corsi of the Mughal mission some time during the 1620s refers to a Venetian named Angelo Gradenigo who had been summoned to Agra to perform on a "monocordio" recently presented to Jahangir.[82] The Mughal Emperor was apparently delighted with his playing. This instrument was either the pair of virginals brought by Roe, or a

[79]Foster, *Letters Received*, 4:289.

[80]Ibid., 5:89.

[81]Guildhall Library, London, Commissary Court of London (London Division), Will Register 9171/23, fol. 204v.

[82]R. C. Temple, *The Travels of Peter Mundy, in Europe and Asia 1608–1667*, vol. 2 (*HS* 2nd series, vol. 35; London, 1914), 208.

harpsichord or clavichord presented by the Portuguese in response to the English embassy. In either case, Jahangir's reported reaction suggests that the thinking behind the East India Company's original decision to send another keyboard instrument was correct, and that bad luck may have played a part in its indifferent reception.

On 19 December 1617, the East India Company in London was offered the chance to purchase an elaborate mechanical instrument of some kind. The Court rejected the instrument on the grounds that it was too large to be shipped to the East:

> A peticion was red preferd by Wm Goslinge Ingener desiringe to putt of a faire instrument in nature of a Cabinett very Ritch in shewe sett wth ritch stones, and full of strannge Inventions and devises, wch maye bee had upon reasonable tearmes Butt beeinge found insupportable by the bulkynes thereof, they held itt unfitt for their use.[83]

The Company was evidently becoming known among instrument makers as a potential purchaser of automata.

If all "diplomatic" recitals were received as indifferently as those sponsored by the East India Company, the practice would soon have been abandoned. In 1601, however, an Italian Jesuit priest scored a remarkable triumph in Peking with a harpsichord he presented to the Chinese Emperor. His success, which was publicized throughout Europe, showed how effective a keyboard recital could still be in promoting western interests in an Eastern court. Matteo Ricci left Lisbon in March 1578 and arrived in India six months later.[84] While stationed at the College of St. Paul in Goa, he witnessed the arrival of Akbar's ambassadors, and observed the dispatch of the organ to Fatehpuhr Sikri, no doubt waiting eagerly for news of its reception. After working in Cochin, Goa (again), Malacca, and Macao, Ricci finally settled in China, where he remained from 1583 until his death in 1610.[85] His first station was the Jesuit house at Zhaoqing to which, according to his own account, many Chinese were attracted by the prospect of viewing European novelties such as clocks, pictures, statues, maps, and musical instruments.[86] A mission to Peking was first suggested in 1597, after Ricci was placed in

[83]Court Book IV, 3.

[84]The best modern edition of Ricci's own account is P. M. d'Elia, *Fonti Ricciane, Storia dell Introduzione del Cristianesimo in Cino* (Rome, 1942–1949).

[85]J. D. Spence, *The Memory Palace of Matteo Ricci* (London, 1985) xiii–xiv.

[86]D'Elia, *Fonti*, 1:259.

charge of the China mission, which had hitherto been under the control of the Rector of the College at Macao. Valignano, the Official Visitor, believed that an attempt should be made to open a residence in Peking in order to place the China mission on a more secure footing. Ricci, perhaps remembering the success of the organ presented to the Mughals, decided that the selection of gifts for the Chinese Emperor should include a keyboard instrument. After many years as a resident in China, he knew that the Chinese did not possess organs ("organi"), harpsichords ("gravicembali"), or clavichords ("manicordi"), and that a keyboard instrument would therefore have the desired element of novelty.[87] His thinking emerges even more clearly in other accounts. Li Zhizao wrote of the instrument as "a beautiful harpsichord" ("un bel clavicembalo"), a "musical instrument of the West" ("strumento musicale dell'Occidente"), "different in form from the musical instruments of China" ("diverso di forma degli strumenti musicali della Cina"), which produced "unusual sounds" ("suoni curiosi") when played.[88] Diego Pantoja, the young priest engaged to play the instrument, likewise stated in his account that the gifts presented by Ricci included "a very good harpsichord because it is an instrument about which the Chinese are very curious" ("un muy buen Monacordio, por ser pieça de que los Chinas se espantan mucho").[89] It was, incidentally, in this report, as translated by Purchas, that English readers learned of Ricci's harpsichord as "a very faire Monocord."[90]

With his colleague, Father Lazzaro Cattaneo, described by Trigault as "skilled in the art of music" ("artis musicae peritus"), Ricci

[87]Ibid., 32.

[88]D'Elia *Fonti*, 2:134, note 6.

[89]Diego de Pantoja, *Relacion de la entrada de algunos padres de la Compañia de Jesus en la China* (Valencia, 1606).

[90]The wide range of terms used by historians and translators for Ricci's harpsichord makes an interesting case study in some of the difficulties posed by the musical terminology used in Jesuit reports. It is a fair assumption that most Jesuits knew the difference between an organ and a string keyboard instrument, though some may have been unclear about the distinction between a harpsichord and a clavichord. With due caution, eyewitness accounts can be relied on for this much. But in the process of second-hand reporting and translating, the original identity of an instrument could quickly become obscured. Ricci's harpsichord, widely reported, gave rise to the following complex of terms, "gravicembolo," "manicordio," "clavicembalo" (It.); "cravo," "monacordio" (Port.). The process of translation produced, "clavicordium," "gravicimbalum" (Lat.); "regales," "grosses cimbales," "espinette" (Fr.); "monocord" (Eng.).

reached Peking in 1598.[91] His gifts included statues, clocks, maps, glass prisms, and a harpsichord ("un gravicembolo").[92] It soon became apparent, however, that there was little chance of their being received, and so they returned to Nanjing. In 1600, it was decided the time was now right for a second try. Father Diaz, Rector of Macao, sent a selection of additional gifts to Ricci, among which was to have been an organ made at Macao.[93] As it arrived too late, it was reserved for the mission at Nanjing. The mission began badly. Ricci and Pantoja, who by now had replaced Cattaneo, were imprisoned during the journey to Peking and their goods confiscated. They were released, however, and entered Peking on 24 January 1601.

The two Jesuits sent their gifts to the palace. The Emperor was delighted with the clocks and ordered four of his musical eunuchs—players of string instruments—to learn to play the harpsichord. Ricci was well prepared for this. At Nanjing, Cattaneo had given Pantoja a short course of intensive instruction in the rudiments of keyboard technique. In particular, he had been taught "several pieces to demonstrate the potential of the instrument" ("alcune sonate per mostra dell'artificio di questo stromento").[94] Within a short space of time, Pantoja had learned not only how to play, but also how "to tune the harpsichord" ("temperare il manicordio"). In response to the Emperor's command, Pantoja made daily visits to the palace to teach the eunuchs. As one of the musicians was 70 years of age and found the acquisition of new skills a laborious process, each eunuch was taught "one piece" ("una sonata"), so that the older man would not lose face. While the Chinese musicians were learning their pieces, Ricci, anticipating a request from the Emperor to hear some songs accompanied on his new harpsichord, composed "eight short songs in Chinese" ("otto compositioni brevi in lettera cinese") on texts which dealt with moral and religious themes. These eight songs were circulated under the title "Canzone del manicordio di Europa voltate

[91]N. Trigault, *De Christiana expeditione apud Sinas suscepta ab Societate Jesu ex P. Matthaei Ricci ejusdem Societatis Commentariis* (1615), 344. Trigault does not give a reliable text of Ricci, but he was responsible for the publicity given to Ricci's achievements in early seventeenth-century Europe. For an English translation of Trigault, see L. J. Gallagher, *China in the Sixteenth Century, The Journals of Matthew Ricci, 1583–1610* (New York, 1953).

[92]D'Elia, *Fonti*, 2:29.

[93]Ibid., 91.

[94]Ibid., 132–34.

in lettera cinese" and became popular with educated men, their high moral tone winning general approval.[95] After this, the success of Ricci's embassy was not in doubt, and the Jesuits were granted permission to reside in Peking.

News of the harpsichord presented at the Chinese court spread quickly throughout the East. Benedict de Goes heard of the instrument in the remote mountain fastnesses of Eastern Turkestan, having been entrusted by the Jesuits of the Mughal mission with the task of trying to discover the location of the legendary kingdom of Cathay. In 1602, he set out from Agra and travelled northwest through Lahore and Kabul. From here, he crossed the Hindu Kush to the river Oxus, which he followed up to its source through the Pamir mountains, crossing the rugged Wakhjir Pass at over 16,000 feet. At one of his stopping places in Turkestan, a small town called "Chalis," Goes met up with two merchants returning from Peking. They told him of Ricci's presents and their favorable reception by the Emperor. Subsequent reports of this meeting, based on information supplied by Goes, refer to the instrument as "cravos pera tanger" and "manicordij."[96] Goes (already convinced that "Cathay" did not exist) struggled on to reach Yarkand in Chinese Turkestan. Ricci heard of his entry into China and sent a servant to help him, but Goes died a few days later, leaving Ricci to preserve details of the journey for posterity.

The harpsichord presented by Ricci remained in Peking for at least four decades. In 1640, the instrument attracted the attention of the last Emperor of the Ming Dynasty. Father Johann Adam Schall was ordered "to mend the harpsichord presented by Ricci and to translate the hymns in praise of God, written by early Western saints, and copied in a European tongue on the harpsichord" ("di accomodare il clavicembalo offerto dal Ricci e di tradurre gli inni di lode di Dio composti dagli antichi Santi occidentali e riprodotti in lingua europa sul clavicembalo").[97] Another Jesuit in the Peking mission, Father Francesco Furdato, referred to this request in a letter from Peking dated 17 May 1640; the Emperor, he wrote, had sent the

[95]The texts of the songs were published in *Prima collezione di libri cristiani* (1629). See D'Elia, *Fonti*, 2:134, note 6.

[96]Ricci is our main source of information about the last days of Goes, see D'Elia, *Fonti*, 2:426. See also, Guerreiro *Relaçam*, 4:24.

[97]D'Elia, *Fonti*, 2:32, note 2. See also G. H. Dunne, *Generation of Giants, The Story of the Jesuits in China in the last Decades of the Ming Dynasty* (Indiana, 1962), 313.

broken instrument to Schall and asked him to mend it and translate and explain "the two verses from the psalms written on the harpsichord in our letters" ("2 versos dos psalmos que estavão escrito no cravo em nossa letras").[98] The verses in question were Psalm 150, verse 5: "LAUDATE [DEUM] IN CYMBALIS BENESONANTIBUS"; and Psalm 149, verse 3: "LAUDATE NOMEN EIUS IN CHORO; IN TYMPANO ET PSALTERIO PSALLANT EI." When, on 8 September, Schall returned Ricci's harpsichord repaired—the broken strings had been replaced—and tuned, he also offered, in a Chinese translation, "a method for playing the harpsichord and a melody from the Psalms to serve as an exercise" ("un metodo per sonare il clavicembalo e una melodia sui salmi da servire come esercizio"). The story of Ricci's harpsichord was remembered for many years by the Jesuits of the Peking mission. An ambassador from the Vatican to China recounts the tale of the instrument's unexpected resurrection in his "Briefve Relation de la China et de la Notable Conversion des Personnes Royales de cet Estat" (1664).[99]

Ricci's intention was to use the curiosity value of the harpsichord as part of his long-term strategy of winning converts at the highest levels of Chinese society. This was an ambitious aim, but one which was not altogether unrealistic. With his "Canzone del Manicordio," he was able to advertise Christian morality in a manner acceptable to Chinese intellectuals. Years later, as a result of the unexpected request to mend the instrument, Schall was able to take advantage of the renewed interest by providing translations of the Latin inscriptions (which had no doubt been copied on the harpsichord with some such outcome in mind) and some new teaching material.

The heyday of the presentation keyboard instrument was the period between *c*1580 and *c*1615. During these years, keyboard recitals were given before the complete first division of oriental potentates: a Sultan of Turkey; a Tsar of Russia; two Mughal Emperors; a Shah of Persia[100]; a Japanese Shogun; and a Chinese Emperor. The East India Company made no further use of this type of diplomatic gift, but the missionary orders of the Catholic Church, perhaps

[98]D'Elia, *Fonti*, 2:132, note 2.

[99]*Relations de Divers Voyages Curieux* (Paris, 1664).

[100]See Gouveia (1611), 209.

inspired by Ricci's widely advertised success, continued the practice throughout the seventeenth century.

During the course of his travels in Persia, Sir John Chardin was invited to a wedding in the city of Tiflis (then under Persian control) where he witnessed a harpsichord recital given by the head of the Capuchin mission before the local ruler.[101] The man was ordered to appear before the assembled company, but seemed reluctant to do so, fearing, with some justification, that Sir John, a potentially hostile Western observer, would give a critical account of his efforts. Having no choice, however, the missionary placed his "espinette" on a dais in the center of the room and began to sing to his own accompaniment the "Te Deum," the "Magnificat," and the "Tantum ergo." As these melodies proved insufficiently lively for the occasion, he then sang "chansons" and "airs de cour" in Italian and Spanish. Chardin poured scorn upon his efforts, reporting that the harpsichord was "very badly out of tune" ("fort mal acordée"). Despite his shortcomings, the missionary entertained his audience for two hours. His success, like that of many a keyboard player appearing before an oriental court, depended less on the aesthetic merit of the music and its interpretation, than on the general impression created by the performer and his novel instrument.

Organs and harpsichords were still being taken out to the East as gifts in the early eighteenth century. In a letter dated 1 April 1700, Father Peter Paul of St. Francis, nephew of Innocent XII, writing of the progress of the Carmelite mission to Persia and India, reported that: "the organs intended by His Holiness as presents for the King of Persia and the Great Mogul have remained for about two years in the customs-house at Aleppo, there being no one there to pay the duties, and still less the cost of transporting these things by land to Isfahan and to India."[102] At least some of the instruments, however, were eventually sent to Persia. It was reported to the ambassador that officials at Isfahan had opened the boxes containing the Shah's presents and taken out an organ ("un organo") and possibly "the two harpsichords" ("li due spinetti") as well. It was suggested that the

[101]The passage is cited in F. Harrison, *Time, Place and Music: An Anthology of Ethnomusicological Observations c. 1550 to c. 1800* (Amsterdam, 1973), 120–33.

[102]*A Chronicle of the Carmelites in Persia* (London, 1937), 491 and 981–82. I am most grateful to Monsignior Francesco Mocchiuti of the Sacra Congregazione for photocopies of the relevant letters.

Pope should write to the Shah and complain. Father Peter Paul died shortly after his arrival in India in 1701. Among his possessions was an organ which was sold a few days later for 500 rupees.

The keyboard recital occupies a distinctive niche in the early history of musical contact between West and East. To emphasize the importance of organs and harpsichords as diplomatic gifts, however, is not to imply there was any real degree of musical communication between the Western musician and his Eastern audience. So long as their cause prospered, it mattered little to the promoters of a recital whether their gift were admired as a work of art, a mechanical contraption, or a musical instrument, or whether their performer was admired for his musicianship, his dress, or for the shape of his thighs. The mere fact of approval was enough. In 1921, Gertrude Bell reported a comment made by a Sheikh after hearing a performance of the "Pathéthique" in Baghdad: "By God," he said, "a good thumping!"[103] Demeaning though it might be for the musician, some such reaction could be the signal to his sponsors that negotiation could begin.

[103]Cited by G. Dodd in the *Newsletter of the Viola da Gamba Society*, 61 (1988), 13.

CHAPTER 14

The Growth of the Factory System

The factory was arguably the single most important element in the commercial strategy of English companies trading in the East. The loss of a ship could be damaging enough in the short term, but the closure of a factory could result in the disappearance of lucrative markets for many generations. The East India Company soon discovered that since the best way to finance Eastern imports into Europe (there being only limited demand for European goods in India) was to engage in local commerce—the so-called "country" trade—a chain of stations throughout the region was an absolute necessity. Some of these "houses" remained small outposts, manned by a mere handful of individuals, but a few grew into larger settlements in which an expatriate musical culture soon began taking root.

When, in 1603, the East India Company opened its first factory in Bantam, the Portuguese had already been in India for more than one hundred years. Their empire, held together by a chain of strong bases around the seaboard of the Indian Ocean—Ormuz, Goa, Cochin and Malacca—had been won in the early years of the sixteenth century. Goa, the magnificent capital of Portuguese India, had, by the late sixteenth century, a population of about 225,000 and was perhaps the most cosmopolitan city in the world.[1] Her people included large numbers of Portuguese fidalgos, some recently arrived, others who had settled and intermarried with local girls, Hindu merchants, Moslem traders from Arabia, Persia, Bengal and Java,

[1]B. Penrose, *Goa, rainha do oriente: Goa, queen of the East* (Lisbon, 1960), 55. See also J. N. Fonesca, *Historical Sketch of the City of Goa* (Bombay, 1878).

Chinese and Siamese merchants, smaller numbers of Venetians, Germans, Flemings and Englishmen, and black slaves from Mozambique. The brilliance of "Golden Goa" at her peak, and the darker side of the city, notably her notorious gaol and brutally active Inquisition, were the subject of much comment in Europe.[2] To those who had never visited, Goa must have seemed the quintessential oriental city, a heady blend of opulence and violence. The splendors of her musical life were amply reported by Pyrard de Laval in his memorable account,[3] and in the extensive series of Jesuit letters edited in *Documenta Indica*. A brief account of music in Portuguese India will provide a useful background against which the activities of the first musicians to work in the English and Dutch factories may be judged.

A flotilla of small craft carrying instrumentalists was the first impression most visitors had of the music of Goa. In a letter dated 30 September 1567, Father Gaspar Dias reported that "shawms and viols" ("charamelas e violas") were played in these boats.[4] Jerónimo Lobo, described how several "shawm trios" ("ternos de charamellas") provided music during the Viceroy's disembarkation at Cochin in 1622.[5] Lobo himself then walked to the Jesuit house behind another "terno de charamellas" who played skillfully and most harmoniously. Bands of wind players on small boats must have been a common sight in the inshore waters of Goa. According to Pyrard de Laval, "a fine band of cornetts, shawms and other instruments" ("une musique excellente de cornets à bouquin, hautbois et autre instrumens") accompanied the Viceroy and the Archbishop of Goa every time they made a journey by water.[6]

The magnificence of the public processions in Goa was a subject of frequent comment. On important feast-days, the Viceroy himself led the procession, "tambours" and "trompettes" having been

[2]The most significant source of information for English and Dutch readers was Jan Huyghen van Linschoten's *Itinerario* (Amsterdam, 1596). An English translation by William Phillip, *J. H. van Linschoten, his Discours of Voyages into ye Easte and West Indies*, was published in London in 1598.

[3]A translation of Pyrard de Laval's description of Goa is in A. Gray, *The Voyage of François Pyrard de Laval*, vol. 2, part 1 (*HS*, vol. 77; London, 1888), 1–130.

[4]J. Wicki, *Documenta Indica*, vol. 7 (1566–1569) (*MHSI*, vol. 89; Rome, 1962), 294.

[5]D. M. Lockhart, M. G. da Costa and C. F. Beckingham, *The Itinerário of Jerónimo Lobo* (*HS*, 2nd series, vol. 162; London, 1984), 44.

[6]*Voyage de François Pyrard de Laval* (Paris, 1619), 92. Gray (1888), 90.

sounded as a signal to assemble.[7] The longest cavalcades included three or four hundred fidalgos on horseback, palanquins (litters), sombreros (parasols), Portuguese pages, Mozambiquan slaves, and bands of musicians. According to a document dating from the time of Don Duarte de Meneses (1584–1588), the Viceroy's personal retinue included ten trumpeters and four musicians.[8] The churches in Goa also maintained bands of musicians for processions, which included players of shawms ("hautbois"), cornetts ("cornets à bouquin"), drums ("tambours"), violins ("violons"), and other instruments.[9] On feast-days, they would join with the Viceroy's own musicians, and those belonging to wealthy fidalgos, in a magnificent display of musical pageantry. Father António da Costa described the scene of the Viceroy's coming to the College of St. Paul's on the Feast of the Virgin in 1558: "there were many kinds of instruments such as shawms, drums, trumpets, flutes, viols and a harpsichord" ("avia muytos generos de instrumentos, assi como charamellas, atabales, trombetas, frautas, violas d'arco e cravo"); after mass there was a solemn procession with the instruments mentioned above, and "more music from the boys of the College."[10]

Of all the varied aspects of musical life in Goa, the one which drew the most frequent admiration was the high standard of music at the Jesuit College of St. Paul's. Built in 1542, the College was consecrated on the Feast of the Conversion of St. Paul. Its purpose was to instruct new converts of all races in the European arts and sciences, with particular emphasis on latin, music, rhetoric, philosophy, and theology. By 1560, the College had established a reputation as the most influential Jesuit institution in the East. The boys of the College were obliged by their masters to adopt a high public profile. Every day, before entering the classrooms, they heard mass, and then all boys under the age of fifteen processed through the streets singing the creed "à haute voix."[11] The use of boy singers to spread the doctrines of the Church was a tactic of evangelism widely favored by the missionary orders of the Catholic Church. Chirino described the practice in his account of the growth of the church in the Philippine

[7]*Voyage* (1619), 78. Gray (1888), 78.

[8]Purchas, 9:168.

[9]*Voyage* (1619), 101. Gray (1888), 99.

[10]*Documenta Indica*, 4 (1557–1560) (*MHSI*, vol. 78; Rome, 1956), 189.

[11]*Voyage* (1619), 99. Gray (1888), 96.

Islands, *Relacion de las Islas Filipinas* (Rome, 1604). Children were taught to read and write, to play musical instruments ("tañer"), and to sing ("cantar"), and were then sent out every week to the small churches in the area to chant the doctrines they had learned.[12]

The musical instructors at St. Paul's taught their pupils the instruments traditionally studied by choirboys in Europe—the organ, the harpsichord and the viol. The young instrumentalists regularly performed in services. In 1559, Frois heard services at Goa performed with "douçainas e violas de arquo."[13] The important place of viol playing in the curriculum of Jesuit colleges in the East was particularly evident in Japan. In 1562, a priest from Bungo wrote that his time was being spent in tending the sick and in teaching fifteen Japanese and Chinese boys to read, write, sing, and play viols ("tanger violas darco").[14] Three years later, another Jesuit from Bungo wrote that, on Saturdays, the Salve was sung "con violas de arco", and, on Sundays and feast days, "violas" were played at mass, everything being done with great solemnity and devotion.[15] In 1567, St. Paul's received a bequest of three "violas d'arcos" from a gentleman of some means. These and other instruments were sometimes played, according to Father Gaspar Dias, by slaves who occupied accommodations close to that of the boys.[16]

Wind instruments—shawms and flutes—were also frequently heard in churches of the Portuguese Indian Empire. They are often described as "playing with" or "accompanying" (possibly, though not necessarily, in the strict musical sense of the term) the singing of the boys. A few examples must suffice. A priest writing from Goa in 1569 described the "charamelas" and "frautas" which accompanied some "motetes" and "cantigas" performed by the boys.[17] Other letters

[12]*Relacion*, Chapter 11. For an English translation of Chirino, see E. H. Blair and J. A. Robertson, *The Philippine Islands 1493–1898*, vols. 12 and 13 (Cleveland, 1904).

[13]A. da Silva Rego, *Documentaçao para a História das Missoes da Padroado Português do Oriente*, India, vol. 7 (1559) (Lisbon, 1952), 309. This series supplements (and to some extent duplicates) the material in *Documenta Indica.* On the use of music in Jesuit missions, see T. D. Culley and C. J. McNaspy, "Music and the early Jesuits," *AHSI*, vol. 80 (1971), 213–45.

[14]*Cartas* (Evora, 1598), vol. 1, fol. 101.

[15]Ibid., fol. 198.

[16]*Documenta Indica*, vol. 7 (1566–1569) (*MHSI*, vol. 89; Rome, 1962), 298.

[17]*Documenta Indica*, vol. 8 (1569–1573) (*MHSI*, vol. 91; Rome, 1964), 87.

from 1570 describe baptisms at Margão (near Goa) with "shawms, flutes and trumpets, and other musical instruments" ("charamelas, frautas e trombetas, e outros instrumentos musicos").[18] A particularly interesting reference is made to the use of "many instruments of music, both Portuguese and native" ("muitos instrumentos musicos assi Portugueses como da terra") which suggests that the instrumental resources of the churches in Goa consisted of a blend of European imports and Indian instruments.[19]

The quality of the music at St. Paul's is a constantly recurring theme in Jesuit letters of this period. On 4 December 1562, Father Balthazar da Costa wrote that the music of St. Paul's was "very sweet" ("muy suave") with both voices and "instrumentos de muziqua." He continued: "there were two of these choirs that alternated in various parts" ("destes coros avia dous que se alternavam de diversas partes").[20] The Jesuits were fully aware of the power of music to inspire new converts and win others, and they placed great faith, at least during the early stages of their mission, in the aural and visual splendor of instrumental participation and the spacial effects of the double choir manner.

The uncritical admiration expressed in so many letters from the early years of the mission at Goa is noteworthy. It should be borne in mind, however, that these reports were compiled by the Jesuits themselves, and since their impartiality ought not to be taken for granted, an assessment of the reliability of this type of evidence is essential.

The charge most often made against the accuracy of missionary reports from the East (and elsewhere) is that their claims were exaggerated. There was every incentive, so the argument runs, to project as vital and positive a picture of their endeavors as was possible without resorting to actual falsehood. It would be easier to attract new recruits and financial backing if the mission was obviously flourishing. (Later there would be other possibilities such as the emotive appeal of the martyr.) It is generally agreed that while an element of wishful thinking certainly colors some Jesuit reporting, the charge that this seriously falsifies their whole story is without foundation.

[18]Ibid., 334.

[19]Ibid., 335.

[20]*Documenta Indica*, vol. 5 (1561–1563) (*MHSI*, vol. 83; Rome, 1958), 594.

The basic veracity of musical reporting in the annual letters from Goa is perhaps best demonstrated by examining the period from the late 1570s through to the 1590s when a debate about the value of music in mission began to surface. Throughout the 1570s and 1580s, the majority of Jesuit correspondents continued to refer to the music of St. Paul's with uncritical admiration. Father Nicholas Spinola, giving his first impressions of the College in a letter dated 26 October 1578, observed that: "on all feast days they sing a sung mass with much music, an organ, many trumpets, shawms and other instruments" ("cantano tutte le feste una missa cantada con grande musica, organo, molte volte trombe, chiaramele et altri instrumenti").[21] In the same year Father Francisco Pasio wrote of the "fine music of the orphans and catechumens" ("buona musica de orfanelli e catechumini") who play the "organ and other instruments of the country" ("organo e altri instrumenti della terra").[22] The most telling remark came from Father Silvestro Pacifico who, in 1584, wrote: "the choir is not inferior to that of Rome [referring, probably, to the choir of the Jesuit seminary] since as well as measured music there is an organ, flutes and trumpets" ("questa capella non è inferiore a quella di Roma perchè fora del canto figurate vi è organo, flauti e trombette").[23]

Significantly, the late 1580s saw the emergence of a dissenting point of view. Adverse comments begin to appear: complaints about the high cost of maintaining a musical establishment and the lack of propriety in some of the performances, even arguments against the basic assumption that music was a valuable tool in mission work. In 1589, a Jesuit writing from Cochin expressed the opinion that far too many musicians were employed in his college: "there is already no musical instrument that we do not have . . . we have musicians ("ministriles") in this college even when totally unnecessary . . . there are a thousand secular people who would willingly take their place . . . ."[24] In 1591, a scandal was caused at Goa by some of the music played during a mass. Songs ("cantigas") were performed, profain in character, of the type known as "chacota," which were accompanied

[21]*Documenta Indica*, vol. 11 (1577–1580) (*MHSI*, vol. 103; Rome, 1970), 319.

[22]Ibid., 359.

[23]*Documenta Indica*, vol. 13 (1583–1585) (*MHSI*, vol. 113; Rome, 1975), 519.

[24]*Documenta Indica*, vol. 15 (1588–1592) (*MHSI*, vol. 123; Rome, 1981), 470.

by instruments such as guitars ("gitaras"), citterns ("cíteras"), and others, and not, as the priest reporting the incident commented, because of any lack of organs in the church.[25]

The lobby against music found its most articulate champion in the formidable Father Francesco Cabral. His experiences in Japan led him eventually to question the wisdom of expending large sums of money on music. When he came to India, he expressed his opinion with vigor. In a memorandum written in 1591, he commented on the seemingly insatiable desire of Jesuit colleges in India to possess shawm trios ("ternos de charamellas"). He wrote:

> We have been flooded with a multitude of shawms; the College at Cochin sent boys here to learn and they have now been taught; the college at Baçaim also asked for permission from the Father Provincial for others . . . Coulão where there are three or four Fathers, for others . . . even Bandorá . . . where there are one or two Fathers . . . the College of St. Paul's has two or three trios, supposedly for the service of God and Christianity . . . but I suspect that there are other reasons; I say this because a few days ago the College sold one of its sets for one thousand pardaos, but a few days later it bought another set much more cheaply . . . .[26]

In 1594, Cabral returned to the subject with a critique of the choral traditions of the Indian colleges. After making a practical point—that the employment of a "mestre da capella" was expensive—he went on to question the arguments originally made in support of music; singing was allowed to help convert pagans, but such people, Cabral pointed out, did not frequent Portuguese churches; moreover, early hopes of attracting converts by means of sung services had yet to be realized.[27] The growth of this school of thought is itself testimony to the vigor of the musical traditions of St. Paul's. Although they disagreed sharply over future policy, there was no dispute between the two sides in their assessment of the robust state of music in the colleges.

[25]Ibid., 721.

[26]Ibid., 629. Concern over the excessive numbers of Indian instrumentalists employed in churches in Mexico led to instructions to curtail their numbers. R. Stevenson, *Music in Aztec and Inca Territory* (Berkeley and Los Angeles, 1968), 154–240, cites a strongly-worded document to this effect issued in 1561.

[27]*Documenta Indica*, vol. 16 (1592–1594) (*MHSI*, vol. 126; Rome, 1984), Doc. 133, Item 19.

Another charge made against the accuracy of musical reports from the East is that their writers had an imperfect knowledge of the technical terminology of music. This argument might be sustained if it could be shown that there were few missionaries with musical training in India, but the evidence suggests otherwise. Substantial salaries were paid to the "mestre da capela" and to the "tangedor dorgãos" at St. Paul's in 1576.[28] The employment of a capable choirmaster and an organist in the largest Jesuit college in India is not perhaps surprising. Of much more interest is a seventeenth-century document describing the skills of the men sent out to India by the rival Augustinians during the late sixteenth and early seventeenth centuries. The mission sent in 1568 included one "Francisco o Arpa," "so called because he played and sang to the instrument very well"; also João da Trinidade, a "very good musician."[29] The mission sent in 1593 included Sebastião de Jesu who could "play the organ and the harp and sing very well."[30] There can be no doubt that the author of this compilation makes inflated claims for the musical talents of his men; the *average* level of ability is one of outstanding excellence! Doubtless there were able musicians in the Augustinian mission, but it might be more realistic to interpret the flow of superlatives—examples include "excellente na arte de muzica"; "muito bom musico"; "muito grande abelidade na arte da Musica"—as evidence of competence for the task in hand rather than brilliance. What this document certainly does confirm, however, is that musical ability was regarded as a very desirable quality in recruits, and that many men with musical training did serve as missionaries in the East. This suggests that, unless there are good reasons for believing otherwise, the technical terms used in the original missionary letters (as distinct from published translations—a fruitful source of error, as we have already seen in the reporting of Ricci's harpsichord) should be regarded as reasonably accurate.

Undoubtedly the most difficult phrases to evaluate properly are those that suggest the performance of polyphony. In 1553, Father Gaspar Barzeu listed the subjects studied by the children of St. Paul's; he included both "canto llano" (plainsong) and "canto de órgano" (measured music).[31] Descriptions of the music performed at St. Paul's

[28]A. da Silva Rego, *Documentaçao*, vol. 12 (1572–1582) (Lisbon, 1958), 343.

[29]Ibid., 123.

[30]Ibid., 130.

[31]A. da Silva Rego, *Documentaçao*, vol. 7 (1559) (Lisbon, 1952), 200.

nearly always use the latter phrase or an equivalent. Valignano wrote from Goa on 25 December 1574 that masses at the College were sung "con canto figurato."[32] The most frequently encountered phrase, however, is the ubiquitous "em canto d'orgão." An interpretation of extreme caution was urged by Harich-Schneider in her assessment of Jesuit reports from sixteenth-century Japan: "The frequently occurring term 'em canto d'orgão' meant at that time in Europe vocal polyphony; in Japan it was probably just monodic plainchant with organ accompaniment in unison."[33] However, in view of the number of musicians active in the mission, it seems unlikely that such a basic error would have been made with such frequency. Moreover, the argument with which she supports this view—that the switch from an essentially monodic musical culture like the Japanese to a polyphonic one would have rendered very difficult the acquisition of the skills needed to perform European polyphony—takes no account of the age of the students. There is no reason to suppose that Japanese boys, exposed as they were to the rigors of Jesuit instruction, could not have mastered the fundamentals of European polyphony and sophisticated musical instruments such as the harpsichord, with as much facility as the young recipients of Susuki training have of European music in the twentieth century. An example may help highlight the difficulty. In a letter from Goa dated 14 November 1576, Father Gomes Vaz described the music of the Easter celebrations that year after the proclamation by the Superior of the words "Surrexit Dominus vere, alleluia!": "They [all the priests and brothers] responded in measured music 'Et apparuit Dominus petro, alleluia'; and they began to ring the bells and to play various instruments of music and the children to sing in various choirs 'Regina Coeli laetare, alleluia' " ("E Ihe respondem em canto d'orgão: Et apparuit Dominus petro, alleluia. E começam a repicar os sinos e tanger diversos instrumentos de musica e a cantar os mininos em diversos choros: 'Regina Coeli laetare, alleluia' ").[34] It seems unlikely that this Easter antiphon would have involved the full complexities of Venetian polychoral writing, yet the choirs surely sang something more than accompanied chant. Possibly the setting was a relatively simple polyphonic one, with instruments and double choir

[32]*Documenta Indica*, vol. 9 (1573–1575) (*MHSI*, vol. 94; Rome, 1966), 492.

[33]E. Harich-Schneider, *A History of Japanese Music* (London, 1973), 460.

[34]*Documenta Indica*, vol. 10 (1575–1577) (*MHSI*, vol. 98; Rome, 1968), 724.

effects to enhance its power. In the sixteenth-century missionary context, then, one suspects that there is sometimes little to choose between translating the term "canto d'orgão" as "harmony" or "polyphony."[35]

The boys of St. Paul's enjoyed a fine reputation, not only for their musical contributions to the daily liturgy, but also, like their counterparts in Europe, for secular entertainments. When, in 1579, Akbar's ambassadors arrived at Goa, the College spared no effort in their reception. According to Ricci's account, they were saluted by "every kind of instrument."[36] On their first visit to the College, they were shown around the Church to the sounds of singing and organ playing. Later, they were entertained by the boys who danced and sang (both in Portuguese and Parsee), and played the harpsichord ("cravo") and viols ("violas"). Ricci doubted whether a better welcome could have been provided in Portugal.

The performance of plays was part of the curriculum of St. Paul's and other Jesuit colleges in the East. In a letter from Cochin dated 6 January 1565, Father Francisco Lopes described the entertainment staged to mark the beginning of the school year. After dances and recitations, there was a play with five acts during which there was music on flutes ("frautas"), shawms ("charamelas"), and viols ("violas d'arco"). [37] The following year, a tragicomedy based on the story of the Prodigal Son was enacted at Cochin. In certain passages, the characters sang to a harp ("arpa") and there was also music from flutes and shawms.[38] As in Europe, music for the choirboy plays probably consisted of songs accompanied by string instruments and incidental music played by wind instruments.

Accounts of music in Goa naturally emphasize the public performances, but music was also a popular pastime amongst the inhabitants. In a passage devoted to the recreations of the Portuguese, Pyrard de Laval described the gambling houses frequented by soldiers where young women were employed, *inter alia*, to play and sing to the company.[39] Of Goan women in general he commented that

[35]Stevenson (1968) cites references which show that cathedral choirs in Mexico were capable of performing polyphony in the second half of the sixteenth century; compositions by Morales are named in one report (p.201).

[36]*Documenta Indica*, vol. 11 (1577–1580) (*MHSI*, vol. 103; Rome, 1970), 840.

[37]*Documenta Indica*, vol. 6 (1563–1566) (*MHSI*, vol. 86; Rome, 1960), 414.

[38]Ibid., 742.

[39]*Voyage* (1619), 116. Gray (1888), 111.

their diversion was "to sing and play instruments all the day long."[40] He further mentioned the lodging houses, where soldiers "sing and play on the guitar ("guiterne") or other instrument.[41]

The Jesuit letters, and Pyrard de Laval's account, leave us with an unforgettable impression of the musical life of Goa at the height of her brilliance. The elements which make up this colorful picture—the flotillas of small boats with musicians sent to escort ships into harbor; the musical processions; the choirs of boys; the blend of western and Indian instruments—are typical of the publicly flamboyant Portuguese Eastern Empire (and also of the Spanish Philippines). It is small wonder, then, that musicians and trumpeters in the service of the English and Dutch East India Companies which challenged Portuguese supremacy in the early seventeenth century, were sometimes lured away from their own uncertain enterprises by the attractions of the still dominant, if now indubitably declining, imperial power.

The first English factory in the East Indies was established at Bantam by a small group of men left by Lancaster when he set sail for England in 1603. Against formidable odds, these hardy adventurers succeeded in preserving the factory until the arrival of the East India Company's next fleet in December 1604. Their experiences are described in Edmund Scott's colorful narrative *An Exact Discourse* (London, 1606). According to Scott, the night watch at Bantam was set, military style, to the sound of the drum and the singing of a psalm:

> The 22 day of August, at night, there were certaine Javans gotten into a great yeard hard by our house; who, when wee were singing of a psalme (which wee did use to doe when wee did set our watch), these rogues threw stones at our windowes, as if they would have beaten downe our house; and some of the stones came in at the windowes, and missed us very narrowly.[42]

The noise of the drum at the end of every watch was an aural sign of their vigilence:

[40] *Voyage* (1619), 117. Gray (1888), 113.

[41] *Voyage* (1619), 137. Gray (1888), 130.

[42] W. Foster, *The Voyage of Sir Henry Middleton to the Moluccas 1604–1606* (*HS*, 2nd series, vol. 88; London, 1943), 92.

> These heathen divels came foorth two or three times, thinking to have executed their bloodie pretence; but God would not suffer them, for so soone as they came within sight of our lights and might heare our drumme sound at the end of every watch, their hearts fayled them.[43]

Of all the manifold dangers surrounding the English factors at Bantam, fire resulting from a general conflagration, or from an arson attack, caused the greatest anxiety. At the mere sound of the word "fire," whether spoken in English, Malay, Chinese, or Javanese, Scott was likely to leap out of bed from a deep slumber! Likewise the other factors:

> And not onelie myselfe but my fellowes, Thomas Tudde and Gabriell Towerson, who, after our watches had been out and wee heavie asleepe, our men many times have sounded a drum at our chamber doores and wee never heard them; yet presently after, they have but whispered to themselves of fire and wee all have runne out of our chambers.[44]

In the autumn of 1603, after the assassinations of several Dutchmen, the English factors felt it prudent to make a demonstration of their independence from the Dutch (a matter upon which the Javanese had been misled). Accordingly, they arranged a celebration of the anniversary of the accession of Elizabeth I. On 17 November, wearing new suits of silk with scarves of red and white taffeta, they set up the flag of St. George on top of their house and paraded to the sound of the drum:

> With our drumme and shott wee marched up and downe within our owne grounde; beeing but fourteene in number, wherefore wee could march but single, one after another; plying our shotte, and casting ourselves in rings and esses.[45]

Despite their vigilance—one plot to burn the factory using an underground tunnel was thwarted and the supposed culprit viciously tortured—the English house sustained severe damage in a fire started by an old woman making candles. During the rebuilding of the compound and its protective fence, the Englishmen were obliged to camp in a small shed in their yard: "with our drumme, shot, and pykes, [we] lyved soldierlike untill our fence was made up, and

[43]Ibid., 95.

[44]Ibid., 98.

[45]Ibid., 100.

afterwards too."[46] During the first precarious years of the Bantam factory, as in so many fledgling overseas settlements, a drum was the only instrument available for displays of military watchfulness.[47]

Daily services in the Bantam factory followed the pattern prescribed for worship at sea. Lancaster concluded his advice to the factors: "Thus I end, desiering you to meete together in the morninges and eveninges in prayer."[48] Psalms would have been sung at these services as a matter of course, and, as is clear from Scott's narrative, at the setting of watches. On Sundays, certain periods were additionally set aside (at least in theory) for personal study. With this in mind the Company provided a small library of devotional books for general use, to supplement the Bibles and Psalters owned by many individual factors. The commission given to Saris stated that: "For the better comforte and recreation of such of our factors as are recideinge in the Indies: wee have sent the workes of that worthie servant of Christe Mr Wm Perkins to enstruct their myndes and feede their soules wth thatt heavenlie foode of the knowledge of the truth of Gods word, and the booke of Martirs in twoe voleumes, as alsoe Mr Hackluits Voyadges to recreate their spiritts with varietie of historie."[49] The books were to be left with the chief merchant, who was to ensure that "they should have espetiall care to sanctifie the Sabboth daye, and to reade upon those devyne books for the instruccion and comforte of all those that shall be there remayning." Such regulations were, in practice, difficult to enforce once employees of the Company had disembarked—a fact of which the authorities in London were only too painfully aware. One does not get the impression from reports of the behavior of young Englishmen in India that theological study or psalm singing were high on their list of recreational delights!

At moments of communal peril, however, psalm singing was widely recognized as an effective means of raising men's spirits. A report describing the conduct of the English factors imprisoned on

[46]Ibid., 135.

[47]A letter from Surat dated October 1609 refers to the deaths of five men in the East India Company's house there, one of them Andrew Evans, the drummer. India Office Library, East India Company, Original Correspondence, No. 13.

[48]W. Foster, *The Voyages of Sir James Lancaster to Brazil and the East Indies 1591–1603* (*HS*, 2nd series, vol. 85; London, 1940), 163.

[49]E. M. Satour, *The Voyage of Captain John Saris to Japan, 1613* (*HS*, 2nd series, vol. 5; London, 1900), xv.

the Island of Amboina in 1623 on the night before their execution (the notorious "Massacre" in which the Dutch authorities, having supposedly discovered a plot against their factory, executed a number of Englishmen) includes the following passage: "After this they spent the rest of that doleful night in prayer, singing of psalms, and comforting one another, though the Dutch that guarded them offered them wine, bidding them drink lusticke [lustily] and drive away their sorrow (according to the custome of their own nation in like case), but contrary to the nature of the English."[50] One of the unfortunate factors, Samuel Colson, was allowed to keep a psalter with him, on the blank leaves of which he penned a pathetic profession of innocence.[51] When this document was returned to London, the Company propagandists claimed it as evidence of the "godly behaviour" of their men.[52]

There is no evidence to suggest that the East India Company maintained a consort of professional musicians in any of its factories during the early seventeenth century, since it was usually possible to hire musicians from visiting ships. On Christmas Eve in 1630, the President of the English Factory at Surat invited the Dutch to share in the festivities, and sent an urgent message to Captain Morton of the *James Royall* to send his musicians: "I pray tell Capt. Morton that the Dutch and all other Christians here are our sollemnely invited guests to morrow and we shall want the Musicke to grace our intertainemt: intreat him therefore to send them up instantly, (or soe many of them as are well) to be here (if not to night) then, erly in the morning, and therein not to faile me . . . ."[53] If Surat, the largest English factory in the East, had to rely on musicians from the Company's ships to provide music at the traditional Christmas entertainment, it is certain that lesser factories would have been equally dependent upon this source of supply.

The English and Dutch often entertained each other to dinner and music, despite the growing coolness between the two nations becoming evident even before the Amboina affair. In a letter from

[50]W. N. Sainsbury, *CSP, Colonial Series, East Indies, China and Japan*, vol. 4 (London, 1878), 314.

[51]Ibid., 312.

[52]Ibid., 319.

[53]India Office Library, East India Company, Original Correspondence, No.1330.

Teco, an employee of the East India Company complained of Sir Thomas Roe's friendship with the Dutch merchants there, despite their recent capture of English ships: "Our Marchant*es* and Mr Rowe, and the Marchant*es* of the Flemishe howse, were within a shorte tyme, that we were taken; bancquittinge and feastinge, one the other; with theire musicke, as if theye had byn greate Friend*es*, and had not received any losse att all."[54] The Dutch were generous in their hospitality too. Cocks, who had been left in charge of the English factory in Japan after the departure of Saris, was asked to a banquet at the Dutch house on 27 November 1621. He enjoyed "great cheare with musick, after our cuntrey fation, singing and dansing."[55] The musical entertainments provided by the Portuguese were noted by Peter Mundy during his voyage to China in 1636. At Goa, the Jesuits laid on dinner for the English visitors and then entertained them "with good Musicke of voices, accompanied with the Harpe and Spanish gitterne."[56] The "English musicke" was present and presumably contributed to the performance. At Macao, Mundy described another dinner at which there was "indifferent good Musick of the voice, harp and guitterne."[57]

Professional consorts on leave from the Company's ships were evidently unable to satisfy the growing demand for musical entertainments and the practice quickly grew up of hiring local Indian bands to supplement their efforts. It is a fair assumption that most of the local bands recruited to perform in English factories were hired to accompany troupes of dancing women and other entertainers. The German traveller Mandelslo, who visited a number of English factories in the late 1630s, was present on several occasions when European musicians and Indian bands were jointly responsible for the provision of an evening's entertainment. In order to mark his departure from the Surat factory in 1638, Mr. Methwold threw a lavish banquet for all the merchants in the area. After a farewell speech of thanks, the musical entertainments began:

[54] Ibid., No. 822.

[55] E. M. Thompson, *The Diary of Richard Cocks*, vol. 2 (*HS*, vol. 67; London, 1883), 225.

[56] R. C. Temple, *The Travels of Peter Mundy, in Europe and Asia, 1608–1667*, vol. 3, part 1: *Travels in England, Western Asia, Achin, Macao, and the Canton River, 1634–1637* (*HS*, 2nd series, vol. 45; London, 1919), 55.

[57] Ibid., 256.

> This Ceremony ended, they went into their Garden without the City, where Mr *Metwold* had prepar'd a magnificent entertainment, consisting of whatever the Country afforded that was excellent and rare, as also a Set of *English* Musick, Violins, another of *Mahumetan*, and a third of *Benjan*, which for our further divertisement, was accompanied by the Women dancers of the Country . . . .[58]

The previous year at the English house at Isfahan, Mandelslo had witnessed a similar contrast of cultures, a "Divertisement of Musick upon the Virginals," followed by the dancing of Indian women.[59]

The number of musical amateurs who took up residence in the East India Company's factories was at first small. The tedium of the long voyage round the Cape was often enlivened for the amateur instrumentalist by the presence on board of like-minded companions, but the prospects for such men after their arrival in the East depended very much upon the size of the factory to which they were attached. Away from the large houses, amateur musicians would have been very fortunate indeed to find congenial company for their chosen recreation. Although, by the 1620s, the East India Company had a large number of men in the East—one list of factors in the Indies, "fowerskoare" in number, was submitted to the Court in London and attracted the comment from some members that the Company had hitherto employed a greater number[60]—there were well over thirty English factories and trading stations in the area, most of which were manned by two or three individuals. A letter, dated 8 March 1629 from an English factor in Macassar on the Island of Celebes (where there were three factors) to a colleague in Japara on Java (where there were two), mentions the following gift to a customs official: "And to the Shabander Malick (to whome pray commend me) a Portugall voyall . . . ."[61] This "voyall" was probably a violão or guitar, as Portuguese instruments were not uncommon in the area. From the point of view of a lone individual in such an isolated situation, a string instrument such as a viol, lute, guitar, or cittern probably represented the best chance of obtaining musical satisfaction.

During the first half of the seventeenth century, there was a steady increase in the size of European factories in the East. The

[58]*The Voyages and Travels of J. Albert Mandelslo* (London, 1669), "Mandelslo's travels in the Indies," Book 1, 47.

[59]Ibid., "Ambassadors of the Duke of Holstein to Muscovy and Persia," Book 5, 206.

[60]India Office Library, East India Company, Court Book VI, 274–78.

[61]India Office Library, East India Company, Original Correspondence, No.1289.

earliest "houses," typically both small in size and precarious in situation, gave way to more permanent settlements. These were certainly not immune from war, pestilence, the vagaries of oriental rulers, and the effects of mutual competition, but were increasingly able to withstand the pressures of external events. With the decline of the Portuguese Empire becoming ever more marked, the English, Dutch, and French East India Companies extended the boundaries of their own spheres of interest throughout the region. By the second half of the century, substantial expatriate communities had grown up in a few major centers. As settlements grew in size, they were able to support a larger and more varied musical community.

The employment of a "noise" of trumpets on a permanent basis may be seen as clear evidence of the growing power and status of the larger factories. The primary duty of the trumpeters was to escort the President's palanquin whenever he appeared in public. In *A New Account of East India and Persia* (London, 1698), John Fryer described the Surat President's manner of conveyance thus: "The President besides these has a Noise of Trumpets, and is carried himself in a Palenkeen, an Horse of State led before him, a *Mirchal* (a Fan of Ostriches Feathers) to keep off the sun, as the *Ombrahs* or Great Men have . . . ."[62] Of the Governor of Fort St. George at Madras he wrote: "His Personal Guard consists of 3 or 400 Blacks; besides a Band of 1500 Men ready on Summons: He never goes abroad without Fifes, Drums, Trumpets, and a Flag with two Balls in a Red Field; accompanied with his Council and Factors on Horseback, with their Ladies in Palenkeens."[63] The sounding of trumpets in public was not something that every Indian official could regard with equanimity, and it seems to have been a cause of persistent friction. The European factors in Surat had several skirmishes with the Governor on this issue. In 1672, the English President, Gerald Aungier, informed the East India Company in London that his factory had been seized and its arms and trumpet confiscated. However: "At length it seems the Governor, being ashamed of what he had done, betwixt 8–9 at night, recalls all his souldiers, returnes all the armes and the trumpet, and leaves the house free."[64] Abbé Carré stated that the Surat Governor

[62]W. Crooke, *John Fryer's East India and Persia*, vol. 1 (*HS*, 2nd series, vol. 19; London, 1909), 218.

[63]Ibid., 107.

[64]C. Fawcett, *The English Factories in India*, new series, vol. 1, *The Western Presidency 1660–1677* (Oxford, 1936), 219.

ordered all three European factories to refrain from having trumpets blown during meal times and when visiting the town, his motive being to oblige them to purchase the privilege.[65] The issue was still the subject of correspondence in 1675, when the Dutch were apparently still insisting upon their traditional practices in this matter: "some punctillios of honour they yet standing upon, as their trumpet sounding before them in the street, which the Governor says he cannot grant, the King's order being to the contrary."[66] The English diplomatically gave ground. Aungier sent back his trumpeter, "as the Governor and other great men [here] are not well pleased with the Sound of an English Trumpet." No depictions of English trumpeters in India have survived from this period, but an illustration of the Dutch factory at Hooghly in Bengal gives a colorful view of a trumpeter leading a ceremonial procession (Plate 27).

Plate 27. The Dutch Factory at Hooghly in Bengal. A trumpeter leading a procession. Hendrick van Schuylenburgh, 1665. Rijksmuseum, Amsterdam.

[65]M. E. Fawcett, C. Fawcett and R. Burn, *The Travels of the Abbé Carré in India and the Near East 1672–1674*, vol. 1 (*HS*, 2nd series, vol. 95; London, 1947), 149.

[66]Fawcett (1936), 251.

If restrictions were imposed for a time, they were evidently soon lifted and, thereafter, as the Company's influence grew, there seem to have been few constraints on the sounding of trumpets. The value of ceremonial music in enhancing a public profile in India was never seriously doubted by the Company. It was acknowledged explicitly by William Hedges, the agent at Hooghly in 1683. Describing the arrival of an interloper, one Captain Alley, he wrote:

> Alley went in a splendid Equipage, habitted in Scarlet richly laced. Ten Englishmen in Blew Capps and Coats edged with Red, all armed with Blunderbusses, went before his pallankeen, 80 Peons before them, and 4 Musicians playing on the Weights, with 2 Flaggs before him, like an Agent. A gawdy shew and great noise adds much to a Public Person's credit in this Country.[67]

A "gawdy shew and great noise" were deemed indispensable when the Company sent an ambassador on a major diplomatic initiative. In order to enhance the musical pomp on such occasions, a wind band was sometimes hired in London. On 27 January 1701, Sir William Norris, the Company's representative, left Surat in the company of sixty Europeans and 300 Indians. His procession is reported to have included "the music, with rich liveries, on horseback . . . one kettle drum, in livery, on horseback . . . three trumpetts in liveries, on horseback . . . ."[68] A manuscript in the British Library (Add. 31,302, fol.8) lists "The Names Stations and Salaries of the Persons to Attend the Ambassador." This includes the musicians: Christian Feltman, Lewis Scott, William Shirlock, and John Cottrell ("Hautboys and double Courtell"); Daniel Hopkins, Samuel Hopkins, and William Prince ("Trumpeters"); Henry Latham ("Bagpyper"); and William Bond ("Kettle Drumer"). All were to receive £36 at the rate of £3 a month. At one stage during his embassy, Norris, intending to send a deputation to an Indian official, was informed that the man had recently forbidden the Dutch to bring musicians with them. The English ambassador was at great pains to insist his men should turn back if any opposition were offered to their musical instruments.[69]

[67]R. Barlow, *The Diary of William Hedges*, vol. 1 (*HS*, vol. 74; London, 1887), 123.

[68]P. Anderson, *The English in Western India* (London, 1856), 323–24.

[69]H. Das, *The Norris Embassy to Aurangzib 1699–1702* (Calcutta, 1959), 150. A similar complement of musicians—four trumpets, four waits and two kettledrums—accompanied a French party from Madras in 1670. See J. S. Cummins, *The Travels and Controversies of Friar Domingo Navarrete 1618–1686*, vol. 2 (*HS*, 2nd series, vol. 119; Cambridge, 1962), 318.

Plate 28. The Dutch Factory at Hooghly in Bengal. A shawm player. Hendrick van Schuylenburgh, 1665. Rijksmuseum, Amsterdam.

The East India Company also made frequent use of Indian musicians in public displays. To the average European of the time, the music produced by an oriental wind band must have seemed discordant in the extreme, but the eye- and ear-catching sights and sounds of a procession, in which the brilliantly contrasting liveries of Indian and European musicians were combined with their different playing styles, could not be denied. There are no seventeenth-century illustrations of Indian musicians in the employ of the East India Company, but the aforementioned picture of the Dutch factory at Hooghly in Bengal shows an Indian musician (possibly employed as a wait) playing a shawm at the entrance (Plate 28).

The records of Fort St. George at Madras contain many references to the "country music" as it was always termed. The accession of James II in 1685, for instance, was celebrated with colorful pageantry and a public procession:

> After that came Peddy Nague [the chief naik] with his Peons . . . bringing with them also Elliphants, Kettle Drums, and all the Country Musick . . . Peddy Nagues Peons, the Chief Merchants and Gentue Inhabitants went first, Elliphants carrying our Flags, the Kettle Drums and Musick playing before them. After that went 12 English Trumpets, with Silk Banners, and 6 Hoeboyes, all in Red Coates, playing by turnes all the way . . . the Proclamation ended with great shouts and joyfull Acclamations, crying God bless King James the Second. Also at every place of reading there was a volley of small shot, the Trumpetts sounding and Hoeboyes playing.[70]

In 1692, ambassadors from Aurangzib's son were received in the Company's new garden with "accustomary ceremony of musick."[71]

By the turn of the century, the Governor of Fort St. George seems to have been accompanied by Indian music whenever he went out. Charles Lockyer wrote: "The Governour seldom goes abroad with less than three or four-score Peons arm'd, besides his English Gards to attend him. He has two Union Flags carry'd before him, and Country Musick enough to frighten a Stranger into a Belief the Men were mad."[72] On 17 August 1727, the reception of the Company's new charter at Madras was celebrated with a public procession with: "Major John Roach on horse-back at the head of a Company of Foot Soldiers, with Kettle drum, Trumpe[ts] and other Musick"; and then: "The Dancing Girls with the Country Musick." A letter to the Company in England, dated 22 September 1727, raised a question which must have been constantly in the minds of the East India Company's officials, namely, the value of the "country music" versus its high cost:

> The Country Musick is a privilidge bought of this government by the old Company [before the new charter] at a very great charge, and is therefore kept up, it being look'd upon here as one of the greatest Marks of Grandure that can be; but if you please to have them discharged, it shall be done, they being far from Agreeable to your President or any of the Europeans . . . .[73]

The Governor of Madras and his colleagues obviously tended to regard Indian bands as a wearisome necessity.

[70]H. D. Love, *Vestiges of Old Madras, 1640–1800* (London, 1913), I:487.

[71]Ibid., 517.

[72]C. Lockyer, *An Account of the Trade in India* (London, 1711), 17.

[73]Love (1913), 2:242.

Finally, in 1754, the East India Company at Fort St. George was offered, at a price, the services of a *naubat*—a ceremonial ensemble responsible for performing at fixed times of the day above the entrances to palaces or shrines in the Mughal Empire. The musicians of the Company's "nobet" are listed, together with their monthly wages:[74]

Table 5

2 Men who beat the Nagar upon the Elephant	(9 rupees per month each)
4 Men who beat the Daukas, or small Kettle Drums, upon 4 Horses	(one at 20 rupees a month, one at 15 and two at 10)
4 Men who play upon the Sourna or the Country pipes, upon four Horses	(two at 24 rupees a month, two at 16)
3 Who blow the Carnas, or Trumpets with a broad Mouth, upon 3 Horses	(10 rupees a month each)
1 Man who blows the Turay, or large Trumpet, upon a Horse	(10 rupees a month)
2 Men who play upon the Jangey, or Gingling Musick	(9 Rupees a month each)
1 Elephant Keeper with his Assistant	(12 rupees a month)
6 Horsekeepers to take care of the 12 Horses	(6 Rupees a month each)

[74]Ibid., 292 and 432. On the function of the naubat ensemble at the height of Mughal power, see B. Wade, "Music as Symbol of Power and Status: The Courts of Mughal India," in *Explorations in Ethnomusicology: Essays in Honor of David P. McAllester*, ed., C. J. Frisbie (Detroit, 1986), 97–109.

In total this amounted to twenty-three men at a monthly cost of 259 rupees. To this had to be added extras: "Feeding 1 Elephant and 12 Horses belonging to the Noubet" (180 rupees a month). This arrangement lasted no longer than it took a ship to make the return journey to England and back. In a letter dated 25 March 1757, the Company in London directed that this "useless piece of Pageantry" be stopped. By then, bands of "country music" had been periodically employed at Madras for over 100 years; paradoxically, their contribution to the advancement of the Company's interests diminished the more secure those interests became.

The flamboyance of the East India Company's secular image did not influence the conduct of religious worship within its sphere of authority. Unaccompanied psalm singing remained the norm throughout the seventeenth century, as it did in the Dutch settlements. The Sunday services of Europeans resident in Ceylon, for instance, included "Lobwasser" (psalms) which were sung before and after the sermon.[75] Just as it did in North America, the practice of psalm singing became a significant element in the public image of Protestants working in the East. The author of "Japan Diary," an account of an isolated attempt by the East India Company in Bantam to re-establish contact with the Japanese in 1673, described how the English crew sang psalms on the *Return*, as she lay at anchor off Nagasaki: "I asked them leave to wear our colors, and sound our trumpets, which they said we might do; and at their departure we sounded . . . we daily went to prayers, with singing of psalms publickly upon the quarter deck."[76] The flags, trumpet calls, and psalm singing seem to have been part of a concerted attempt by the Englishmen to convince the Japanese of their identity—in a piece of astute diplomacy, the Dutch had already informed the authorities of Charles II's Portuguese marriage.[77]

Organs were probably introduced into English churches in India some time towards the end of the century. An instrument was

[75] S. P. L'H. Naber, *Christoph Schweitzer Reise nach Java und Ceylon 1675–1682* (Reisebeschreibungen von Deutschen Beamten und Kriegsleuten in Dienst der Niederländischen West- und Ost-Indischen Kompagnien 1602–1797, vol. 11; The Hague, 1931), 82. "Lobwasser" refers to the popular German translation of Marot's psalter by Ambrosius Lobwasser.

[76] J. Pinkerton, *A General Collection of the best and most interesting voyages and travels* (London, 1808–1814), VII:641.

[77] Thompson (1883), 1:xlvi–xlviii.

purchased for St. Mary's at Madras in 1687.[78] It was mentioned by Charles Lockyer, in 1711, in his brief description of the church, which, he commented, was "inferiour to the churches of *London* in nothing but Bells."[79] One of the duties of the organist at Madras was to play during the entry of the Governor—the only ceremonial element in public worship: "On the Governour's Approach, the Organs strike up and continue a Welcome till he is seated."[80] The Madras organ was apparently replaced in 1718. In the Court Minutes for 22 October, it was ordered that: "the Committee of Shipping be desired to give Permission for Sending on one of the Ships outward-bound an Organ for the use of the Church of Fort St. George together with an Organist." In 1746, an organ (presumably this one) was stolen by the French and taken away to Pondicherry.[81] Then, in 1751, an unnamed gentleman contributed £300 to replace the instrument. Mr. Bridge (or, in his absence, Mr. Byfield) was ordered to build an organ and to procure an organist to come out with it.[82] The Court of Directors in London was asked to give the instrument and the player passage in one of their ships, in 1752, and to pay the £300 to the maker upon completion of the order. However, it did not finally arrive in India until 1759, only two years before the return of the instrument originally taken by the French.

An organ built for the first English church in Bombay (which was never completed as a result of the embezzlement of funds) was still in the Fort in 1715, according to the Reverend Richard Cobbe. On 24 December 1716, George Bowcher, a merchant at Surat, wrote to him that his predecessor "had finished a stately organ" which he had seen in the fort.[83] To which Cobbe replied: "As to the organ you were speaking of, it is still in the fort, but quite out of order, broken and useless."[84] Cobbe does not say whether a new instrument had yet been purchased. It was evidently one thing to ship an organ out to India, but quite another to maintain it in good working order for any

[78]Love (1913), 1:425.

[79]Lockyer (1711), 18.

[80]Ibid., 19.

[81]Love (1913), 2:433. See also F. Penny, *The Church in Madras*, vol. 1 (London, 1904), 308.

[82]Probably the London organ-builders Richard Bridge and John Byfield.

[83]R. Cobbe, *Bombay Church* (London, 1766), 42.

[84]Ibid., 47.

length of time. Apart from problems of heat and humidity, insect damage could prove fatal. In 1751, there was a report in Calcutta of an organ being "eaten up" by white ants.[85]

The increased resources available for musical entertainments in European factories in the late seventeenth century are evident in many accounts. Several visitors to Dutch settlements at the Cape and Batavia commented favorably on the quality of the music provided at the Governor's table. Robert Knox recalled the "exceeding great Varieties of Food, Wine and sweet Meats, and Musick" at Batavia.[86] François Valentijn, returning to Holland from the East Indies in 1695, was feasted at the Cape, to the accompaniment of "a very fine consort of voices and instruments" ("een zeer fraey Muzycq van Stemmen, en Instrumenten"), at which a gentleman "sang very well" ("zeer fraey zong").[87] The more important English factories were similarly well served. At Madras, rather than rely upon the services of visiting ensembles as had been the practice hitherto, governors began to maintain a small resident ensemble of musicians. In 1716, Joseph Collet wrote to his mother from Fort St. George: "The Company keep a handsome Table and for my own part I keep a very good Concert of Musick and purpose now and then to treat the Ladys with a Ball and sometimes bear a part with them."[88] In his will, dated 13 November 1721, Governor Francis Hastings bequeathed 500 pagodas to his "Musick"—William Zinzan and Michael Deakins.[89]

Freelance professional musicians from Europe who opted to work in the East are a fascinating but elusive group of men. For much of the seventeenth century, they retained an obvious scarcity value and, like clockmakers, apothecaries, gunners, and engineers, were often able to market their skills to good effect. A Carmelite, writing from Persia in 1608, commented that the Shah would be willing to employ clockmakers, musicians, painters, and those who could construct fountains or similar

[85]H. Yule and A. C. Burnell, *Hobson-Jobson: A glossary of colloquial Anglo-Indian words and phrases*, rev. ed., by W. Crooke (London, 1903), 32.

[86]R. Knox, *An Historical Relation of the Island Ceylon* (London, 1681), 173.

[87]F. Valentijn, *Oud en Nieuw Oost-Indien* (Dordrecht, 1724–1726). The passages in Valentijn concerning the Cape of Good Hope have been edited by R. Raven-Hart, *Description of the Cape of Good Hope, with matters concerning it*, vol. 1, ed., P. Serton (*VRS*, 2nd series, vol. 2; Cape Town, 1971); vol. 2, ed., E. H. Raidt (*VRS*, 2nd series, vol. 4; Cape Town, 1973).

[88]H. H. Dodwell, *The Private Letter Books of Joseph Collet* (London, 1933), 139.

[89]Love (1913), 2:185.

mechanical devices.[90] Tales of the fabulous wealth of oriental potentates abound at this period. Some portray the capricious generosity of these men towards favored servants. In *A True Historicall discourse of Muley Hamets rising to the three Kingdomes of Morvecos, Fes and Sus* (London, 1609), the Moroccan ruler is depicted handing over a fortune to a musician during periodic bouts of drunkenness:

> And such was his lavish manner of spending and consuming of his treasure, that in his humors hee neither regarded what hee gave nor to whome; in so much that a Jew, who was a musitian and used to play before him in his drunken fits, what with the gifts given him by the prince and what else he gotte out of his house, had gotten, together in money and jewels, in the space of foure or five yeares, to the value of foure hundred thousand duckets, which is about fortie thousand pound sterling.[91]

True or not, such tales doubtless attracted some to stake everything on an eastern voyage. For English musician-adventurers, the easiest place to reach was India. The Mughal Court was in any case far more receptive to Europeans than any other major oriental power. In order to reach the subcontinent, freelance musicians had little option but to enlist in the service of the Company, as few were willing or able to emulate Thomas Coryat and walk! At an opportune moment they could discharge themselves by agreement or simply desert. The East India Company was probably not averse to a few of its employees attempting to make their own way. If an individual did manage to achieve a position of some influence, the Company could then, as it did with William Adams in Japan, attempt to make use of his good offices. A musician who achieved a position close to the personage of a ruler—the center of power in an oriental court—had a unique opportunity to study the customs and practices of diplomatic interchange. This kind of knowledge was highly prized by ambassadors. During Norris's embassy to Aurangzib in 1700, the English ambassador, well aware of the need to identify someone conversant with the manners and customs of the Mughals, inquired where he could find a knowledgeable informant. The man suggested to him was one Johannes Pottvleet, "a ffleminge musitian."[92] By the very nature of their way of life, freelance professional musicians rarely surface in

[90] *A Chronicle of the Carmelites in Persia* (London, 1937), 165.

[91] There are several references in this work to English engineers and soldiers employed in Morocco at this period.

[92] H Das, *The Norris Embassy to Aurangzib 1699–1702* (Calcutta, 1959), 211.

published accounts of voyages. Robert Trully, whose exploits we have already encountered, is the only musician of this kind about whom anything substantive is known. Withington's account of him is of particular interest as it briefly records the fortunes of several Englishmen who entered the service of the ruler of the Deccan after failing at the Mughal Court. Apart from India, the most receptive areas for freelance European musicians seem to have been Persia—a traveller who visited Isfahan in *c* 1668 noted that one of the Shah's French servants could "play on ye violin"[93]—North Africa, the Levant, and Arabia.

As well as Europeans seeking their fortune, the pool of independent professionals resident in the East included numerous Indian musicians from Portuguese territories, many of whom had received some training on European instruments. The ebb tide of the once-dominant European nation stranded whole populations of rootless persons from whose ranks came many a would-be musician, desperate to improve his lot. Abbé Carré described one such band at the Dutch factory near Golconda in 1673. He was utterly contemptuous of their efforts:

> The Dutch employ many of that class of people, among others a fine troop of musicians. These are poor Christians from Kanara, near Goa. They had passed their youth in slavery with some Portuguese nobles, where they had learnt to strum a guitar and sing some airs, almost as melodious as penitential psalms. They have become so proud of their accomplishments that, finding nothing to attract them in their own country, they visit the oriental courts, as they think there is nothing more charming and melodious than their music. I had this diversion at all our meals. One tortured a harp, another strummed a guitar, a third scaped a violin, and two others, having no instruments but their voices, joined in with the rest in such a way that one could not listen to their harmonies without pity and compassion. There was nothing but repetition of *helás, háa, híns, hús*, and such like sounds, which lasted about a quarter of an hour. After the meal, they came and asked me proudly what I thought of their fine concert, and enquired if we had anything so charming and agreeable in our European countries. "No," I replied, "we certainly have nothing like it, and I can assure you that, if in France we had a troop like yours, we would enjoy it with much more pleasure and amusement than all the tunes we use. But what of

[93]R. C. Temple, "The Travels of Richard Bell (and John Campbell) in the East Indies, Persia and Palestine, 1654–1670," *The Indian Antiquary*, XXXVI:126.

> it? Every country has its own modes." They were so delighted at hearing me speak in this manner that they imagined they were the best musicians in the world. They had never found anyone to praise them as they thought I had done; and when I was not chatting with the Dutch, they came running into any room where I was, and gave me so much of their society that my people had great difficulty in turning them out at night, to enable me to get a little repose.[94]

In its heyday, the Portuguese Empire attracted musicians from other European countries; now it contributed in no small measure to the degraded lower reaches of the music profession in the East.

The growing strength of expatriate European musical culture in the East is most clearly evident in the emergence of networks of amateur musicians in the environs of the larger settlements. A pleasant account of music-making in the English factory at Constantinople during the late 1640s is given in Robert Bargrave's "A Relation of sundry voyages and Journeys."[95] Bargrave travelled to Constantinople in the retinue Sir Thomas Bendyshe. During the outward voyage, there were "many handsom divertisments of musick and dancing" among the young ladies and gentlemen.[96] Bargrave was himself a viol player, and during his years in the Levant, he sometimes incurred the displeasure of his master, James Modyford, as a result of his hobby: "and if sometimes I did perhapps overcome my busyness, and was employing my spare time in Study or in musique, to find me so, seemd very unpleasing to him."[97] Modyford's proposed marriage to Lady Abigail Bendyshe inspired Bargrave to compose an entertainment consisting of "Dialogues, Songs, Masques, and Anticks." The rubric to one of the pieces, "A Dialogue between Art and Nature in the habits of a Court Lady and a Shepheardess composd for two Trebles to an Instrument and taught the Lady Abigail," gives a fair idea of the resources available.[98] The tunes he composed include a series of dance melodies for a "Masque for Fower persons to be habited like the 4 Seasons of the Yeer"; they are trivial, yet interesting as examples of the sort of recreational music composed for entertainment in an English factory.

[94]Fawcett, Fawcett and Burn (1947), 2:350.

[95]M. Tilmouth, "Music on the Travels of an English Merchant: Robert Bargrave (1628–61)," *ML*, vol. 53 (1972), 143–59.

[96]Ibid., 145.

[97]Ibid., 147.

[98]Ibid., 149.

The best account of amateur music-making in the East Indies (there is unfortunately no English source of comparable value) is Valentijn's *Oud en Nieuw Oost-Indien*. At the age of nineteen, Valentijn was engaged as a minister by the Dutch East India Company. He was a keen amateur musician and took with him a violin ("Hand-viool") and a harpsichord ("Klavecimbaal"). During the outward journey, Valentijn, a self-confessed "great lover of music" ("een groot Liefhebber der Muzycq") commented favorably on the musical entertainment available on board, referring in particular to "a fine performance on the viola da gamba" ("een fraey Muzycq-stuk op de Viool da Gamba") by a certain Herr Verryn.[99] At the Cape, Valentijn, who was evidently an impressionable young man, was persuaded to part with his harpsichord by the Lady-of-the House at his lodging place.[100]

After his arrival at Batavia, Valentijn joined enthusiastically in the activities of the circle of music lovers resident there. He took part in "a fine musical performance" ("een zeer fraey Muzycq") in which Abraham van Riebeeck played "basso continuo," he himself sang tenor, the Notary played a recorder ("Flute douce"), and several others played the violin ("Hand-viool").[101] Excellent though this was, he witnessed an even finer performance at the house of the merchant in charge of trade with Japan. This was given by slaves, who "played in a masterly fashion on all instruments" ("meesterlyk op alle Instrumenten speelden"). Valentijn also regularly played upon "a very fine organ" ("een zeer fraeyen Orgel") in the home of Cornelis van Outhoorn, whose daughter was a good player, who kept "a marvellous harp-player" ("een heerlyk Harpslager").

In January 1686, Valentijn was appointed minister to the Island of Amboina. There he was able to enjoy the musical sessions that were held at the home of the Governor, Robert Padbrugge. Having obviously learned nothing from the loss of his harpsichord at the Cape, he describes how he was persuaded to part with his violin:

> Master Lobs paid a special visit to me too; but his sole aim, being a gentleman who fancied anything that cost him nothing, was my fine violin ["myn fraey Hand-viool"] and Dutch strings ["Vaderlandse Snaren"], of which he knew I had a reasonable stock of good quality. So he requested me kindly and casually to let him have them, making

[99]Valentijn (1724–1726), vol. 4, part 2, 98.

[100]Ibid., 105.

[101]Ibid., 107.

> light of my unwillingness, promising only the enjoyment of a musical evening ["een Muzycqje"] at Master Padbrugge's home, and a thousand promises that came to nothing.[102]

Valentijn's *Oud en Nieuw Oost-Indien* provides interesting glimpses into the musical life of Dutch East-Indian society in the late seventeenth century. The circle of active amateur musicians in important centers such as Batavia and Amboina included the employees of the Company, their wives, daughters, and servants. Musical slaves, who in some cases were performers of considerable skill, could also be hired. There was a similar growth of amateur music-making in the English settlements. By the early years of the new century, inventories of goods belonging to Englishmen who had died in India quite often contain evidence of their musical interests. Even in a small collection of wills, such as that preserved in Volume 23 of the East India Company's Factory Records (Miscellaneous), two individuals are recorded as having owned musical instruments: Mr. Hanslopp (1710), "One Old Hoboy" and "A Jappan Flute"; Mr. Shelton (1725), "2 Musick Books," "a flute," and "2 [flutes] and a Hautboy."

The patterns of musical life that emerged in the English and Dutch factories by the end of the seventeenth century were strikingly unlike those of the old Portuguese colonies. At the heart of Portuguese India—and indeed of the two Hispanic empires in both the Old World and the New—lay the heroic and indefatigable labors of the missionary orders. Much of what is distinctive about music in Portuguese India—the extravagant religious processions; the colorful instrumental participation in services; the intensive instruction of new converts in the techniques of musical instruments—relates to the conscious deployment of music as an evangelistic tool. In marked contrast, there was no equivalent missionary effort on the part of ministers of the English and Dutch East India Companies. Such musical pageantry, as was promoted in the English and Dutch settlements, resulted instead from a commercial consideration—the need to present an image of prosperity. The common denominator between old colonial order and the new was of course the military music. For as long as the European nations remained in India, trumpets and drums remained potent musical symbols of their power.

[102]Ibid., 111. I am most grateful to Peter King for the translation.

PART III

REACTIONS AND ATTITUDES

CHAPTER 15

Geographical and Commercial Themes in English Music

With the growing availability of travel literature in late Elizabethan England and the involvement of many musicians in the voyages of discovery, it was perhaps inevitable that the wonders of the newly discovered parts of the world should attract the attention of composers and writers of madrigal and song lyrics. To claim that the subject was an important influence on English composition at this period would be absurd, and yet seafaring, overseas trade or geography occasionally provide the theme of a madrigal or lutesong lyric. The achievements of English explorers were embraced more openly by the popular ballad-makers of the day, but their interests were understandably jingoistic, and they did not venture much beyond stereotyped celebrations of the exploits of naval heroes like Sir Francis Drake.

John Wilbye was the first English composer to set a text based on the imagery of far-flung places and their treasures. The seventh and eighth pieces in *The First Set of English Madrigals to 3. 4. 5. and 6. voices* are a linked pair:

> What needeth all this travail and turmoiling,
> Shortening the life's sweet pleasure
> To seek this far-fetched treasure
> In those hot climates under Phoebus broiling?
> O fools, can you not see a traffic nearer,
> In my sweet lady's face, where Nature showeth
> Whatever treasure eye sees or heart knoweth?
> Rubies and diamonds dainty,

And orient pearls such plenty,
Coral and ambergris sweeter and dearer
Than which the South Seas or Moluccas lend us,
Or either Indies, East or West, do send us.[1]

As Fellowes pointed out, the inspiration for this text was probably the fifteenth sonnet of Spenser's *Amoretti* (London, 1595), "Ye tradeful merchants that with weary toil,"[2] which was in turn a reworking of a sonnet from *Les Amours de Diane*.[3] In all three pieces, the poet wonders why merchants strive so hard to bring back treasure from distant lands when, in Spenser's words:

For loe my love doth in herselfe containe,
all the worlds riches that farre be found.

The author of the madrigal lyric takes up Spenser's image of the Indies, East and West, as well as a more specific location—the Moluccas, the famed Portuguese spice islands.

The exotic goods mentioned in the madrigal—coral, ambergris and precious stones—are strongly redolent of the Portuguese East Indian trade. All are described in Linschoten's *Itinerario*, an English translation of which was published in the same year as the madrigal.[4] According to this influential work, the southeast coast of Africa, around the ports of Sofala and Malindi, was the source of plentiful supplies of ambergris. Defined in the *Oxford English Dictionary* as "a wax-like substance of marbled ashy colour, found floating in tropical seas, and as a morbid secretion in the intestines of the sperm-whale," ambergris was sold by Portuguese merchants both in India and Europe. Linschoten's description of the substance draws attention to its supposed medicinal properties and emphasizes its sweetness: "This Ambar, by reason of the sweet and pleasant smell, doth comfort the head and the heart."[5] In the East, ambergris was one of the substances mixed with betel leaves, which "beeing so prepared, is

[1]E. H. Fellowes, *English Madrigal Verse 1588–1632*, revised and enlarged by F. W. Sternfeld and D. Greer (Oxford, 1967), 305.

[2]E. H. Fellowes, *The English Madrigal Composers* (Oxford, 1921), 142.

[3]Fellowes (1967), 720.

[4]A. C. Burnell, *The Voyage of John Huyghen van Linschoten to the East Indies*, vol. 1 (*HS*, vol. 70; London, 1885). P. A. Tiele, *The Voyages of John Huyghen van Linschoten to the East Indies*, vol. 2 (*HS*, vol. 71; London, 1885).

[5]Ibid., 94.

pleasant of taste and maketh a sweet breath."[6] Coral was also found in the Mozambique area, where it was both an article of trade[7] and a hazard to shipping.[8] Precious stones are extensively discussed in the *Itinerario* which devotes chapters to the valuation of diamonds and rubies. In the chapter entitled "Of Oriental Pearles," Linschoten claimed that pearls from the East "are better then those of the Spanish Indies, and have great difference in the price; for they are worth more, and have a better glasse, being clearer and fairer."[9] Interesting and topical though the commercial allusions in the madrigal text were, they did not suggest to Wilbye any specific musical response, words such as "ambergris" and "coral" being unlikely subjects for the techniques of word painting!

In 1600, Thomas Weelkes published his celebrated geographical madrigal "Thule," a brilliantly successful attempt to convey the sense of excitement in the expanding world of Elizabethan exploration in a musical miniature. Few would disagree with Brown's verdict on the piece: "the listener surely cannot fail to wonder, and having once experienced its fascination, he cannot but return to it again and again to marvel."[10] A case could be made for seeing in "Thule," and its second part "The Andalusian Merchant," a response to the earlier Wilbye pieces. The text set by Weelkes has much more impact with its choice of colorful imagery and its use of the personal pronoun "I," but its message is, in essence, that of the Wilbye lyric: that the human condition is indeed stranger than the most exotic novelties of distant climes. There are other, possibly fortuitous, points of comparison: both madrigals comprise a linked pair; both occupy the same position in their respective collections.

The text of "Thule" is every bit as remarkable as the musical setting, memorable for its word painting and strange but effective chromaticism. It contains an abundance of allusions, historical and contemporary, which deserve careful scrutiny:

[6]Ibid., 67.

[7]For references to amber in Mozambique, see C. R. Boxer, *The Tragic History of the Sea 1589–1622* (*HS*, 2nd series, vol. 112; Cambridge, 1959), 66, 265–70.

[8]Tiele (1885), 177.

[9]Ibid., 157.

[10]D. Brown, *Thomas Weelkes: a Biographical and Critical Study* (London, 1969).

Thule, the period of cosmography,
Doth vaunt of Hecla, whose sulphurious fire
Doth melt the frozen clime and thaw the sky;
Trinacrian AEtna's flames ascend not higher.
These things seems wondrous, yet more wondrous I,
Whose heart with fear doth freeze, with love doth fry.

The Andalusian merchant, that returns
Laden with cochineal and China dishes,
Reports in Spain how strangely Fogo burns
Amidst an ocean full of flying fishes.
These things seem wondrous, yet more wondrous I,
Whose heart with fear doth freeze, with love doth fry.[11]

The concept of a remote northern island known as Thule, or Thyle to the classical civilizations, was well known in the late sixteenth century. Its origins can be traced back to a voyage made by Pytheas of Marseilles in the fourth century B.C.[12] Details of this historic journey are shrouded in mystery, but it seems to be agreed that Pytheas coasted up the western seaboard of Europe, crossed from France to Cornwall, and then circumnavigated Great Britain. His contact with Thule, which he is reported to have described as six days to the north of Britain, only a day from the frozen sea, is much debated. It is not known for certain whether he made the journey himself, or whether he heard of the island while in northern Scotland. Despite the contemptuous rejection of Pytheas as an out-and-out liar by the geographer Strabo[13], the belief that there was an island located at the utmost part of the northern world gained widespread credence. Ptolemy placed Thule unambiguously on the parallel 63° North, the boundary of his *terra cognita*.[14] The tradition persisted through the Middle Ages in the writings of Bede, Roger Bacon, and Pierre d'Ailly[15]. Then, in the sixteenth century, translations of the works of Greek and Roman writers gave it renewed currency. Elizabethan readers might have encountered it in Pliny, Seneca, or Virgil,

[11]Fellowes (1967), 293.

[12]J. O. Thomson, *History of Ancient Geography* (Cambridge, 1948), 143–51.

[13]Ibid., 194.

[14]D. B. Quinn, *New American World: A Documentary History of North America to 1612;* vol. 1, *America from Concept to Discovery. Early Exploration of North America* (London, 1979), 10.

[15]Ibid., 29.

or in citations from such authors in the contemporary literature of cosmography. Seneca's allusion to Thule in Act 2 of *Medea* was particularly intriguing because of its apparently prescient hint of lands to be discovered beyond the known world. The following translation by Sir John Heywood was published in 1581:

> And Typhis will some newe founde Land survay
> Some travelers shall the Countreys farre escrye,
> Beyonde small Thule, knowen furthest at this day.[16]

But above all it was a widely cited phrase from Virgil's *Georgics* (I, 30) which represented for Elizabethan cosmographers classical Thule. In the English translation of 1589, the words are rendered "the utmost island *Thule*."[17] Virgil's "ultima Thule" was perhaps the direct inspiration for the first line of the madrigal.

Maps of the world drawn up according to the principles of Ptolemy often positioned Thule at the very top.[18] These visual representations, widely circulated in the fifteenth and sixteenth centuries, powerfully reinforced the aura of remoteness associated with the island, and yet it must be stressed they bore no resemblance to the world as it was known in Weelkes's day. Recent explorations by Davis in Greenland, and by Barentz in Novaya Zemlya and Spitzbergen, had opened up areas far to the north of Iceland, and maps showing the current state of knowledge were readily available. Michael Lok's map, published by Hakluyt in *Divers Voyages touching the discoverie of America* (London, 1582), shows how much was known even before the aforementioned explorers set out. A popular little manual of geography, published the year before Weelkes's madrigal, put the classical tradition of Thule in its true perspective. George Abbot wrote in his *A Briefe Description of the Whole World* (London, 1599):

> Very farre to the North in the same clymate, almost with Sweeden that is under the very circle arctick, lyeth *Izeland*, called in olde time *Thulae*, which was then supposed to be the farthest part of the world Northward, and therefore is called by Virgil, *Ultima Thule*.[19]

[16]Ibid., 8.

[17]*The Georgiks of Publius Virgilius Maro* (London, 1589), 2.

[18]Quinn (1979).

[19]fol. D.

The first line of Weelkes's madrigal text thus invokes not the real world of 1600, but the world of traditional cosmography with its blend of legend and reality as represented by classical geographers and medieval tradition.

The subject of the first part of the madrigal is the great volcano of Hecla. Early descriptions of the mountain in English sources rely on fantastic medieval legends of the kind propounded by Sebastian Münster and Jacob Ziegler. The following excerpt from William Cuningham's *The Cosmographical Glasse* (London, 1559) is typical:

> Island called of Ptolomy Thyle, is an Ilande subiecte to the king of Denmarke: it is full of marvailous thinges to beholde. Amonge which ther are iij. mountaines of an incredible height: the toppes of which ar continually covered with snow . . . Hecla, which continually (like to the mountaine [E]tna) doeth burne, casting with violence (as it were out of a Gunne) greate stones from it. And this fire can not be quenched, and that which is to be wondred, although the fire be marveylus great and of force, by reason of the sulphure, yet haye strawe, or rede, is not of it consumed.[20]

A strikingly similar passage in Richard Eden's *The Decades of the newe worlde or west India* (London, 1555) describes the "strange miracles of nature" to be found on Hecla.[21] Everywhere in these descriptions are echoes of Weelkes's lyric: the sulphurious fire; the frozen clime; the traditional comparison with Etna; and above all the tone of wonder.

The traditional view of Iceland's geography remained unchallenged until, in 1598, Hakluyt published an English translation of Arngrim Jonas's discourse on Iceland under the title: "A Briefe Commentarie of Island: wherin the errors of such as have written concerning this Island, are detected, and the slanders, and reproches of certaine strangers, which they have used over-boldly against the people of Island are confuted."[22] As an inhabitant of Iceland, he writes with indignation at the persistent misrepresentation of his country. His polemic represents the final confrontation between the myths of medieval cosmography and the realities of late renaissance geography. In the words of Taylor, "continuously flaming mountains, strange fountains and mouths of hell must make way for authentic volcanoes, geysers, and lava streams."[23] Step by step, Jonas strips

[20]fol. 175.

[21]E. Arber, *The first three English books on America* (London, 1895), 300.

[22]Hakluyt, 4:89–194.

[23]E. G. R. Taylor, *Late Tudor and Early Stuart Geography 1583–1650* (London, 1934), 31.

away the accumulation of myth. Hecla is not continually burning: "whosoever they be that have ascribed unto Hecla perpetuall belching out of flames, they are farre besides the marke."[24] Icelandic chronicles, he reports, record major eruptions only two or three times a century. He is contemptuously dismissive of the belief that straw will not burn in the fire: "there is no man with us so rashly and fondly curious, that dareth for his life, the hill being on fire, trie any such conclusions, or (to our knowledge) that ever durst."[25] He turns the traditional comparison between Hecla and Etna very effectively against those who claim supernatural causes for the Icelandic phenomena: "But to returne to Munster, who endevouring to search out the causes of the great and strange fire of that famous hill Aetna, is it not monstrous that the very same thing which he there maketh natural, he should here imagine to be preternaturall, yea infernal?"[26] The publication of this vigorous tirade against the hallowed myths of Iceland made her great volcano a subject of much discussion in late Elizabethan England. The madrigal lyric, one manifestation of this interest, inclines, doubtless for poetic reasons, towards the traditional view—"These things seem wondrous."

In the second part of the madrigal, the world of traditional cosmography gives way to the realities of late sixteenth-century voyaging, with a Spanish merchant returning home with news of another volcano. The location of "Fogo," a fiery island in a tropical sea, has already received some scholarly attention. Fellowes interpreted the passage as "the mysterious scene of the distant volcano in remote Terra del Fuego as viewed from the sea."[27] This suggestion was rejected by Milne [28] on the grounds that: (i) there are no volcanoes in this region known to have been active in historic times; (ii) it is far too cold in the Cape Horn region for flying fish; (iii) merchants did not use that route to China in the sixteenth century. (This last point seems to be based on the assumption that China dishes were imported into Europe only via the Cape of Good Hope, which is untrue.) Milne listed nine places called "Fogo" or "Fuego" and argued correctly that Weelkes's "Fogo" was the island of that name

[24]Hakluyt, 4:109.

[25]Ibid., 110.

[26]Ibid., 116.

[27]Fellowes (1921), 203.

[28]J. G. C. Milne, "On the Identity of Weelkes 'Fogo'," *RMARC*, vol. 10 (1972), 98.

in the Cape Verde group, off the tip of West Africa, an identification previously made by Tovey.[29]

Even a cursory glance at Elizabethan travel literature shows that Fuego Island, a spectacular near-perfect volcanic cone rising out of the Atlantic some 9,000 feet, was very well known indeed to English sailors. The first English ships to pass the island regularly were probably the Guinea traders of the 1560s. In his account of a voyage to Guinea and the Cape Verde Islands in 1566, George Fenner wrote:

> In this Island is a marveilous high hill which doth burne continually, and the inhabitants reported that about three yeeres past the whole Island was like to be burned with the abundance of fire that came out of it.[30]

Descriptions of the island's fiery wonders occur in several accounts of Elizabethan ships bound for the West Indies or the South Seas, as indeed (often in close proximity) do reports of flying fish. In narratives of Drake's circumnavigation, references to flying fish follow the description of the volcano:

> The same night wee came with the Island called by the Portugals, Ilha del fogo, that is, the burning Island: in the Northside whereof is a consuming fire, the matter is sayde to be of sulphure, but notwithstanding it is like to bee a commodious Island, because the Portugals have built, and doe inhabit there. . . . Being departed from these Islands, we drew towards the line, where wee were becalmed the space of 3. weekes, but yet subject to divers great stormes, terrible lightnings and much thunder; but with this miserie we had the commoditie of great store of fish as Dolphins, Bonitos and flying fishes, whereof some fell into our shippes, wherehence they could not rise againe for want of moisture, for when their wings are drie, they cannot flie.[31]

Edward Cliffe's account follows very similar lines. He refers to Fogo Island "so called, because it casteth continually flames of fire, and smoake out of the top thereof," and to "flying fishes in great abundance, some a foote long, some lesse."[32] By the end of the century, the volcano and the spectacle of flying fish had become com-

[29] D. F. Tovey, *Essays in Musical Analysis*; vol. 5, *Vocal Music* (London, 1937), 10.

[30] Hakluyt, 6:279.

[31] Hakluyt, 11:106.

[32] Ibid., 152.

monplace in the catalogue of sights associated with voyaging through the tropical regions of the Atlantic. Many Elizabethans would have recognized the madrigal lyric's subject matter from their general reading, even, in some cases, from their own experiences.

Of the two commodities with which Weelkes's "Andalusian merchant" was laden, cochineal was the more significant by far in economic terms.[33] A brilliant red dye produced from insects found only on a species of cactus indigenous to Central America, cochineal was superior to any of the red dyes previously available in Europe and was thus a greatly prized product. It was imported from the New World into Seville and Cadiz on Spanish ships. Lee describes cochineal as "one of the best-kept trade secrets of all time." In the late sixteenth-century, Englishmen could only guess at how it was produced. The instructions for Frobisher's 1578 expedition, drawn up by the elder Hakluyt, made the common mistake of assuming it to be the product of a berry: "if you can find the berrie of Cochinile with which we colour stammelles, or any Root, Berrie, Fruite wood or earth fit for dying, you win a notable thing fitte for our state of cloathing." The English cloth industry had a voracious appetite for cochineal, and although some legitimate trade in the dye continued during the period after the defeat of the Armada in 1588, cochineal became one of the targets of English privateers who preyed upon Spanish shipping from the West Indies. Seizures of cochineal were thus a subject of great topical interest in the 1590s. Among many references which might be cited, there are several in Hakluyt. In a report of the capture of a Spanish ship in 1591, for example, Robert Flicke refers to his prize as "laden with hides cochonillio, and certaine raw silke."[34] He later took on board "two and forty chestes of Cochonillio and silkes." In a translation of Linschoten's account of the privateering exploits of Cumberland, Frobisher, and Grenville, we read of fourteen ships from the Spanish West Indies arriving at Tercera "laden with Cochenile, Hides, Gold, Silver, Pearles, and other rich wares."[35] Although some cochineal was taken from Portuguese ships returning from the East (such as the *Madre de Dios* captured in 1592), the great bulk of the trade was conducted across the Atlantic.

[33]The following details about cochineal come from R. L. Lee, "American Cochineal in European Commerce, 1526–1625," *JMH*, vol. 23 (1951), 205–24.

[34]Hakluyt, 7:59.

[35]Ibid., 66.

The traditional view—that the "China dishes" carried by the merchant ship of the madrigal text indicate the author had in mind a ship returning from the East—is at first sight plausible. At this period, the word "china" referred to the country of origin of porcelain, not, as it later did, to its method of manufacture. China dishes, moreover, were indeed being imported on Portuguese ships from the East Indies. The *Madre de Dios*, for instance, was carrying "porcellan vessels of China."[36] It is a surprising fact, however, that much of the porcelain picked up by English privateers, came from the Spanish West Indies or from ships returning thence. In 1565, Andres de Urdaneta made the first successful passage from the Spanish colony in the Philippines across the Pacific to Mexico. As a direct result of this voyage, the Spanish authorities instituted the Acapulco Galleon, an annual sailing between Manila and Mexico, which was doubtless the source of most of the China dishes seen by Englishmen there. In 1572, Henry Hawkes, an English merchant who lived for several years in New Spain, wrote a report of the commodities of the country only seven years after the trade across the Pacific had been established. He makes it very clear that the newly-imported Chinaware was very highly prized:

> They have in this port of Navidad ordinarily their ships, which goe to the Islands of China which are certaine Islands which they have found within these 7. yeres. They have brought from thence gold, and much Cinamon, and dishes of earth, and cups of the same, so fine, that every man that may have a piece of them, will give the weight of silver for it.[37]

In 1579, Drake captured a cargo from China while sailing up the west coast of South America: "not long after [we] met with a ship laden with linnen cloth and fine China-dishes of white earth, and great store of China-silks, of all which things wee tooke as we listed."[38] By the time of Drake's West Indian venture of 1585, porcelain was widely used in the area. The author of *A Summarie and True Discourse* (London, 1589) describes the use of Chinaware on the Island of Hispaniola:

[36]Ibid., 117.

[37]Hakluyt, 9:392.

[38]Hakluyt, 11:117.

> There was but little plate or vessell of silver, in comparison of the great pride in other things of this towne, because in these hote countreyes they use much of these earthen dishes finely painted or varnished, which they call Parsellina, and is had out of the East India . . . .

The allusions to the Island of Fuego, cochineal, and porcelain in the second part of Weelkes's madrigal lyric are strongly redolent of the world of Elizabethan privateering at the height of the Anglo-Spanish war during the 1590s, a period which saw Cumberland, Frobisher, Grenville, Raleigh, and others preying upon treasure ships of the Portuguese and Spanish fleets as they made their way along the trade routes, past the Azores and the Cape Verde Islands. Having evoked the very different worlds of geographical myth and contemporary privateering, the author of "Thule" makes his point with a flourish; the images of fire and ice fade before the yet greater wonders of the human heart.

The authenticity of these two small pen-portraits raises the possibility that their author was someone with personal knowledge of late Elizabethan privateering. Biographical details of Weelkes's early years are scanty, but it has long been surmised that the composer was connected in some way with the influential London circle of Sir Walter Raleigh. The evidence comes in the *Balletts and Madrigals* of 1598, in which Weelkes, addressing Edward Darcy, a prominent member of the Raleigh faction, acknowledged "one of your worship's least labours . . . the entertaining into your service the least proficient in music . . . ."[39] The exact length of time Weelkes spent in Darcy's service is unknown, but it presumably came to an end with his Winchester appointment in late 1598. As one of Raleigh's most active lieutenants, Darcy occupied rooms in Durham House, his leader's London residence, which in the late 1590s would have been a hotbed of activity in the cause of Raleigh's Atlantic voyaging. This was reaching its peak with the Expedition to Cadiz (1596) and the Islands Voyage (1597), and the explorations of Guiana in 1595, 1596, and 1597. As a servant of Darcy—that is how the composer described himself in the 1598 dedication—Weelkes would certainly have come into contact with the Durham House clique, and it is even conceivable he could have been engaged as a musician on one of the voyages. His age (he was about twenty) and his musical experience (he had been

[39]G. A. Philipps, "Patronage in the Career of Thomas Weelkes," *MQ*, vol. 62 (1976), 46.

studying music for about ten years) would certainly have qualified him for a post in an Elizabethan flagship. Whether or not he ever set foot in a sailing ship, we shall never know, but what does seem probable is that the author of the madrigal text, probably someone in the same circle, was inspired by two events which would have been the talk of Durham House in early 1598.

In September 1597, towards the end of the Islands Voyage, Raleigh captured three Spanish ships returning from Havana which were, according to the account in Purchas, "laden with Cochynella and other rich Merchandize."[40] This seizure of cochineal was by far the largest made in the sixteenth century, and it enabled the Queen to reward Essex, who led the expedition with Raleigh, with a valuable concession. It was the talk of London. On 26 January 1598, Robert Whyte wrote enviously to Sir Robert Sidney that Essex had been given all the "cuccinelloe" at 18s per pound, its true value being 30s or 40s.[41] So great was the haul, enough to supply London merchants for several years, that Essex was granted a two-year monopoly. During the period of the concession, any cochineal entering the Port of London had either to be re-exported or else was impounded.[42] The capture of the Havana cochineal fleet may very well have been the inspiration for the "Andalusian merchant" of the madrigal text. The poet John Donne, who sailed on this voyage, also alluded to the cochineal seizure in his fourth *Satyre*:

> As Pirats, which doe know
> That there come weak ships fraught with
> Cutchanell
> The men board them.[43]

The poem has been dated to the period of the Islands Voyage in 1597 with the help of its—for Donne—unusually topical reference to the "losse of Amyens."[44]

[40]Purchas, 19:128.

[41]*HMC: Report on the Manuscripts of Lord de L'Isle and Dudley*, vol. 2 (London, 1934), 311.

[42]*HMC: Calendar of the Manuscripts of the Most Hon. Marquis of Salisbury*, vol. 8 (London, 1899), 36.

[43]W. Milgate, ed., *John Donne: The Satires, Epigrams and Verse Letters* (Oxford, 1967), 20.

[44]H. J. C. Grierson, *The Poems of John Donne* (Oxford, 1912), II:104.

Interestingly enough, there is reason to believe that the Island of Fuego would also have been the subject of comment in Raleigh's circle at this period. As part of his continuing interest in the exploration of Guiana, Raleigh sent a single ship across the Atlantic early in 1597. As his men made their way down the coast of Africa prior to the crossing, they met up with Benjamin Wood's ships bound for the Straits of Magellan, and two French ships of the West Indian fleet. The English captains were invited to a feast on board the French flagship where, apparently on the spur of the moment, "after great cheere and kinde entertainment" it was decided "to take the Isle of Fogo, if God would give us leave."[45] After a day or two, however, the effects of the alcohol having worn off, wiser councils prevailed, and the fleets went their various ways. The merits of this abortive plan to seize Fuego from the Portuguese would surely have been debated by Raleigh's henchmen when his ship returned from Guiana in June 1597.

In Weelkes's *Ayeres or Phantasticke Spirites* (1608), there are further hints of his connections with the Raleigh faction. The air "Come, sirrah Jack, ho!" mentions a type of tobacco imported from Trinidad:

> I swear that this tobacco
> It's perfect Trinidado.[46]

Lying off the mouth of the Orinoco, the island featured in Raleigh's Guiana schemes was visited by his ships in 1595 and 1596.[47] There is also, as Craig Monson has pointed out, a reference to a "Friday Street" in the enigmatic piece "The Ape, the Monkey and the Baboon," which could be interpreted as an allusion to the Mermaid Tavern, a well-known haunt of Raleigh's sympathizers. That Weelkes knew of the tavern (and possibly even frequented it) is suggested not only by this allusion, but by the fact that his madrigal "Grace my lovely one" is dedicated to Sir Frances Stewart of whom Anthony à Wood wrote: "He was a learned Gentleman was one of Sir *Walt. Raleigh's* Club at the *Meremaid* Tavern in *Fryday-Street* in *London*.[48] Taking together the evidence of his patrons and the possible allusions in his music, there

[45]Hakluyt, 11:2.

[46]Fellowes (1967), 296.

[47]Long before Raleigh's explorations, Guiana had become the assumed location of the mythical golden-clad man—"El Dorado." Upon the slenderest evidence which was in no way borne out by contemporary exploration, Guiana had become synonomous with opulence. Wilbye's madrigal in *The Triumphs of Oriana* (1601), for example: "The Lady Oriana was dight all in the treasures of Guiana."

[48]C. Monson, "Thomas Weelkes: a new Fa-la," *MT*, vol. 113 (1972), 133.

now seems a very strong, if still circumstantial case for the composer's Raleigh connections.

The geographical imagery so brilliantly set by Weelkes in "Thule" might have inspired other composers to draw upon what could have been a fruitful source of material for word painting, but there were no imitations. The very originality of the underlying idea and the individuality of its treatment perhaps deterred others. In his *Second Set of Madrigales* (1609), Wilbye did not return to the subject of Eastern trade. The only allusion to the riches of the Orient—a conventional one—comes when the repose of the human soul is likened to a jewel "which no Indian mines, Can buy . . . ."[49]

A desultory interest in matters maritime surfaces on a more popular level in Ravenscroft's *Pammelia* and *Deuteromelia* of 1609. Two of the three traditional recreations of the sailor—drink and dance—are the subjects of "O Portsmouth it is a gallant town" and "We be three poor mariners."[50] The colorful technical vocabulary of the sailor is deployed in one song:

> The wind blows out of the west, thou gentle mariner-a;
> Look to the luff well, beware the lee still,
> For deadly rocks do now appear-a.
> Look to thy tack!
> Let bowling go slack!
> So shall we 'scape them and go clear.
> Tarra tan tarra!
> Steer well thy course, sirra!
> The wind waxeth large, the sheets do thou veer,
> Go fill the can, give us some beer;
> I'll drink thee,
> I'll brinks thee,
> My mates, what cheer![51]

But composed polyphony of any kind, even as light-hearted as this, was not the natural outlet for the musical celebration of England's achievements as a naval power; the broadside ballad served this function.

[49]Fellowes, 312.
[50]Ibid., 213 and 223.
[51]Ibid., 210.

The subjects of naval and military ballads were predictably patriotic—expressions of joy at victory or of outrage at any "bloody massacre" perpetrated by the enemy. Trumpeters, drummers, and fifers feature prominently. In *The Queen's Visiting of the Camp at Tilbury* (1588), sung to the tune of Wilson's Wild, a "noise" of trumpets pays homage:

> The Sargeant trumpet with his mase
> And nyne with trumpets after him;
> Bare headed went before her grace,
> In coats of scarlet colour trim.[52]

The value of martial music in improving morale is a pervasive theme. *Of ioyful triumphs I must speak* (1599), which relates the doings of the Earl of Essex in Ireland, is typical:

> The drummes and fyfts, with ioyfull sound,
> Did make much musicke on that ground,
> Wherby no feare[ful] heart was found
> amongst our souldiers of *England*.[53]

The true and perfecte Newes of the woorthy and valiaunt exploytes, performed and doone by that valiant Knight Syr Francis Drake (1587) takes up another favorite theme—the musical reception of the conquering hero—in this instance, Drake returning from Santo Domingo:

> Then when aboord their shippes they come,
> They were receyved ioyfully:
> A peale of Gunnes with thundring soune,
> For one houre space even pearst the skie.
> Theyr Drumes strooke up their Trumpets sound
> Theyr victories which doo abound.

The heroic fantasy of the life of trumpeters and drummers purveyed in such ballads represents the one-sided view of the propagandist. Naval ballads doubtless played some part in recruitment—volunteers being, as always, preferable to pressed men.

[52]F. O. Mann, *The Works of Thomas Deloney* (Oxford, 1912), 474.

[53]A. Clark, *The Shirburn Ballads 1585–1616* (Oxford, 1907), 325.

CHAPTER 16

Attitudes to Non-European Cultures in Travellers' Reports

In a long list of sights to be noted by travellers in their journals, the author of *Certaine briefe and speciall Instructions* (London, 1589) includes "musicall instrumentes, publicke and private, with their inventions, varieties, names, sweetenesse of harmonie, and first authors." Descriptions of the music and musical instruments of the peoples of America, Africa and Asia do indeed survive in abundance in the journals of Englishmen at this period, if rarely with the degree of detail envisaged in this manual, and they constitute an important resource for the ethnomusicologist. Descriptive material of this kind requires care in its interpretation. As Harrison pointed out in the introduction to his anthology of source readings[1], the criteria for judging the accuracy of such reports must include an assessment of the observer's motives, opportunities, qualifications and methods. In particular, it is necessary to identify and take into account any out-moded presuppositions—concepts, for example, of "purity" or "progress"—that colour the views of earlier observers, while at the same time acknowledging that quality of description is not related to absence of prejudice. Perhaps the factor most strongly influencing the tone and content of travellers' reports is the motivation of the writer. Harrison identified the major categories: professional and proselytising christians; and men seeking information for the purposes of trade or settlement.

[1]F. Harrison, *Time, Place and Music: An Anthology of Ethnomusicological Observations c. 1550 to c. 1800* (Amsterdam, 1973), preface. See also P.V. Bohlman: "Missionaries, Magical Muses, and Magnificent Menageries: Image and Imagination in the Early History of Ethnomusicology," *The World of Music*, vol. 30, no. 3 (1988), 5–27.

The medieval traditions of pilgrimage to the Holy Land had given Englishmen a certain level of familiarity with instruments of the Near East. Their first sustained experience of musical cultures further afield, however, did not come until the mid 16th century. The motivation behind English exploration at this period was the quest for eastern trade, an ever more urgent preoccupation of the advocates of a colonial policy. Of the four possible sea routes, the first to be tried was the north-eastern passage. It was realised soon enough that China could not be reached in this direction, but as a result of Chancellor's somewhat fortuitous arrival at Moscow, the Russia Company was formed to promote trade in the area. The musical cultures of Russia and the peoples to the north were thus among the first to be reported by English travellers.

One of the most remarkable expeditions of the period was Stephen Borough's north-eastern voyage. With only eight men, he sailed up to Novaya Zemlya. One of his crew, Richard Johnson, left certain notes, "unperfectly written" which contain an extended description of the ritual of the Samish people of Lapland:

> And first the Priest doeth beginne to playe upon a thing like to a great sieve, with a skinne on the one ende like a drumme: and the sticke that he playeth with is about a spanne long, and one ende is round like a ball, covered with the skinne of an Harte. Also the Priest hath upon his head a thing of white like a garlande, and his face is covered with a piece of a shirt of maile, with manie small ribbes, and teeth of fishes, and wilde beastes hanging on the same maile. Then hee singeth as wee use heere in Englande to hallow, whope, or showte at houndes, and the reste of the company answere him with this Owtis, Igha, Igha, Igha, and then the Priest replieth againe with his voyces. And they answere him with the selfesame wordes so manie times, that in the ende he becommeth as it were madde, and falling downe as hee were dead, having nothing on him but a shirt, lying upon his backe I might perceive him to breathe. I asked them why hee lay so, and they answered mee, Nowe doth our God tell him what wee shall doe, and whither wee shall goe. And when he had lyen still a litle while, they cried thus three times together, Oghao, Oghao, Oghao, and as they use these three calles, hee riseth with his head and lieth downe againe, and then hee rose up and sang with like voyces as hee did before: and his audience answered him Igha, Igha, Igha.[2]

[2]Hakluyt, 2:347.

In many ways this lengthy account of a shamanic ritual (only an extract is given here) is typical of the kind of report made by poorly educated seamen. Doubtless Johnson would have concurred with his editor's use of the phrase "devilish rites" to describe what he had seen, yet the vivid, unpretentious language and its author's eye for detail make for an eyewitness account of value. Emphasis is placed on the physical description of the drum and its place in the ritual. An effort is made, through the analogy with English hunting cries and the attempted transcription of the calls, to convey the distinctive Samish manner of singing, which is characterised by the frequent use of glottal stops.[3] What Johnson does not essay—few writers do—is to describe the music itself. Even trained musicians rarely felt able to comment on the technical details of an unfamiliar musical language.

Mid 16th-century English travellers to the Russian capital were fascinated by the liturgy of the Orthodox church, a subject of obvious interest in contemporary England. Chancellor's account of his voyage in 1553 betrays a forthright protestant attitude which is characteristic of its period. Russian religion, he opines, is conducted with "such excesse of superstition, as the like hathe not bene heard of." He notes the importance of icons and observes that during the services men do not sit "but gagle and ducke like so many Geese."[4] The author of the account of the return home of the Russian ambassador in 1557 amusingly comments that people bow and knock their heads so often "that some will have knobbes upon their foreheads with knocking, as great as egges."[5]

The best Elizabethan account of Russia is Giles Fletcher's *The Russe Common Wealth* (London, 1591) which is based on the author's personal experiences of the country. Fletcher is a candid observer—so much so that the Russia Company tried to have his work suppressed, as endangering their interests[6]—and he makes no secret of what he considers the errors of the Orthodox church, but his descriptions of ceremonial are matter-of-fact in tone and do not seem

[3] A. Lüderwaldt, "Samish music," *The New Grove*, ed. S. Sadie (London, 1980), XVI:449.

[4] Hakluyt, 2:236.

[5] Ibid., 443.

[6] E. A. Bond, *Russia at the Close of the Sixteenth Century* (*HS*, vol. 20; London, 1856), 352–55.

to be unduly influenced by his own religious persuasion. He has little to say of the music itself but is greatly impressed by the manner of chanting and singing. Readings are sung "with a playne singing note, not unlike to the Popish tune when they soung their gospels."[7] On festival days, the Te Deum is sung "with a more solemne and curious note." After the Magnificat: "the priest, deacons, and people, all with one voice sing, '*Aspody Pomelui*,' or 'Lord have mercy upon us' thirty times together. Whereunto the boyes that are in the church answere all with one voyce, rowling it up so fast as their lippes can goe: - 'Verij, verij, verij, verij,' or, 'Prayse, prayse, prayse, prayse,' etc., thirty times together, with a very straunge noyse."[8] In his detailed account of the coronation ceremonies of the Russian Tzar, Fletcher's attention is once again caught by the vocal quality of the singing, especially when anything unusual or dramatic is heard, such as when the priests and deacons "chaunt and thunder out, singing: *Many years to the noble Theodore*."[9]

The most visible and audible musical performances in 16th-century Russia were provided by military bands. For obvious reasons, the disposition of armed forces was a subject of interest to travellers of all kinds, and descriptions of military musicians abound. Fletcher comments briefly on their instruments:

> They have drummes besides of a huge bignesse, which they carry with them upon a boarde layde on foure horses, that are sparred together with chaines, every drumme having eight strikers or drummers, besides trumpets and shawmes, which they sounde after a wilde manner, much different from ours. When they give any charge, or make any invasion, they make a great hallowe or shoute altogether as loude as they can, which with the sound of their trumpets, shawmes, and drummes, maketh a confused and horrible noyse.[10]

From the Middle Ages onwards, English travellers in the Near East had periodically encountered the (to them) frightening stridency of shawm bands. But with ancestral memories of the Crusades lingering long, it remained a sound that inspired fear rather than admiration.

[7]Ibid., 120.

[8]Ibid., 121.

[9]Ibid., 24–25.

[10]Ibid., 78.

Strange though its liturgical and ceremonial practices seemed to Elizabethan visitors, Russia was unmistakably a Christian country. Not so North America, where Englishmen were, for the first time, confronted with a totally alien musical world. The most striking feature of Amerindian music was its reliance on a range of unfamiliar percussive instruments, and it is not surprising that idiophones and drums feature prominently in early accounts. The only detailed description of Indian instruments comes in a report from the Virginian settlement:

> Their chief instruments are rattles made of small gourdes or pompion shells; of these they have base, tenor, counter tenor, meane and treble; these myngled with their voices, sometymes twenty or thirty togither, make such a terrible howling as would rather affright then give pleasure to any man ..... For their drums they have a great deepe platter of wood, the mouth whereof covering with a skyn, at each corner they ty a walnutt, which meeting on the back side neere the bottome, with a small cord they twitch them together untill they be so tough and stiffe, that they maye beat upon them as doe wee upon a drum, and they yield a reasonable rattling sound.[11]

As is so often the case in English accounts, the writer here is authoritative only on the technical details of construction; on the wider aspects of musical performance, the lack of specific detail betrays a lack of real comprehension. It is of course axiomatic that this kind of report tells us as much about the attitude of the observer as it does about the observed. Occasionally, as in Henry Spelman's *Relation of Virginia* one senses a sympathetic tone. He compares Indian dancing to "our darbysher Hornepipe," men and women alternating, with one man in the centre playing a pipe and a rattle.[12] On the whole, however, the music, dance and ritual of American Indians seems to have repelled early settlers. The choice of language in their reports—singing is frequently described as howling or shrieking, less commonly as "tunable"—suggests that they believed themselves to be listening to the products of a "savage" culture.[13]

With the foundation of the East India Company and the opening of a regular trade route to India, Englishmen, a century later than

[11]R. H. Major, *The Historie of Travaile into Virginia Britannia* (*HS*, vol. 6; London, 1849), 79 and 107.

[12]H. Spelman: *Relation of Virginia* (London, 1609).

[13]Major (1849), 79.

the Portuguese, encountered the equally alien but much more highly developed musical cultures of the East. Both in the coastal regions of Africa along the Company's trade routes and throughout the area of its operation in the East, as far afield as Japan, a range of exotic, hitherto unfamiliar instrumental types were "discovered" by English travellers. Their descriptions are sometimes sympathetic in tone, implying at least a recognition of the sophistication of what they heard.

Among the best early 17th-century English descriptions of African instruments are those of Richard Jobson, who prospected for gold in Gambia and published an interesting account under the title *The Golden Trade* in 1623. He refers first to an arched harp: "the most common Instrument is made of a great Gourd, and a Necke therto fastened, in some sort resembling our Bandora, the strings meane, and unfit, without frets, yet with Pinnes wound and fitted to some Harmonie." Next the drums: "with this they have a little Drum, whereon with a crooked sticke in the right hand, and the Fingers on the left, they play wringing the mouth and gaping very Deformedly." This playing method, the drums "beaten with the left hand and a pencil-sized stick in the right," is still in use today.[14] Above all, it was the gourd-resonated xylophones which attracted Jobson's attention:

> Under everie great tree, and among all their houses at night were fires without doores, and in especiall places dancing, the Musicall Instruments made with Keyes like unto Virginals, whereupon one playes with two stickes which have round Balls of leather at the end, about their wrists Iron Bracelets. They are called Ballardes, and contayne some seventeene Keyes.[15]

Elsewhere he remarks that the sound of the instrument ("one of their most ingenious Artifices") could be heard a mile away.

As a temporary visitor prospecting for gold, Jobson had neither the opportunity nor the motive for investigating more thoroughly the unusual instruments that he encountered. Longer-term Portuguese residents in Africa had both. Acceptance of certain aspects of native culture might be a matter for debate in missionary orders, but the need to understand the societies in which they lived was universally regarded as a prerequisite for successful mission. In the

[14] R. C. Knight, "Gambia," *The New Grove*, ed. S. Sadie (London, 1980), VII:140.

[15] Purchas, 6:244.

works of the two best-known Portuguese writers on African music we therefore find not only meticulous attention to the details of instrumental construction, but also an attempt to understand the function of musicians in African society. João dos Santos, a Dominican friar who spent nine years in Sofala on the east coast of Africa, exhibits in his comments on two instruments of the Mozambique area the inquisitive cast of mind, characteristic of the best missionary reporting. Writing of the gourd-resonated xylophone, he gives details of the gourds, the keys and the sticks. Of the mbira, he comments that it is: "all of iron wedges, flat and narrow, a span long, tempered in the fire to differing sounds." The wedges are "but nine set in a rew, with the ends in a piece of wood as in the necke of a viole, and hollow, on which they play with their thumbe nailes, which they weare long therefore, as lightly as men with us on the Virginals."[16]

The most perceptive observer of African music was not in fact a missionary but a colonist. Duarte de Lopes, whose account of Congo was noted down in Rome by the papal chamberlain, Filippo Pigafetta, is well known to historians of African music.[17] He describes three instruments of war—a drum, a type of triangular gong, and a wind instrument made from an elephant's tusk.[18] He further comments on their actual use in battle, to signal instructions from a captain to his subordinates and to receive back information about the disposition, weaponry and tactics of the enemy. Needless to say, this kind of information was of no mere academic interest; it would have been collected and examined by Portuguese military planners for use in future conflicts. Lopes gives a wonderfully detailed description of a lute which is worth citing at length, if only to place Jobson's account of an arched harp in a proper perspective:

> Touching their assembling together at Feasts, or other meetings of joy, as for example, when they are marryed, they sing Verses and Ballads of Love, and play upon certaine Lutes that are made after a strange

[16]Purchas, 9:209. The original source is J. dos Santos, *Ethiopia oriental e varia historia de cousas notaveis do Oriente* (Evora, 1609). On the Mbira, see, P. R. Kirby, *The Musical Instruments of South Africa* (Johannesburg, 1968), 47. See also G. Kubik, "Lamellaphone," *The New Grove*, ed. S. Sadie (London, 1980), X:401.

[17]F. Pigafetta, *Relatione del Reame di Congo* (Rome, 1591). See, A. P. Merriam, "Zaire," *The New Grove*, ed. S. Sadie (London, 1980), XX:621.

[18]Purchas, 6:434.

> fashion. For in the hollow part and in the necke they are somewhat like unto our Lutes, but for the flat side (where wee use to carve a Rose, or a Rundle to let the sound goe inward) that is made not of wood, but of a skinne, as thinne as a Bladder, and the strings are made of haires, which they draw out of the Elephants tayle, and are very strong and bright: and of certaine Threeds made of the wood of Palme-tree, which from the bottome of the Instrument do reach and ascend to the top of the handle, and are tied every one of them to his several ring. For towards the necke or handle of this Lute, there are certaine rings placed some higher and some lower, whereat there hang divers plates of Iron and Silver, which are very thinne, and in bignesse different one from another, accordinge to the proportion of the Instrument. These rings doe make a sound of sundry tunes, according to the striking of the strings. For the strings when they are stricken, doe cause the rings to shake, and then doe the plates that hang at them, helpe them to utter a certaine mingled and confused noyse. Those that play upon this Instrument, doe tune the strings in good proportion, and strike them with their fingers, like a Harpe, but without any quill very cunningly: so that they make thereby (I cannot tell whether I should call it a melodie or no, but) such a sound as pleaseth and delighteth their sences well enough. Besides all this (which is a thing very admirable) by this Instrument they doe utter the conceits of their minds, and doe understand one another so plainly, that every thing almost which may be explaned with the Tongue, they can declare with their hand in touching and striking this Instrument. To the sound thereof they doe dance in good measure with their feet, and follow the just time of that Musicke, with clapping the palmes of their hands one against the other.[19]

The point to stress here is Lopes's attempt to explain something of the significance of the instrument in Congolese society, an unusual stage beyond mere physical description.

While it is undoubtedly true that the best descriptions of non-European music in the 16th and 17th centuries are to be found in the works of missionaries and other residents with long-term interests, there are exceptions. A disinterested observer with an open mind and a quick eye for detail could provide valuable information. Such a man was Peter Mundy, the widely-travelled Cornish sea captain. From his keen interest in the construction of unfamiliar musical instruments, it might be assumed that he was an amateur musician, and this is confirmed by a passing reference to the loss of his lute

[19]Ibid., 501.

book.[20] With some musical knowledge, an inquisitive mind and a vivid writing style, Mundy produced a journal that is correctly regarded as one of the most valuable travel documents of the 17th century. In the following extract which dates from 1636, he describes the tube zither of Madagascar, the valiha:

> They are nott alltogether void off Musicke, For beesides their ordinary singuing, they have a little Instrumentt aboutt a Foote in length named Ambolo, made of a Cane. The Said Instrumentts and strings all of one peece, cutt outt off the same, being certaine thrids raised outt off the grayne off the Cane which runne from Joint to Joint, which as they would have to sound higher or lower so accordingly they Force uppe certaine little wedges, thatt are under the ends of the strings.[21]

Mundy's journal also includes a drawing of the instrument.

The relatively dispassionate approach adopted by Mundy and some other early English auditors of African music contrasts favorably with the prejudice displayed by later writers. The effect that prolonged participation in the slave trade had on English attitudes is beyond the scope of this study, but its general effect must have been to degrade African culture in the eyes of those who took part. The slaver Thomas Phillips could not conceal his contempt for what he heard in a Dutch factory on the Gold Coast and wrote with real venom: "soon after I came the musick, being three black fellows, with the like number of hollow elephants teeth ... made a hideous bellowing, another in the mean time beating a hollow piece of brass with a stick."[22] There are similar passages elsewhere in this unpleasant diary.

The first Englishmen to experience the distinctive sounds of Javanese music were the sailors of the *Golden Hind*. An account of how, in response to performances by the English consort, Drake received the Javanese "country musick" on board is tantalisingly vague: "though it were of a very strange kind; yet the sound was pleasant and delightfull." Could this have been a gamelan? Gong-chimes were the first Javanese instruments to be described in an

[20] R. C. Temple, *The Travels of Peter Mundy in Europe and Asia, 1608–1667*, vol. 5, *Travels in South-West England and Western India* (*HS*, 2nd series, vol. 78; London, 1936), 123.

[21] R. C. Temple, *The Travels of Peter Mundy in Europe and Asia, 1608–1667*, vol. 3, part 1, *Travels in England, Western India, Achin, Macao, and the Canton River, 1634–1637* (*HS*, 2nd series, vol. 45; London, 1919), 273.

[22] A. and J. Churchill, *A Collection of Voyages and Travels*, vol. 6 (London, 1732), 287.

English source. Scott, one of the factors who took up residence in Bantam in 1602 wrote:

> Their musique, which was ten or twelve pannes of Tombaga, carried upon a coulstaffe between two; these were tuneable, and every one a note above another, and alwayes two went by them which were skillfull in their Country musique, and played on them having things in their hands of purpose to strike them.[23]

His comment that these "pannes" made a "hellish sound" is perhaps reflective of the general mood of paranoia that gripped the residents of the English factory during their first precarious year.

Gongs and metallophones invariably attracted the attention of early European visitors to the East Indies. Published accounts of the first Dutch voyage to Bali include several illustrations (Plates 29 and 30). Peter Mundy, visiting Sumatra, recorded his impression of the sound of the gong:

> Another Copper Instrument called a gung, wheron they strike with a little woodden Clubbe, and although it bee butt a small Instrumentt, not much More then 1 Foote over and 1/2 Foot Deepe, yett it maketh a Deepe hollow humming sound Resembling thatt of a great bell: all the afforesaid musick Discordantt, Clamorous and full of Noise.[24]

There are relatively few detailed descriptions of Indian instruments in the many journals kept by employees of the East India Company in the early years of the 17th century. The ceremonial ensemble of the Mughals, the Naubat, which performed at set times of the day, impressed by its sheer volume of sound. As usual, Mundy's account, written during a stay in Agra, is the best by an Englishman:

> The Naubatt Conna or place where his drummes are beatinge in the Amcasse [audience chamber], over against the place where hee sitts, which att some tymes of the daye are stricken upp 20 or 25 together which makes such a noyse that the place seemes to shake with it, they being of them 4 foote diameter. There also stand his musick, as Trumpetts, pipes or hauboys.[25]

[23]Purchas, 2:484.

[24]Temple (1919), 123.

[25]R. C. Temple, *The Travels of Peter Mundy in Europe and Asia, 1608–1667*, vol. 2, *Travels in Asia, 1628–1634* (*HS*, 2nd series, vol. 35; London, 1914), 210.

Plate 29: Indonesian gongs and chime gongs seen by the Dutch expedition of 1595–1597. *D'Eerste Boeck* (Amsterdam, 1598) fol. s3. By permission of the British Library.

Plate 30. Indonesian dancers and a performer on a tube-resonated metallophone seen on the Dutch expedition of 1595–1597. *D'Eerste Boek* (Amsterdam, 1598) fol. s4. By permission of the British Library.

Mundy's eye for the telling detail is also evident in his account of the musical instruments that accompanied Shah Jehan:

> After theis came 12 paire of Copper Drummes on 12 Eliphants, the heads of some of them are 4 foote dyameter, covered with redd Cloth, which they went beatinge a leasurely stroake, jumpeing altogether. With theis went the Trumpetts of att least 8 foote long and 1 1/2 broad att the [pummell] or end, with which they make a base, hoarse hollow sound, neither riseinge nor fallinge.[26]

While he was in Agra in 1632, Mundy made a rough sketch of some dancing girls and musicians.[27] The "dauncinge wenches" are shown accompanied by a "tabor" player, "an old woman which doth only singe and clapp her hands keeping a kinde of tyme," "a fellow beating on both sides of a Drumme" and "a woman Clapping two things like Sawcers of brasse, keeping tyme also." Mundy concludes: "It is to be understood they all singe, aswell those that daunce as those that playe, all of one note, except the man who is the Diapason. Noe thirds nor fifts in Musick as I could heere." Elementary though his observation now seems, Mundy's attempt to understand the basis of Indian music shows an unusual degree of perception for the time.

The short-lived English factory in Japan provided the first opportunities for English merchants to experience the musical cultures of the Far East. Captain Saris, the first representative of the East India Company to visit Japan, observed intelligently a four-string lute, its playing method and tablature notation (see p. 161). Richard Cocks, the first resident factor, was on one occasion invited to a Noh drama. He described the great audience that assembled and then commented on the music of the bamboo flute and kotsuzumi drum:

> Their acting Musique and singing (as also their Poetry) is very harsh to us, yet they keepe due time both with hands and feet. Their Musique is little Tabers, made great at both ends, and smal in the middest, like to an Houre-glasse, they beating on the end with one hand, and straine the cords which goe about it, with the other, which maketh it to sound great or small as they list, according their voices with it, one playing on a Phife or Flute; but all harsh, and not pleasant to our hearing.[28]

[26]Ibid., 199.

[27]Ibid., 217.

[28]Purchas, 3:543. For an introduction to the music of the Noh, see W. P. Malm, *Japanese Music and Musical Instruments* (Rutland, Vermont and Tokyo, 1959), 105–31.

From 1615 Cocks kept a detailed diary which shows that he had many opportunities to listen to Japanese and Chinese musicians. On 8 September 1616 he dined at the house of a Japanese merchant who provided "women plears, who danced and songe."[29] On 23 November he was again entertained by women "with their musick."[30] At Nagasaki, Cocks was present at a performance of Chinese music, organised by a merchant known to the Englishmen as Captain Whaw or Whow. On 27 February 1618 Cocks wrote: "We were envited to Capt. Whaw, the China, to dyner, where we were extraordenarely entertayned, with musick at our entry, with the lyke at first, second, and therd course, where there wanted not wyne of all sortes..."[31] A few days later Cocks sent a gift "to the China musitions which plaid at Capt. Whows when we weare at dyner."[32]

Two attitudes may be discerned in the reports of English travellers in their accounts of non-European musical cultures, the one essentially positive, the other wholly negative. Peter Mundy's journal is a fine example of the former, adopted by those for whom the strangeness of the new was its main delight. Much more common, however, especially once the novelty of the overseas experience began to wear off, was an attitude of contemptuous rejection. A ripe specimen of this point of view was the English traveller Thomas Coryat. Admittedly an eccentric, the laughing-stock, indeed, of his age, Coryat delighted in pouring scorn on the "very ridiculous and squeaking musicke" that he encountered during his wanderings. His language is comical. He complains of some singers that their "yelling and disorderly squeaking did even grate mine ears."[33] That such an attitude, expressed albeit in less exaggerated terms, should have come to predominate, is partly explained by the scale of the barriers to understanding an unfamiliar musical culture. Casual attempts to investigate further were doomed in the absence of any workable methodology. Just how ludicrous amateur "research" could be is shown by Henry Blount's farcical attempt to investigate the musicality of Turkish string players:

[29]E. M. Thompson, *The Diary of Richard Cocks*, vol. 1 (*HS*, vol. 66; London, 1883), 173.

[30]Ibid., 211.

[31]Ibid., 2:19.

[32]Ibid., 21.

[33]Purchas, 10:418.

> The *Musicke* of *Turkey* is worth consideration; through all those vast Dominions there runnes one tune, and for ought I hard, no more, nor can every man play that; yet scarce any but hath a *fiddle,* with two strings, and at Feasts, and other meetings, will confidently play upon it, but hee knowes not to what tune, nor can play the same twice over; this I'm sure of; for to make experiment, I have ventured to play at divers meetings, pretending the ayers of my Countrey, to note whether they had skill or no, and tooke so well as they have often made me play againe; then I found their skill and mine alike, for I never understood the least touch of any instrument; Nothing could more disguise their *Genius* unto me, who was used to guesse at the *fansies* of men by the ayres wherewith I found them most taken, almost as much as by their discourse.[34]

Needless to say, we learn nothing of Turkish string playing from this other than the fact of its existence.

[34]H. Blount, *A Voyage into the Levant* (London, 1636), 106.

CHAPTER 17

An Episode of Acculturation: The "Hindostannie Air"

One final issue remains to be discussed in this study of English musicians overseas: the question of whether the geographical proximity of colonial English musical culture to the civilisations of the New World and the East produced any lasting change in either. The phenomenon to be considered here is that of "acculturation," the process whereby one culture adopts and assimilates elements from another. The following definition was accepted by the American Social Science Research Council: "Acculturation comprehends those phenomena which result when groups of individuals having different cultures come into continuous first-hand contact with subsequent changes in the original cultural patterns of either or both groups."[1] Throughout the Hispanic world, acculturation was unquestionably the most significant musical consequence of the age of colonization, with a vigorous process of interchange between settler, black slave and native inhabitant. Yet, with one interesting exception to be discussed below, in the English settlements the process seems hardly to have started.[2] The worldwide influence of English and American popular culture is a phenomenon of the age of mass communication only. Even in the nineteenth century, when the commercial, military and political influence of the English nation was approaching its zenith, cross-fertilization with the musical cultures of her Empire was still negligible.

[1]G. Chase, *A Guide to the Music of Latin America*, 2nd ed. (Washington, 1962), 14.
[2]Ibid., 16.

Mission was, as we have seen time and again throughout this study, crucial to the process. In the Catholic colonies generations of young people at their most impressionable age received instruction in the Christian faith and its associated music. After intensive and sustained efforts of this kind, which in effect provided the conditions in which representatives of two cultures could "come into continuous first-hand contact," musical instruments, forms and styles did begin to cross ethnic boundaries, becoming in some cases genuine and valued parts of the cultural heritage of recipient societies. Anthropologists have drawn attention to the unacceptable methods (bribery and intimidation) adopted by some members of missionary orders, but the process of change itself is neither regarded as a moral evil nor (necessarily) as a factor contributing to impoverishment.[3]

Experience in the Hispanic colonies showed that political dominance was essential to the success of mission and thus to the process of acculturation itself. Where a powerful presence was established, as in Latin America, missionaries, despite periods of conflict with the state, did eventually succeed in imposing theirs as the dominant faith; where missions had to work without political influence, as was often the case in the East, their success was correspondingly limited. For a time in the late 16th century, Portuguese missions in Japan seemed to be on the point of creating the conditions necessary for significant and long-lasting European influence on Japanese society, yet they lacked effective support in the centres of political power and were thus extremely vulnerable. With the advent of politically hostile forces, the edifice was utterly shattered in the space of a few years, and only the faintest traces of a covert Christian legacy were discovered when Japan finally re-opened her frontiers in the nineteenth century.[4] In India it was only in the coastal territories actually administered by Portugal that the process of acculturation had any long-term effect, with the Goanese adopting Portuguese instruments, song-forms and dances. Further inland, the Jesuit missions in the heartlands of Mughal power at Agra and Lahore made but a fleeting impression during the reigns of Akbar and Jahangir. As their congregations dwindled, so did their cultural influence.

[3]C. Seeger, *Studies in Musicology 1935–1975* (University of California Press, 1977), 206–7.

[4]E. Harich-Schneider, *A History of Japanese Music* (London, 1973), 484.

The lack of interchange between the musical culture of the English colonists and the many indigenous musical cultures within her Empire is of course explained by the absence of this kind of systematic missionary effort. The English came to trade, to settle or to enslave, but only rarely to convert. Not until the late eighteenth century was overseas mission organized by the Protestant churches on a significant scale. It is true that individuals and small groups sometimes attempted programmes of evangelism, and also that when this occured, there were sometimes musical transfers. John Josselyn, describing the musical accomplishments of Indians on the coast of Maine in 1663, referred directly to their facility in copying string instruments and learning to play on them:

> Musical too, they be, having pretty odd barbarous tunes which they make use of vocally at marriages and feastings; but Instruments they had none before the English came amongst them, since they have imitated them and will make Kitts and string them as neatly and as Artificially as the best Fiddle-maker amongst us; and will play our plain lessons very exactly . . . . "[5]

It is necessary to stress, however, that when, as here, Indians were seen copying instruments and learning hymn tunes ("plain lessons"), it was the short-term result of a period of educational or evangelistic endeavor associated with a particular trading post or mission station. English bowed instruments may have been taught to some Indians, but the instruments did not succeed in crossing the cultural boundary to find acceptance in Amerindian culture itself. As Seeger pointed out, the likelihood of significant acculturation taking place in English-speaking North America was in any case never very great, with the Indians as a rule being increasingly pushed back into wilderness areas and, ultimately, reservations.[6] As for Amerindian influence on English music, there was none, the general contempt with which their music was regarded, precluding any desire to imitate.

In a later age, the mutual influence of the music of the white settlers and the black slaves and their descendants was profound, but in the seventeenth century this process could hardly be said to have started. The attitude of English settlers towards the music of their

[5]J. Josselyn, *Two Voyages to New England* (Boston, 1865), 103.

[6]Seeger (1977), 187.

African slaves was at best condescending, as exemplified by Ligon's account of an incident on Barbados when a black overseer came into his house:

> He found me playing on a Theorbo, and singing to it, which he hearkened very attentively to; and when I had done, he took the Theorbo in his hand, and strook one string, stopping it by degrees upon every fret, and finding the notes to varie, till it came to the body of the instrument; and that the nearer the body of the instrument he stopt, the smaller or higher the sound was, which he found was by shortning of the string, considered with himself, how he might make some tryal of this experiment upon such an instrument as he could come by; having no hope ever to have any instrument of this kind to practice on.

A few days later, Ligon came across the man sitting at a xylophone, and he made a half-hearted attempt to demonstrate the difference between sharps and flats. "I say this much," he concludes, "to let you see that some of these people are capable of learning Arts."[7] With such a degree of prejudice, mutual influence was again most unlikely.

In the eastern trading stations and settlements the situation was rather different. Throughout the seventeenth century, the practice of hiring Indian ensembles for reasons of prestige and the employment of local musicians to accompany dancers produced a musical environment that might in one sense be described as multi-cultural with its striking mélange of English, Dutch, Portuguese, Chinese, Indian and African musicians, but even in these circumstances there is no evidence at all of any interchange. Indeed, it is clear that different groups performed as distinct units: in a procession, the European trumpeters and the "country" music would occupy different places in the marching order; in an evening's entertainment at a factory, different sets of musicians would perform like separate "acts" on a circus bill. The only ethnic transfers across these boundaries came with the occasional use of slaves or native servants trained on European instruments, but, at least in the seventeenth century, this practice was far commoner in Portuguese and Dutch settlements. In the eighteenth century the gulf between English and Indian culture was as great as ever. Calcutta had now developed into an important centre of expatriate English culture, and its musical life was that of

[7]C. D. S. Field, "Musical Observations from Barbados, 1647–50," *MT* (1974), 567.

an English provincial city, with an oratorio season, a regular series of subscription concerts and an enthusiastic body of amateur musicians. The political dominance of the East India Company in Bengal was such that the need to hire Indian musicians for diplomatic reasons was fast diminishing. The separation between Indian and English culture seemed complete, and yet, quite suddenly in the 1780s, there occurred a remarkable development—an intense and sympathetic interest in Indian music, during which, for the first time, the English began to take seriously the highly sophisticated but the (to them) musically impenetrable styles and genres of the subcontintent. The origins of this fascinating episode lie in the Cult of the Picturesque, a movement that swept across eighteenth-century Europe. Its chief characteristic was a fascination with the wilder aspects of nature and with people in realistic local settings. Anything with exotic subject matter, especially anything oriental, was certain of a sympathetic hearing. The movement was influential in India and undoubtedly played a part in shaping English attitudes towards Indian culture.[8] Another positive factor was the growing trend towards the serious study of oriental cultures. A small but by no means uninfluential group of Englishmen became deeply interested in Indian languages, religions and customs. The Asiatic Society, founded by the leaders of this group, was to make a particularly valuable contribution. It was against this background that there was a period of genuine interaction between the music of the English and that of India—an episode of acculturation.

As was often the case, it was the musical instruments of an unfamiliar culture that provided the best starting point for outside observation. A document in the Hastings papers (British Library, Add. 29233, fol.106) describes how a group of Englishmen in Rungpore [Rangpur] observed and tested the circular breathing of a musician from Bhutan. It is in the form of an affadavit dated 27 February 1780, in which George Bogle and others certified that they had witnessed a certain Tamchen "play upon a Baotan Pipe, made of a Reed, in the manner of a German Flute (though with only six Holes) and that he continued to sound it for the space of five minutes by a watch, with a continued uninterrupted Sound." To test for possible deception, a feather was held under the musician's nose, which was

[8]On the Cult of the Picturesque in India, see M. and W. G. Archer, *Indian Painting for the British, 1770–1880* (Oxford, 1955).

seen to move whenever breath was drawn. Next the man was handed a French horn, an instrument he had never seen before. He was able to blow it for three minutes "though only one note, and the sound being sometimes louder than at others." The musician then described how the art could be acquired by blowing through a pipe immersed in water. A bowl of water was duly fetched and a demonstration given. The open-minded spirit of inquiry and the quasi-scientific methods adopted by these Englishmen typify attitudes at this period. A much better known example is Francis Fowke's description of a *bin* in the first volume of *Asiatick Researches* (Calcutta, 1788). Fowke's informants were two players called "Jeewan Shah" and "Pear Cawn." He gives details of tuning, fretting, playing position and fingering. From his comments on the music, it is clear that he had listened carefully to the performances of these players. He describes their style as being one "of great execution," but he was unable to discern any "regular air or subject"—a commonly made point. The music, he continued, "seems to consist of a number of detatched passages, some very regular in their "ascent and descent." He noted that the open wires were struck from time to time "in a manner that prepares the ear for a change of modulation," but that "the ear is always disappointed." Any move from the principal key seemed to him to be of short duration only. Although he was understandably unable to comprehend so radically different a musical language, the quality of his observation is above average for the period.

Interest in unfamiliar instruments was not of course unusual. What is much more remarkable about this phase of Anglo-Indian musical exchange is the attempt to transcribe and arrange Indian music for European performance. Once again there are clear European models, in particular the vogue for writing sets of variations on "national" airs. Fashionable Calcutta was well up-to-date with London taste. J. C. Bach's concerto on the Scotch tune of "The Golden haired laddie" is documented in Calcutta only six years after its publication in London in 1777.[9] The success of such pieces doubtless stimulated English musicians in India to investigate what was available to them. They faced a formidable task. London-based composers had materials from Scotland available in relatively accessible

[9]D. Johnson, *Music and Society in Lowland Scotland during the 18th Century* (London, 1972), 196. India Office Library, Fowke Mss, Eur. E4, fol. 262.

form, but English musicians in India had first to transcribe the music and translate the texts of the Indian originals, and then to arrange them in an acceptable European manner. Letters and journals of the period provide detailed evidence of how the rather improbable transition from Indian song to English concert piece—the results were popularly known as "Hindostannie airs"—was managed.[10]

We learn a great deal about methods of collecting and arranging Indian songs from extant musical sources. The Fitzwilliam Museum in Cambridge possesses a manuscript of Indian song arrangements (Ms. 380) compiled under the direction of Sophia Plowden during her time in Lucknow. It consists of a volume of seventy-seven pieces, mostly untitled, but there are also thirty-nine loose sheets containing the titles and words of Persian and Urdu songs. The borders of these sheets are decorated with patterns on gold or silver backgrounds, and they contain a fine series of depictions of musicians and dancers drawn by Sophia's own Indian artists. A note in a nineteenth-century hand is attached to the volume of music, which explains that the songs were collected by Sophia Plowden in Lucknow during 1786 from the songs of "Khannum, Dile Sooth (?), Morade (?) Bux, Higinay (?), Kareem Bux, Noñal, Asaph al (?) Dowla and Colonel Polier." The note also says that the borders were designed by Sophia herself and executed by her own painters, that the words of the songs were collected by her Moonshee, that the musical lines were drawn by her own painters and that the notes were "fairly written" by John Braganza.[11] The background to the compilation of this manuscript is to be found in a diary which records Sophia Plowden's journey up the Ganges to the Kingdom of Oudh in 1787.[12] This source confirms in almost every respect (other than the minor discrepancy in the date) the accuracy of the note attached to the music book. What is clear is that although Indian tunes were frequently exchanged, copied and performed in Calcutta, they were

[10]R. Head, "Corelli in Calcutta: Colonial music-making in India during the 17th and 18th centuries," *EM*, vol. 13 (1985), 548–53. Head gives a brief account of the phenomenon, based on the Fowke materials. For a detailed examination of this subject, see I. Woodfield, "The 'Hindostannie Air': English Attempts to Understand Indian Music in the Late 18th Century," *JRMA* (1994).

[11]F. Wormald and P. M. Giles, *A Descriptive Catalogue of the Additional Illuminated Manuscripts in the Fitzwilliam Museum acquired between 1895 and 1979* (Cambridge, 1982), I, 394–5.

[12]India Office Library, Mss, Eur. F127/94.

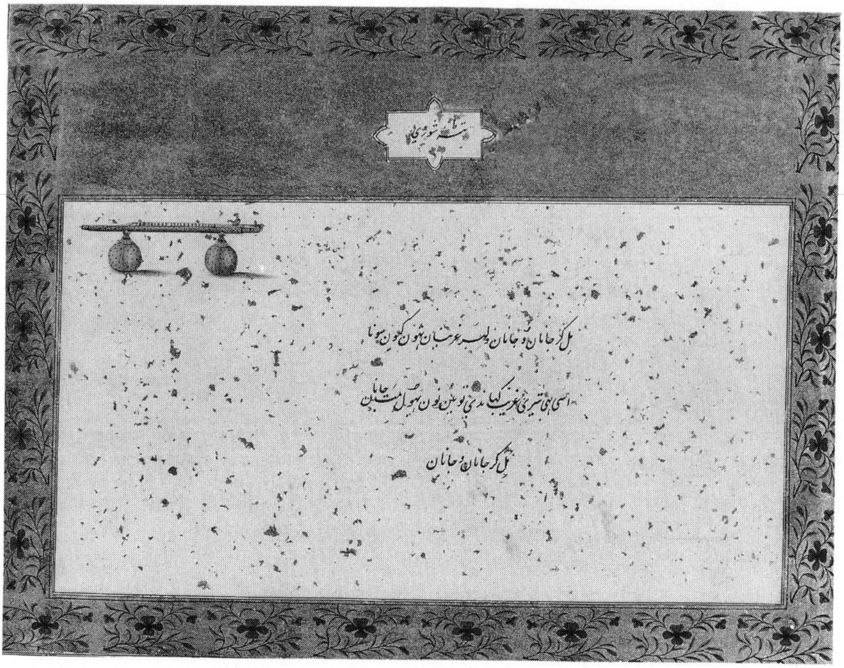

Plate 31. A *bin* painted by an Indian artist for Sophia Plowden at Lucknow in the late 1780s. Fitzwilliam Museum, Cambridge, Ms 380, loose sheet, no. 10. Reproduction by permission of the Syndics of the Fitzwilliam Museum, Cambridge.

actually collected in the two principal cities of Oudh—Lucknow and Benares. While she was in Calcutta, Sophia's diary records only the usual round of plays and concert parties. She began her journey up-country to Lucknow in September 1787 and it almost ended in distaster on the Ganges when one of the boats began to roll badly: "the alarm was now universal, and the confusion indescribable. Chests, bottles, books, millinery, a harpsichord, eatables, drinkables, bundles of cloths all thrown together on the shore . . . . "[13] Having survived this frightening debacle, she reached Lucknow, where her diary starts to record her attempts to collect Indian songs.

It is clear from Sophia's diary that nautch dancers and their musicians were the source of her Indian songs. The meticulously drawn miniatures of dancers and musicians in the Fitzwilliam manuscript constitute a resource of major importance for the study of

[13]Mss, Eur. F127/94. Entry for 2 November 1787.

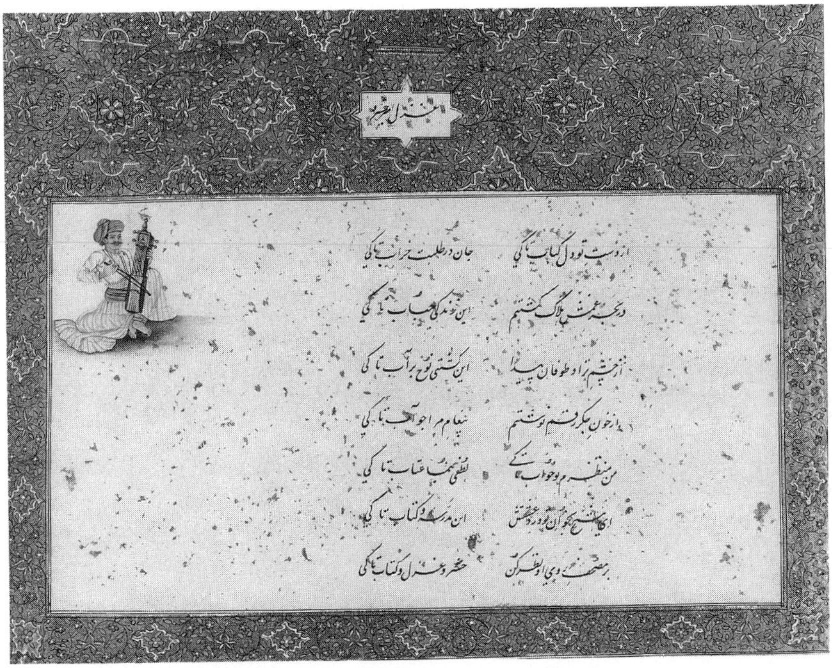

Plate 32. A four-string sarangi painted by an Indian artist for Sophia Plowden at Lucknow in the late 1780s. Fitzwilliam Museum, Cambridge, MS 380, loose sheet, no. 13. Reproduction by permission of the Syndics of the Fitzwilliam Museum, Cambridge.

music in late eighteenth-century Lucknow. Among the instruments depicted are the *bin* (Plate 31), a four-string *sarangi* (Plate 32), *tabla* (Plate 33)—this is one of the earliest known depictions of the instrument—a four-string, fretless *tambura* (Plate 34) and a group consisting of two dancers, a drummer and a fretted Persian *setar* (Plate 35). It is entirely characteristic of the age that while men approached Indian instruments in a scientific fashion, women collected artistic depictions of them.[14] The diary names two nautch performers, "Morade Bax" and "Khanam"; both are cited as sources for songs in the Fitzwilliam manuscript. There seems very little doubt that Khanam was the leading exponent of nautch in the Lucknow of the 1780's; there are several references to her "set"—a "set" was a troupe

[14]Fowke Mss, Eur. E4, fol. 556. Benares, 22 March 1785, "Hogan supped here last night. He has obligingly offered me the time of his ingenious pacuter. I accepted of it very gratefully as I intend to have the Hindostanny instruments drawn by him."

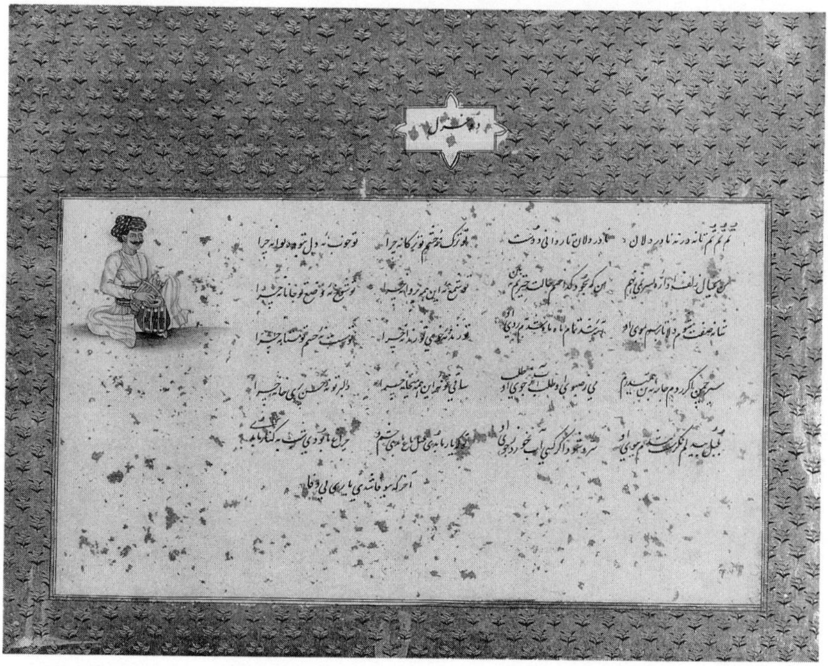

Plate 33. *Tabla* painted by an Indian artist for Sophia Plowden at Lucknow in the late 1780s. Fitzwilliam Museum, Cambridge, Ms 380, loose sheet, no. 19. Reproduced by permission of the Syndics of the Fitzwilliam Museum, Cambridge.

of dancers and musicians—coming "to notch,"[15] and she seems sometimes to have been invited specifically for the purpose of song dictation. On 12 January 1788, for example: "Had a Notch, Khennom here in the morning. Bellas wrote me down an Hindostanny tune." Again on 11 February, Khanam was invited and "Bellas wrote down a Persian song." Such was her regard for the Indian singer that she even commissioned a portrait from the artist Zoffany, who was then in Lucknow.[16] Only once does Sophia actually describe a nautch performance in detail. On 18 February she was invited to breakfast by Hydr Beg Khan [the chief minister of Oudh] on the occasion of his daughter's marriage. She described the Nautch women as "well

[15]Ibid., 23, 24, 26 December.

[16]Ibid., 21 April 1788, "Mr Zoffany began Shaw Khannons picture for me." On Zoffany in India, see M. Webster, *Johann Zoffany 1733–1810* (London, 1976), 14–16, 74–81 (Exhibition Catalogue for the National Portrait Gallery).

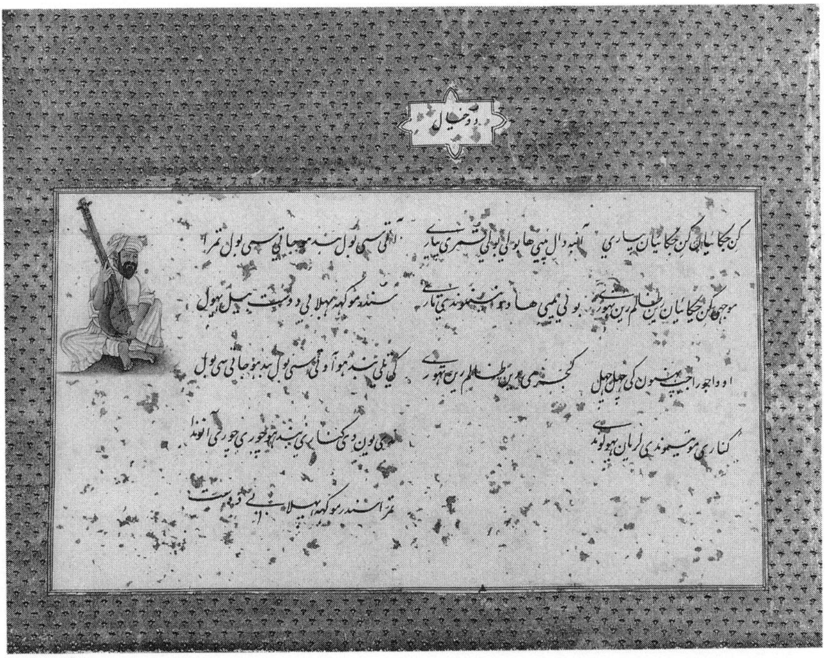

Plate 34. A four-string fretless *tambura* painted by an Indian artist for Sophia Plowden at Lucknow in the late 1780s. Fitzwilliam Museum, Cambridge, Ms. 380, loose sheet, no. 7. Reproduction by permission of the Syndics of the Fitzwilliam Museum, Cambridge.

dress'd but most ugly and some very fat and old." "Their voices," she continued,"were held in estimation, but as they only sang Tappas, a sort of wild harsh music without any air I was not much pleas'd..."[17]

Asuf-ud-daulah, the Nawab of Oudh, was well aware of the interest being shown by English collectors in Indian music and seems to have encouraged it. On 3 March he was invited to the house of the English Resident, Mr. Ives, whose wife performed on the harpsichord. Sophia Plowden was then asked by the Nawab to sing a Persian song.[18] On September 18 she was invited to breakfast with the Nawab, and the entertainment was as usual "notching." She requested the nautch girls to sing the song of "Jo Kamshere Levy Allum Deaktey," upon which the Nawab told her that the poetry of

[17]Mss, Eur. F127/94. Entry for 18 February 1788.

[18]Ibid., 3 March.

Plate 35. A four-string *setar*, a drum and two dancers painted by an Indian artist for Sophia Plowden in Lucknow in the late 1780s. Fitzwilliam Museum, Cambridge, Ms. 380, loose sheet, no. 24. Reproduction by permission of the Syndics of the Fitzwilliam Museum, Cambridge.

the song was his own composition. As she had not yet got a correct copy, she asked permission to send someone for one, and the Nawab agreed to repeat the words to him.[19] This confirms the note on the Fitzwilliam manuscript that "Asuph al Dowla" provided material for Sophia's collection.

The circle of devotees of Indian music at Lucknow included not only Mrs. Plowden and Colonel Polier from whom she obtained a number of songs,[20] but also William Hamilton Bird. On one occasion Sophia Plowden recorded in her diary that Bird had accompanied her on the harpsichord in a performance of some of her airs, and on another that he had provided her with settings of two Indian airs.[21]

[19]Ibid., 18 September.

[20]On Zoffany's portrait of Colonel Polier illustrating his oriental interests, see Webster (1976), 79.

[21]Mss, Eur. F127/94. Entries for 8, 9 March 1788.

In 1789 he published a collection entitled *The Oriental Miscellany*.[22] He wrote to Warren Hastings (British Library, Add. 29171, fol. 363) begging him "to deign to receive" copies of the publication. In his introduction Bird claims to have adhered strictly to the original compositions, although, not surprisingly, it cost him great pains "to bring them into any form as to TIME, which the music of Hindostan is extremely deficient in." He identifies the airs of Kashmir and Rohilkand—the tract of land to the north-west of Oudh—as being particularly perfect and regular, but even these, in performance, "need the grace of a Chanam (a famous woman singer) and the expression of a Dillsook (a male singer of great eminence) to render them pleasing." Khanam, we know, and Dillsook may be identified with the "Dile Sooth" of the Fitzwilliam manuscript.

Bird is particularly informative on the genres of Indian music preferred by English collectors. He names four. *Raagnies* are "void of meaning and regularity" and are therefore "impossible to bring into a form for performance by any singers but those of their country (Hindostan)." He concludes that they appear to be "the efforts of men enraptured by words, to which they have added notes as their fancy and amorous flights have dictated." *Teranas* are performances of the Rohillas [Afgans living in Rohilkand], sung by men only. The two genres which provide almost all the material for Bird's volume are the *Rekhtah* and the *Tuppah*. The *Rekhtah* is the most comprehensible type of Indian music and exceeds other forms in regularity. The *Tuppah* is "wild but pleasing when understood." The *rekhtah* is now described as a type of *thumri*, while the *tappa* involves figurative and ornamental variations performed at rapid speed,[23] which perhaps accounts for Sophia Plowden's comment that they seemed "wild" and "harsh." Both these genres, which are categorized as light-classical or semiclassical, seem to have been especially popular in Lucknow in the late eighteenth century. Kippen writes of Lucknow under the nawabs as a melting pot of influences "from which emerged new instruments and styles of music, catering to the predilection of the Kings and courtiers for the light and superficial."[24] It was very probably elements of this repertory that took the fancy of

[22]W. H. Bird, *The Oriental Miscellany* (Calcutta, 1789). See Head (1985).

[23]E. Te Nijenhuis, *Indian Music: History and Structure* (*Handbuch der Orientalistik*, Series 2, vol. 6: Leiden and Cologne, 1974), 93 and 96.

[24]J. Kippen, *The Tabla of Lucknow* (Cambridge, 1988), 20.

English collectors. It was accessible to them through the leading nautch performers and it was evidently considered comprehensible enough for transcription.

In attempting to transcribe Indian music into the European idiom of the day, English musicians were faced with an impossible task. The examples published by Bird are supplied with key signatures, time signatures and harmonizations, with the result that the Indian airs appear in a form in which doubtless almost every trace of their original character has been lost, except perhaps their general melodic contour. The Fitzwilliam manuscript, however, is more interesting. Its scribe, the Portuguese musician John Braganza struggles bravely and imaginatively with the problem. He tries to harmonize some melodies with an alberti bass figure or in parallel tenths, but more often than not, recognising the futility of this, he resorts to a drone bass or to parallel octaves. He does not always force melodies into regular, metrically consistent phrases, which suggests an attempt to remain faithful to his perception of the original. In some of the decorative roulades and rapid repeated notes of the melodies there seem distant echoes of Indian originals. Once Braganza goes so far as to use an irregular key signature—a piece with b flats and f sharps. The results of his efforts are bizarre indeed, but what is of real interest is not the inadequacy of the transcription but the fact the attempt was made.[25]

Two strands of opinion have always characterized European perceptions of indigenous musical cultures. On the one hand, interest, growing sometimes upwards into respect and even admiration; on the other, indifference, declining frequently into contempt and open hostility. During the fashion for "Hindostannie airs" in the1780s the positive attitude was prevalent. The scientific examination of Indian instruments, the patronage of leading Indian performers, the commissioning of portraits of Indian singers and instrumentalists, and the attempted transcription of Indian songs, together represent a rapprochement with Indian music that may fairly be termed an episode of acculturation. Although the fashion waned around the turn of the century, some effects lingered on. Nautch songs remained popular in certain sections of Indian society,[26] and they were used effectively as symbols of the

[25] I. Woodfield: "Collecting Indian Songs in Late 18th-Century Lucknow: Problems of Transcription," *British Journal of Ethnomusicology* (1995).

[26] K. K. Dyson, *A Various Universe* (Our; Bombay, Calcutta and Madras, 1978), 256, reports the evidence of Miss Emma Roberts that the Armenian community in Calcutta sang Hindustani songs to the piano.

colorful orient by composers of opera and popular song in England.[27] But the history of English attitudes towards Indian music during the nineteenth century represents the steady triumph of the opposing point of view.[28] Once a socially acceptable activity supported enthusiastically by its devotees, the nautch was now usually viewed with boredom or scorn. English writers in India continue to describe the nautch—it was, after all, one of the clichés of the Indian experience—but their tone changes unmistakeably, even before the Mutiny.[29] Attempts to introduce Indian instruments or music into the concert parties of the Raj were now likely to be rebuffed. Mrs. Fanny Parks wrote how she had "favored the party with some Hindustani airs on the sitar," which she "could not persuade them to admire."[29] Even someone like Solvyns, whose four-volume *Les Hindús* contains valuable pictorial evidence of the instruments in use in early nineteenth-century India, wrote, as Hood pointed out, in a manner that shows his "complete lack of understanding of the music as well as of the character of the people."[31] Once erected, the barrier of prejudice proved durable. It persisted through to the departure of the English and beyond.

[27]Head (1985). The song heard by Sophia Plowden in Lucknow was especially popular: *Taza ba taza, nao ba nao, The famous Song of the Persian Poet Hafiz, translated from the original melody by O. G. Phipps* was published in London in 1857. See also Dyson (1978), 343, 345. J. Bor, "The Rise of Ethnomusicology: sources on Indian music c. 1780–c. 1890," *Yearbook for Traditional Music*, vol. 20 (1988), 51–73, gives further examples of Indian songs published in London.

[28]The eventual dominance of this attitude leads sometimes to an underestimation of the earlier open-mindedness. See R. Leppert and S. McClary, *Music and Society: The Politics of Composition, Performance and Reception* (Cambridge, 1987).

[29]Dyson (1978), Appendix B.

[30]Ibid., 350.

[31]F. Ll. Harrison, M. Hood and C. Palisca, *Musicology* (New Jersey, 1963), 220.

Index

This index consists mainly of places and individual people, but it also includes the following collected headings: music; musicians i; musicians ii; trumpeters; drummers and fifers; instruments i; instruments ii; consorts, ensembles and bands; ships. Geographical locations in the text are indexed: towns, cities, islands, rivers, regions, provinces, states, island groups, countries, sub-continents, continents, seas (but not oceans). Place names of towns and cities outside Europe are identified by a region or country, except in the most obvious cases; thus: "Vijanayagar, India" and "Nanjing, China," but "Calcutta" and "Peking." In a few instances, place names are indexed under the spelling generally current in the 16th- and 17th-century sources upon which this study is based; thus: "Benares." Where a place name has changed unrecognizably and the modern name is well known, it is given in square brackets; thus: "Batavia [Jacarta]." Names of European professional musicians, trumpeters and drummers and those whose job required some musical competence (mainly priests and missionaries) are indexed in the relevant collected entries. The names of amateur musicians are indexed in the alphabetical sequence. The few native musicians referred to by name are indexed in the alphabetical sequence in the spelling by which they were known to Europeans, for example, "Dillsook, Indian musician." Also in the alphabetical sequence are names of non-musicians, ranging from monarchs down to minor company officials, captains and pilots. A few names have not been indexed; individuals of no significance, whose appearance in the text is fortuitous (within a quoted extract, for example) are ignored. Primary and secondary authorities mentioned by name in the text are indexed.